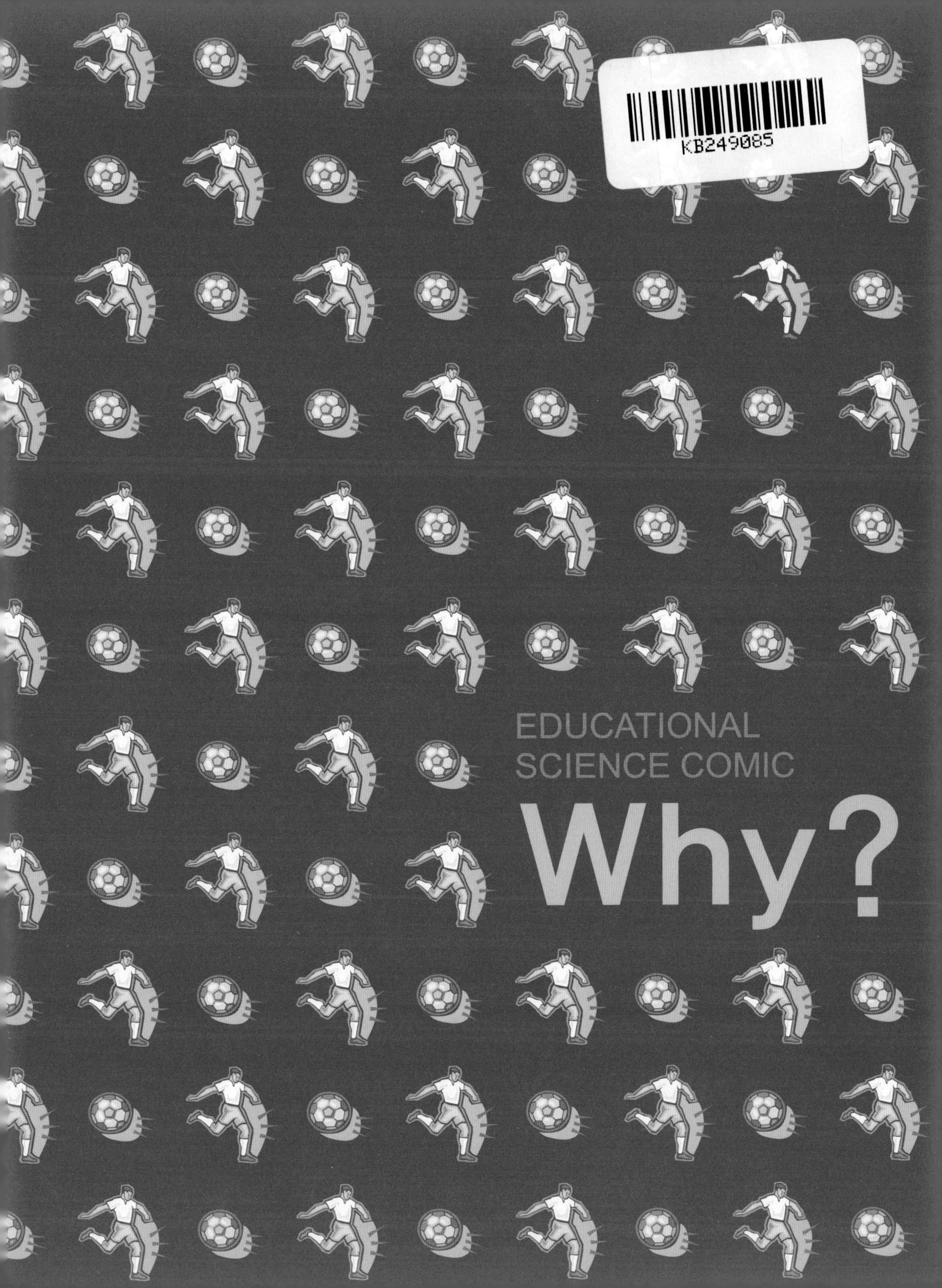
KB249085
EDUCATIONAL
SCIENCE COMIC
Why?

Why?

Sports Science

English Edition

Scientific Consultant
Jinsil Mock

Jinsil Mock graduated from University of Illinois at Urbana Champaign with a B.S. in elementary education. She worked as a middle school math and science teacher in Illinois. To further her studies in education, she received a master's degree in Learning and Teaching from Harvard University in Cambridge, Massachusetts and is now working on her PhD in Education at Vanderbilt University's Peabody College of Education and Human Development in Nashville, Tennessee.

Chief Editor
Scott Lichtenstein

Born and raised in California, Scott graduated from Harvard University with a degree in Chemistry and was President of the Harvard Parliamentary Debate Society. After graduation, Scott wrote textbooks and taught test preparation seminars as a Managing Director of DemiDec, an educational publishing company. In 2007, he co-founded Imperial Publishing, an educational content provider and publishing company based in San Francisco. He is currently the CEO of Imperial Publishing.

Editor
David Vincent Kimel

Born in Israel and raised in Connecticut, David attended Harvard at the same time as Scott. David graduated from Harvard Summa Cum Laude and Phi Beta Kappa with a degree in Classics. He co-founded Imperial Publishing and provides educational content to companies around the world. In addition to his duties as President of Imperial Publishing, David is currently the coach of the Yale Debate Team.

Why? Sports Science

Second edition published in Republic of Korea in 2007
English edition published in 2013 by
YeaRimDang Publishing Co., Ltd
Yearim Bldg, 153, Samseong-dong, Gangnam-gu, Seoul, 135-090

Copyright © YeaRimDang Publishing Co., Ltd

ISBN 978-89-302-1357-8 18690

Introduction to
Why? Sports Science

It was heartwarming news when Tae-Hwan Park, a young swimmer from Korea, won the gold medal in the Men's 400 m Freestyle race at the FINA World Aquatics Championships in 2007, competing against world-renowned swimmers. The victory was even more significant in that it disproved the prejudice that Asian athletes are physically inferior to Western athletes. The reason that Asian athletes scored poorly in the past in sports games such as track and swimming lay more in a lack of scientific training than in physical differences. And the reason that Tae-Hwan Park was able to win the championship was because he had trained himself persistently through scientific methods.

And in 2002 Korean soccer players had the possibility of winning the world championship. They, too, had had scientific training by coaches with expertise.

Why should sports be scientific? It's because sports are science. Various scientific principles in disciplines such as physiology, chemistry, and biology are hidden in each sport. In other words, scientific factors combine together to create a sport. Thus, those who understand the principles behind a sport can master the techniques more quickly and set higher records.

"Why? Sports Science" discusses fascinating scientific principles behind various sports such as basketball, badminton, golf, and judo.

It is hoped that this book will help you grow closer to sports by integrating sports and science.

Korean Edition

Editorial Supervisor
Jinho Baek

Jinho Baek received a doctorate in science at Sungkyunkwan University. He is currently a principal research engineer at the Korea Institute of Sports Science at Korea Sports Promotion Foundation, a member of the Sports Science Committee of the Korea Association of Athletics Federations, and a member of the research committee at the Korea Gymnastic Association. His works include the theses, *The Fundamental Biomechanics of Sports* and *An Analysis of the Kinematic Characteristics of the Starting Position in the 500 m Short Track*.

Author
Youngsun Jo

Youngsun Jo has written the texts for various graphic novels including *Micro Expedition Volumes 1 and 2, Scientific Principles that Make You Smarter, Power Up Word Master Volumes 1 and 2, Children Crime Scene Investigators Volumes 1 and 2, The Raincoat Weather Expedition, The Little Prince,* and *Catch the I.Q. Thief Volumes 1,2, and 3.* Currently, he writes stories for *Funny C.*

Cartoonist
Youngho Lee

Youngho Lee has illustrated various children's books and graphic novels including *Going to an Amusement Park by Myself, Market Economy is My Friend, Power Up Word Master Volumes 1 and 2,* and *The Raincoat Weather Expedition.* Currently, he illustrates for *Funny C.*

CHARACTERS

Gomji

A boy who likes to play games but hates to exercise. He is weaker than Omji because he doesn't exercise, but becomes stronger little by little through his training with Spot, the robot.

Omji

A strong, healthy girl who exercises on a regular basis. Spot and Dr. Teunteun greatly respect her because of her knowledge of sports and science.

Dr. Teunteun

A scientist who successfully developed a universal sports robot. He is abducted by villains who try to steal the robot.

Spot

A universal sports robot who undertakes the special mission of training Gomji. He rescues Dr. Teunteun from the villains.

CONTENTS

CD-3

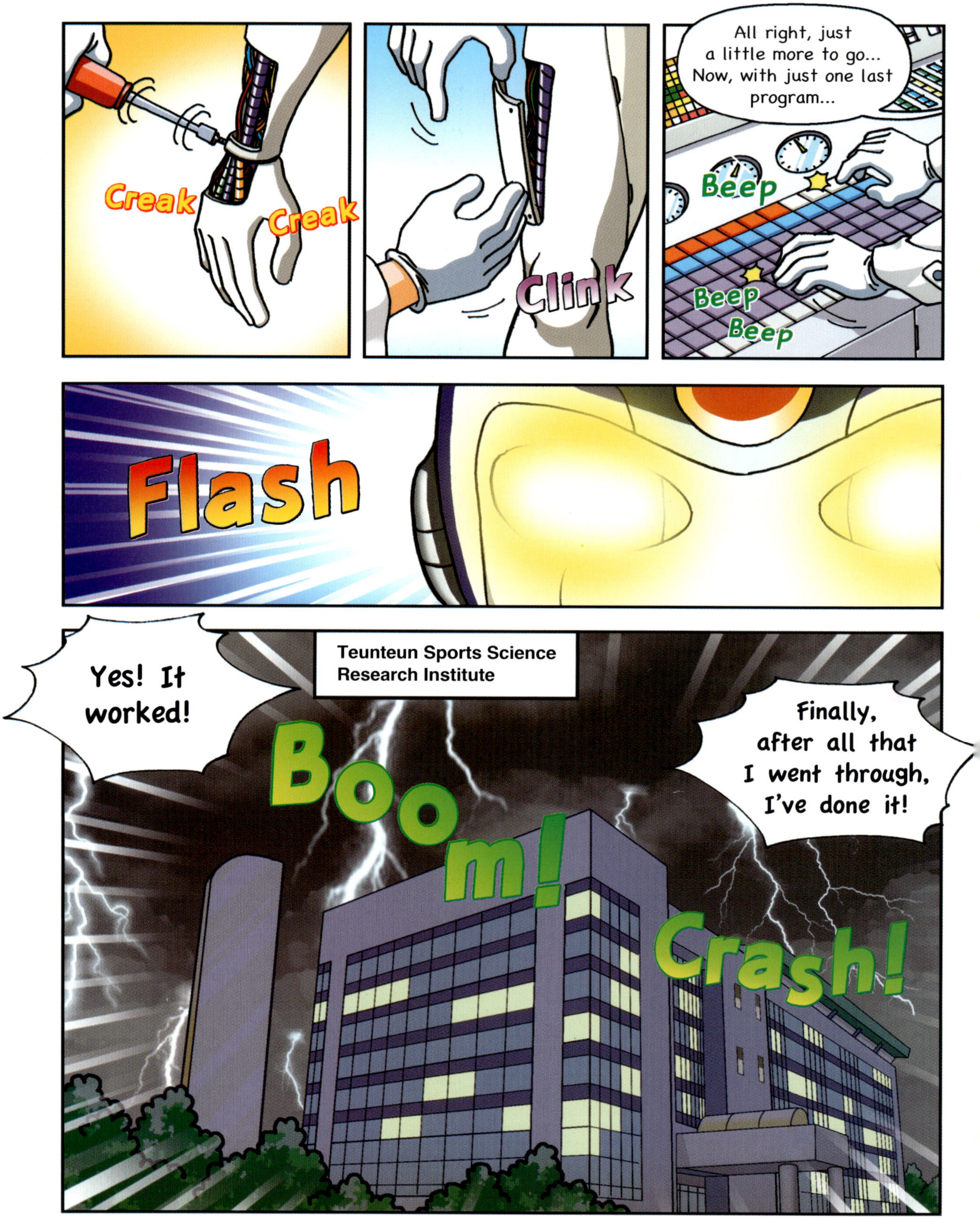

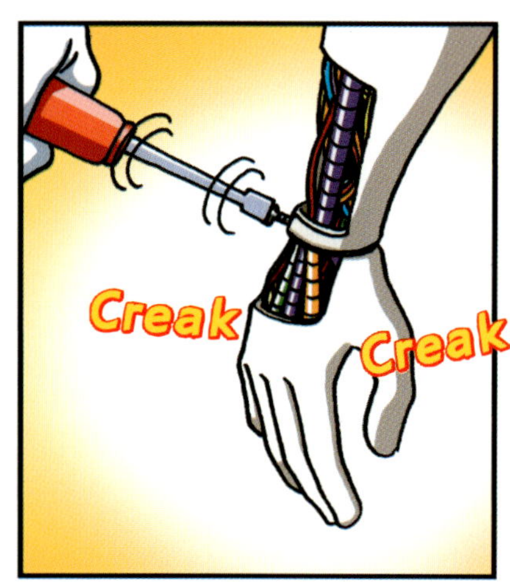

Creak
Creak

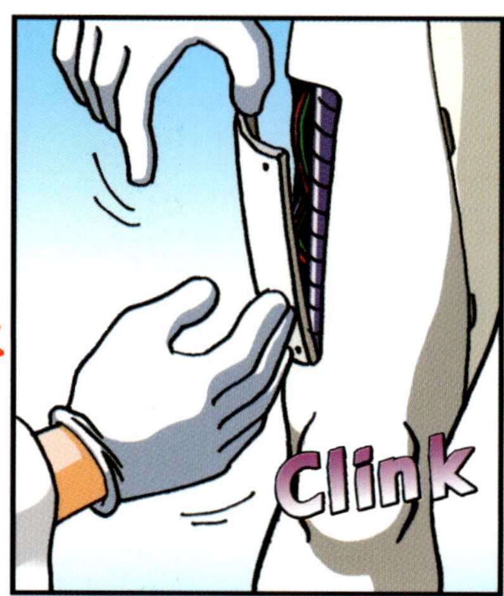

Clink

All right, just a little more to go... Now, with just one last program...
Beep
Beep
Beep

Flash

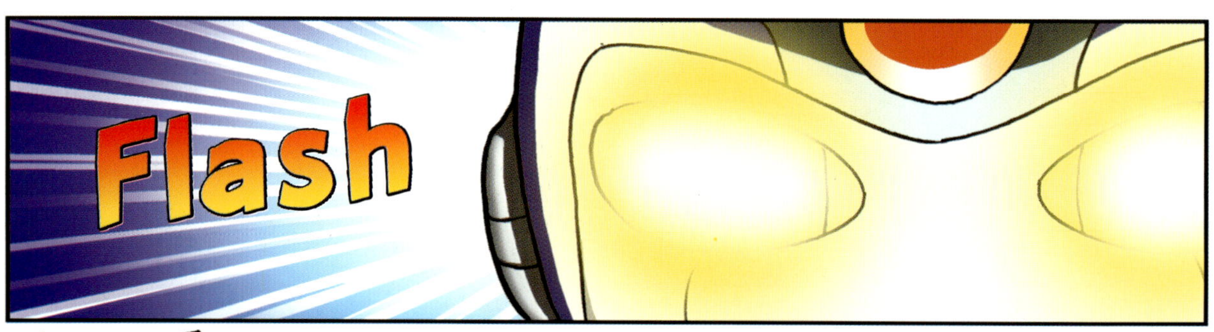

Yes! It worked!
Teunteun Sports Science Research Institute
Finally, after all that I went through, I've done it!
Boom!
Crash!

Sports is a Science

Gomji's Evaluation

How to Measure Ideal Weight

(Height - 100) x 0.9

If the number exceeds your weight by:
10% → Overweight
20% → Obese
100% or 45 kg → Morbidly obese

*An ideal weight does not always indicate sound health.

*Sports Science: A discipline that studies various sports-related principles and scientific knowledge on the biological, psychological, and physio-dynamical aspects of sports activities.

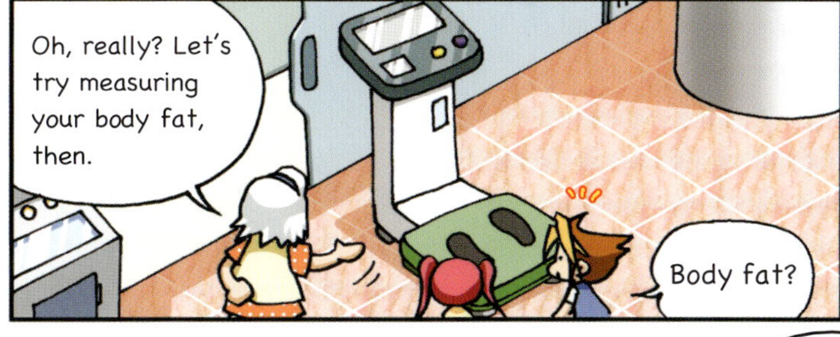

Body Fat and Obesity

Body fat percentage refers to the amount of fat in a person's total weight. Even if you're thin, you're obese if you have too much fat.

Adult male   Normal : 15-18%
       Obese : Over 25%

Adult female   Normal : 20-25%
       Obese : Over 30%

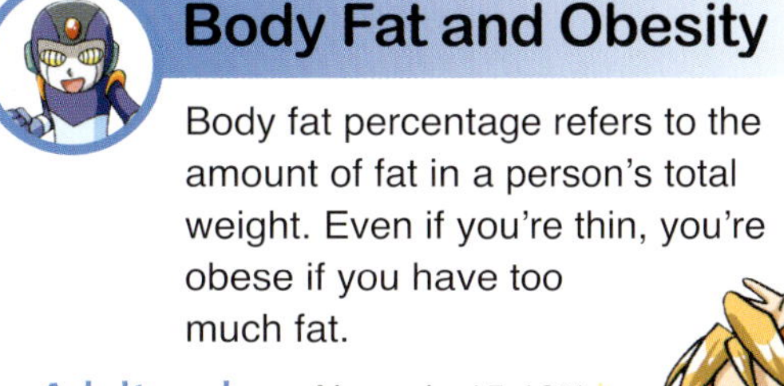

How Body Fat Scales Work

How can you measure body fat just by standing on a scale? The components that make up the human body have different electrical resistances. Fat offers higher resistance to electrical currents than muscle. This is because electrical currents pass easily through the high volume of fluids that muscle tissue contains. Therefore, comparing the electrical resistance will give you the body fat percentage.

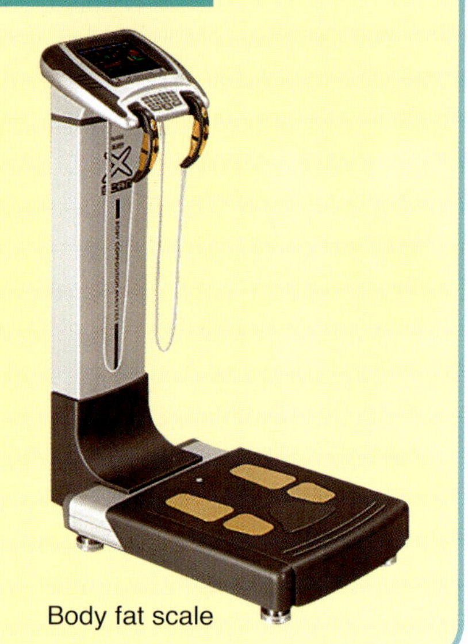

Body fat scale

Items of Evaluation

- Reflex and Agility – 50 m run
- Endurance – 1,200 m long run
- Reflex – Standing long jump
- Muscular Strength, Muscular Endurance – Sit-ups
- Flexibility – Sitting up and bending the upper body forward

Poor bodily function indicates poor immune function as well.

How do People Grow in Height?

An increase in height indicates the growth of bones in the body. Height increases when the growth plate at the end of a bone expands. Growth plates gradually turn into solid bones as a child grows into an adult. Though it varies from person to person, the increase of height in men continues until ages 25-28, and in women, until ages 23-24.

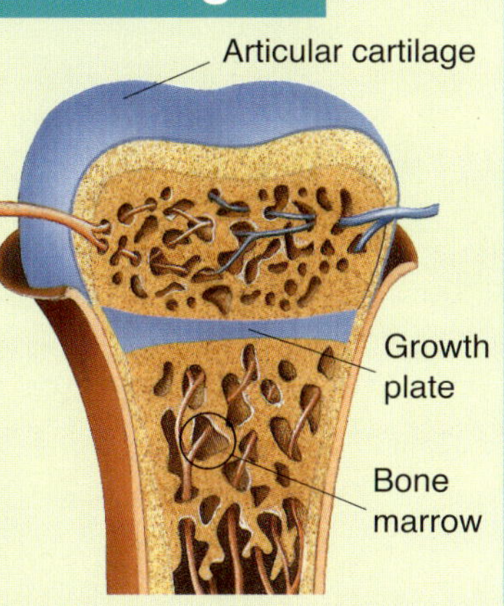

The Structure of a Bone

Growth and Exercise

Exercises that Contribute to Growth

An appropriate amount of exercise stimulates growth plates and contributes to a growth in height.

Exercises that Hinder Growth

Excessive muscular exercise interferes with the supplying of nutrition to the bones and hinders growth.

Exercising Scientifically

1. The Principle of Overload

In order to strengthen an organ or body function, more than the usual amount of exercise is required. Such exercise is hard on the body at first, but the body soon adjusts and strengthens.

2. The Principle of Gradualness

If you start exercising excessively all of a sudden, your body will become exhausted. Start with a light exercise routine, then gradually increase the level of intensity.

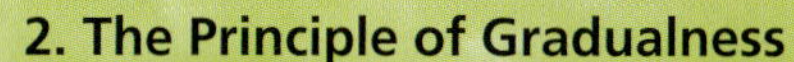

3. The Principle of Repetition

Exercising all at once or exercising on an irregular basis isn't effective, and can even hurt the body.

4. The Principle of Individuality

Because everyone is different in their physical capacity, the level of exercise must be determined accordingly.

5. The Principle of Singularity

Different kinds of exercise bring different results, so choose the right kind of exercise by determining what you would like to improve.

*Stamina: The ability for the body to take in oxygen and continue with exercise

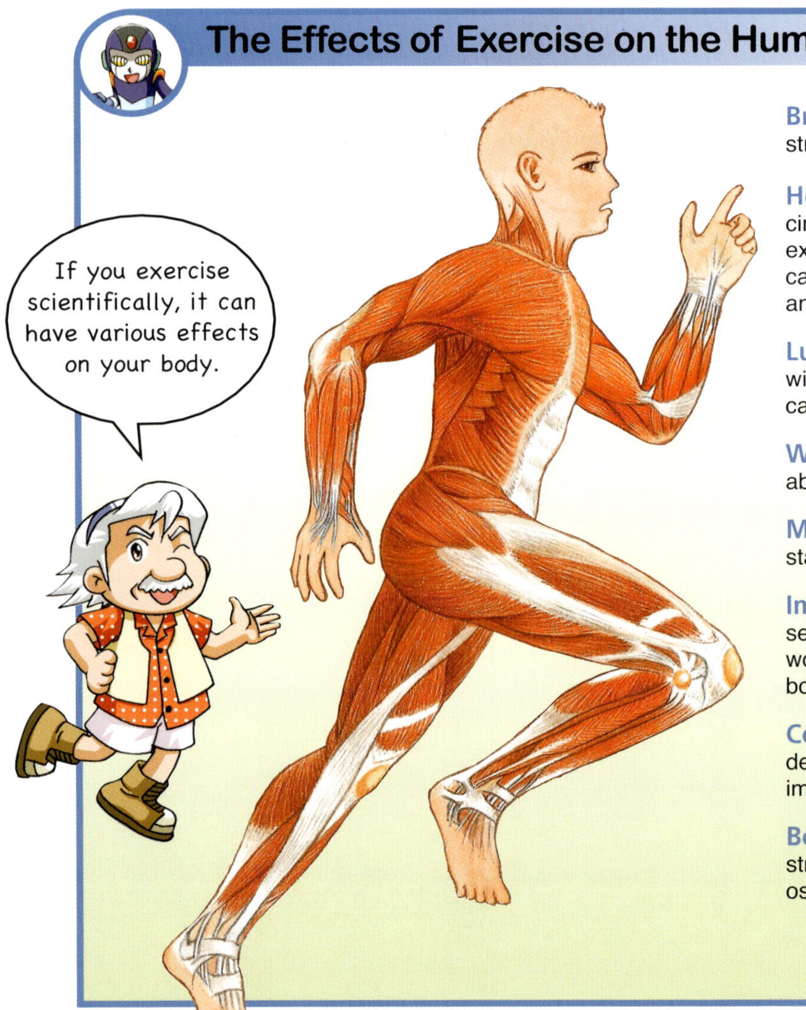

The Effects of Exercise on the Human Body

Brain You will feel refreshed, and your stress level will decrease.

Heart Improved function will facilitate the circulation of the blood. You will be able to exercise for longer periods of time, and it can prevent the hardening of the arteries and heart diseases.

Lungs The muscles that help respiration will become stronger, increasing lung capacity and oxygen consumption.

Waist A decrease in body fat and abdominal fat prevents obesity.

Muscles Strengthened muscles increase stamina.

Immune System Exercise results in the secretion of hormones that facilitate the workings of the various organs in the body, improving the immune system.

Colon The risks of colorectal cancer decreases, and bowel movement improves.

Bones The density of bones increases, strengthening the bones and preventing osteoporosis.

Aerobic and Anaerobic Exercises

Aerobic Exercise Aerobic exercise is light exercise that can be done for a long period of time, such as walking, biking, and swimming. Prolonged exercise is possible in aerobic exercise, as sufficient energy is supplied to the muscle tissue through respiration which converts carbohydrates into energy without making lactic acid*. Aerobic exercise is effective for weight loss.

Anaerobic Exercise Anaerobic exercise, such as short distance running, weightlifting, and pushups, requires exertion of a large amount of energy in a short period of time. The sudden demand for energy results in a rapid production of energy through the breaking down of the glycogen*, without oxygen, in Muscles. Lactic acids are created in this process, exhausting the muscles, which makes prolonged exercise difficult. Anaerobic exercise increases muscles and strength.

*Lactic Acid: A substance that is produced during strenuous exercise. The production of lactic acid is responsible for muscle fatigue during exercise.
*Glycogen: A substance that stores glucose, a cellular energy source, in a form that can be used immediately.

Oxygen
Fat cells break down.
The fat in the human body breaks down only when it fuses with oxygen. That's why aerobic exercise is effective in weight loss.

Fat is used as an energy source and begins to break down after twenty minutes of light to medium aerobic exercise.

There's a good reason why I'm so thin.

You may be thin, but you're a midget.
What? A midget?
Seethe

I'm a guy, so I'm going to focus on anaerobic exercise to gain muscles!
You should get rid of your potbelly first!

It's better to do both aerobic and anaerobic exercises together than to focus on just one.
Nyah!

If aerobic exercise is done before muscular exercise, proteins are used as an energy source because carbohydrates, the main energy source, have been used up.

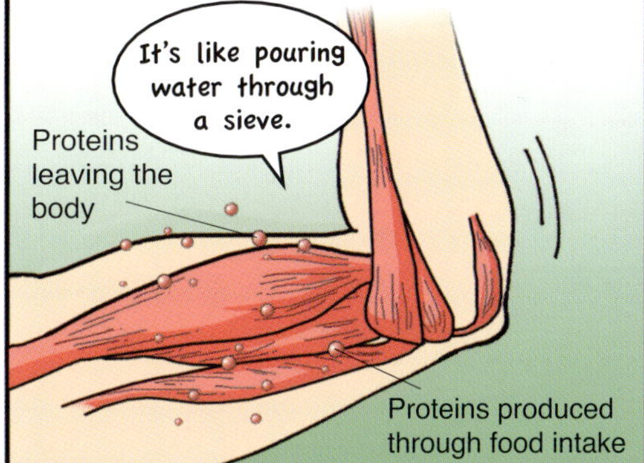
In other words, muscles can't grow due to a lack of proteins, which are the main component of muscles.

It is more effective to do aerobic exercise after muscular exercise, because there will be no decrease in muscles while more fat is broken down.

Weight training is the most typical anaerobic exercise.

Jogging is the most typical aerobic exercise.

Lactic Acids, the Cause of Muscle Fatigue

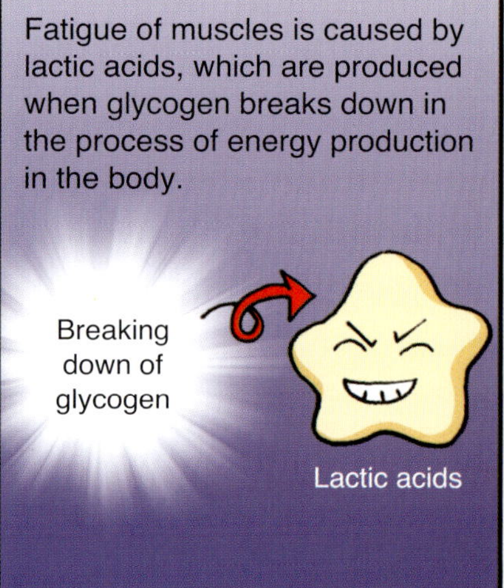

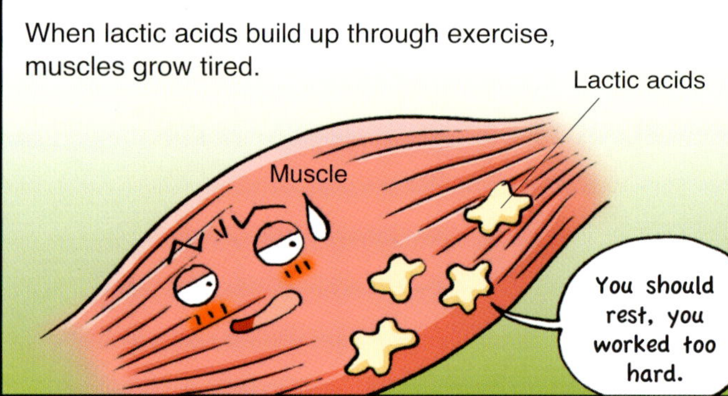

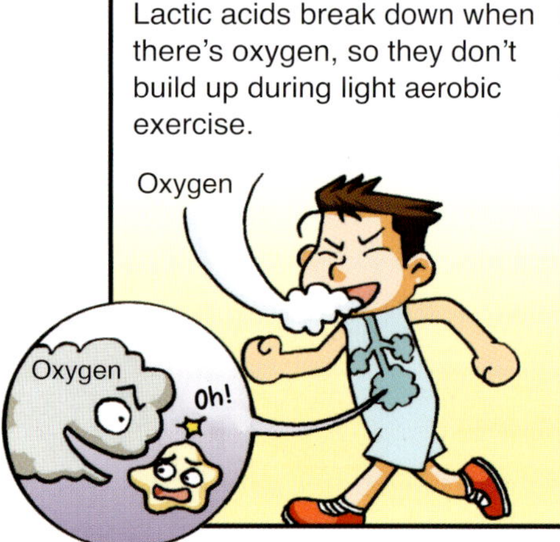

Athletes wrap themselves up in a towel after a game to help their muscles relax by keeping their bodies from cooling down.

Increased lung capacity leads to an increased oxygen consumption and a decrease of lactic acid accumulation.

Sports and the Heart

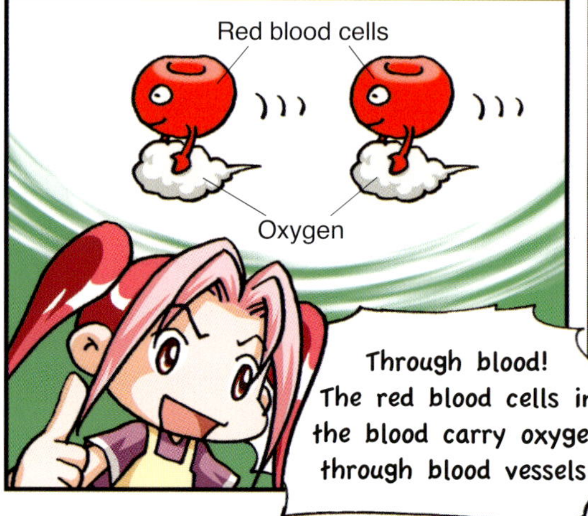

An Ordinary Heart and an Athletic Heart

The heart needs to pump about 5 liters of blood per minute throughout the body for people to carry out daily activities. Most people meet the required amount with 70-80 heartbeats, but athletes meet the same amount with only 40-50 heartbeats. In other words, athletes are more fit for intense exercise because they can produce more energy than ordinary people as they can supply a greater amount of oxygen and blood in a short period of time.

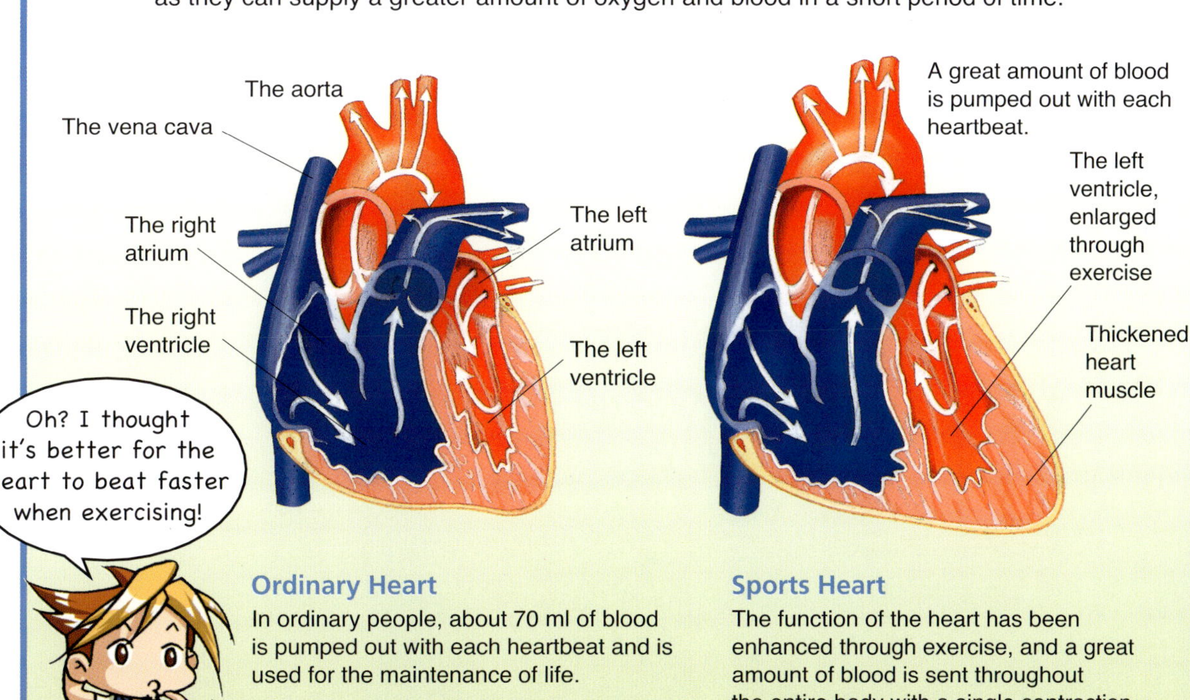

Ordinary Heart

In ordinary people, about 70 ml of blood is pumped out with each heartbeat and is used for the maintenance of life.

Sports Heart

The function of the heart has been enhanced through exercise, and a great amount of blood is sent throughout the entire body with a single contraction.

Power Walking

People gain weight because they don't spend as much energy as they consume.

**Amount of activity = Amount of food consumed
→ Weight maintained**

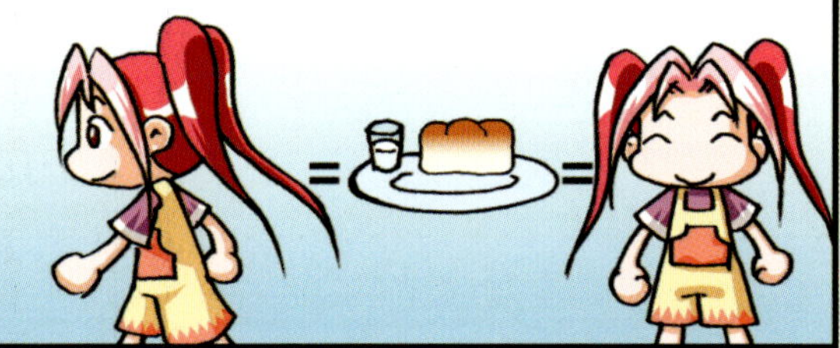

People who are not very active and like to sit or lie down tend to gain weight.

**Amount of activity < Amount of food consumed
→ Obesity**

If you walk vigorously in an upright position, you'll be able to maintain a straight figure, and your muscular strength and cardiopulmonary function will improve.

Walking vigorously will lead to greater energy consumption.

The bones will support the body with stability.

A stooped posture is hard on the bones and will result in an abnormal figure.

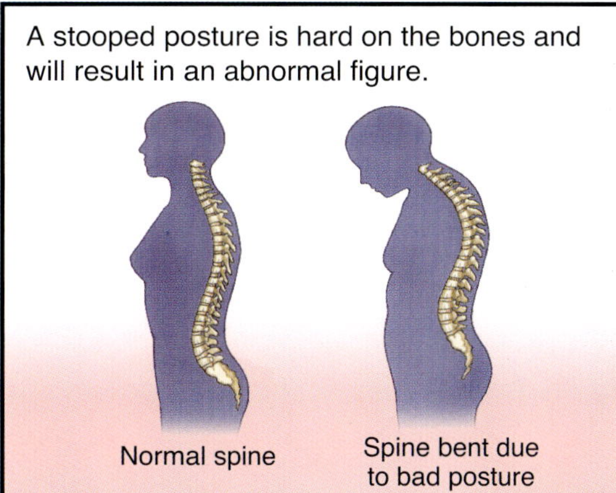

The Basic Posture for Power Walking

- Walk at 6.4-8.9 km/h.
- Don't turn your waist excessively.
- Raise your arms high and swing them briskly.

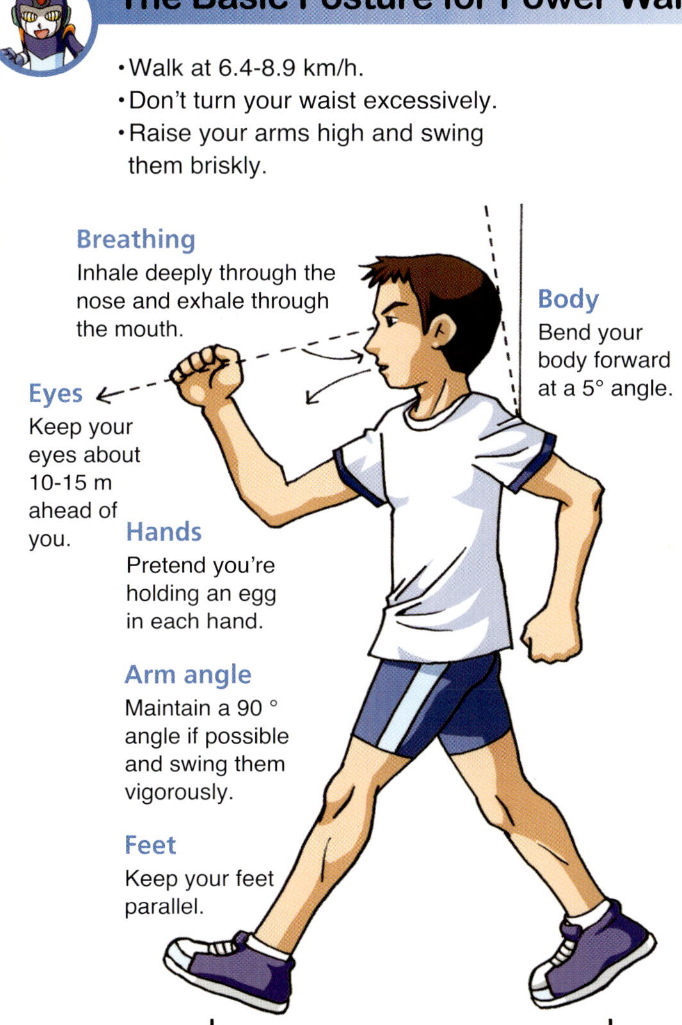

Breathing
Inhale deeply through the nose and exhale through the mouth.

Eyes
Keep your eyes about 10-15 m ahead of you.

Hands
Pretend you're holding an egg in each hand.

Arm angle
Maintain a 90 ° angle if possible and swing them vigorously.

Feet
Keep your feet parallel.

Body
Bend your body forward at a 5° angle.

Stride (cm) = Height (cm) − 100

Walking is better than running for cutting down on body fat, because it's easier and can be done for a longer amount of time.

The Order of a Step

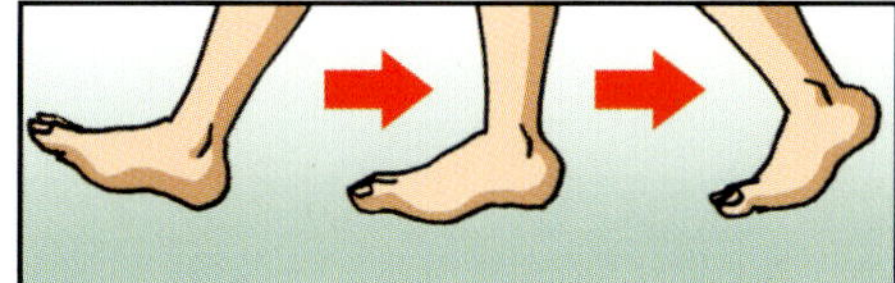

An Attack by Unidentified Assailants

You'd better not run away.
Of course not...

Oh... I should've exercised regularly.

I don't like scary gym instructors...
Drip Drip

Oh, no!
?!

Omji! What's going on?
The...the doctor, the doctor...
Rush

The doctor has been abducted!
What?

Ha ha ha
Vroom

We're going to be the richest men in the world, now that we have the sports robot and the doctor!

Groan Groan
Vroom

But is this really the universal sports robot? It looks too simple, somehow...
Float
The newer the product, the simpler the design! Be quiet if you don't know!
Float

The phone line is down, and I don't see any security guards.
Sob
Grandpa!
Tap
Tap

Huh? What's this?

I think it's Grandpa's key to the laboratory...

The First Encounter with Spot

Target detected! The name is Gomji!
Huh? I... I'm the target?

Whirr
Snap
Snap
Oh, it's a monster! Run!

Wait!
Sprint

Wow, it's so fast!
Slide
Screech

Ha ha ha! Gomji! Where do you think you're going, without your training?

I am programmed to train Gomji, no matter what. The name is Spot! I'm Spot, a universal sports robot.
Train?

The Hidden Sports in Science

Stretching and Physical Balance

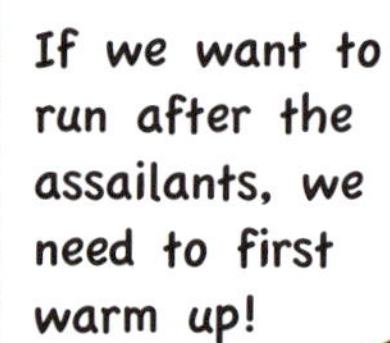

Simple stretching can dramatically increase the effect of exercise.

Stretching loosens up the tension in bones and muscles, and facilitates movement.
One, two!
One, two!

Warming up before exercise can prevent spasms or injury, such as a stretched ligament.
Oh, I have cramps in my leg...

By warming up, you can prepare your body for exercise, and use your capacity to its fullest.
I'm ready!

That's true! When I warm up before swimming, I don't get cramps in my legs easily.
One, two!
One, two!

Oh, that's why athletes warm up before a race!

In addition, stretching helps you maintain a normal body shape.

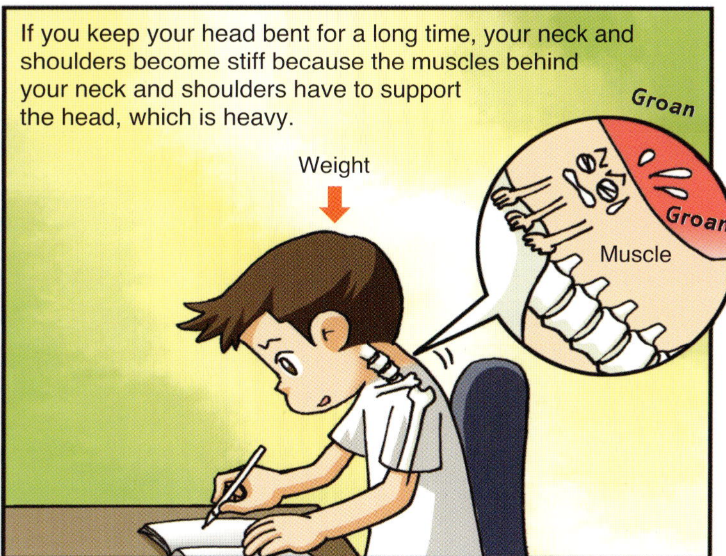

If you keep your head bent for a long time, your neck and shoulders become stiff because the muscles behind your neck and shoulders have to support the head, which is heavy.
Weight
Groan
Groan
Muscle

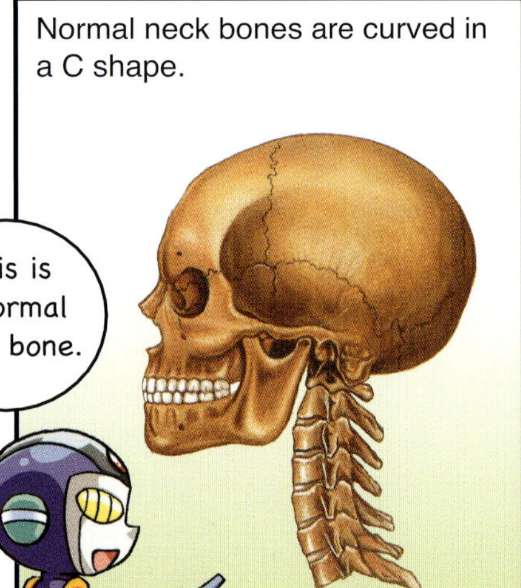

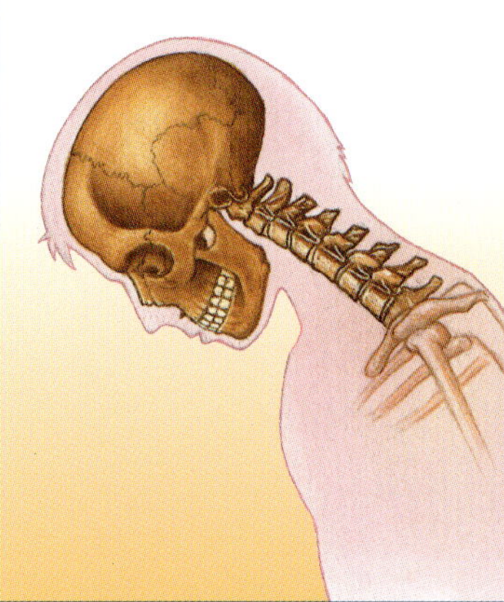

Various Types of Stretching

Stretching, in addition to being a warm-up exercise, helps you overcome fatigue and loosens up tense muscles by accelerating the breakdown of lactic acids after exercise.

Sideways shoulder stretching

Upper arm stretching

Shoulder and chest stretching

Shoulder stretching

Back and buttock stretching

Waist and shoulder stretching

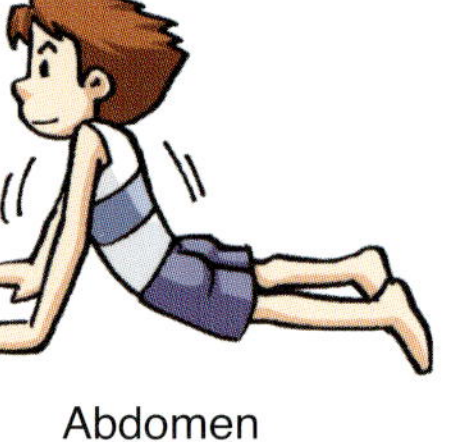

Abdomen stretching

The Science in Sprinting

The Starting Posture in Short Distance Running

In short distance running, starting speed is crucial for setting the record. You bend your body forward when you start out because when your waist is bent, the center of gravity becomes lower, decreasing inertia and allowing you to run faster in a stable posture. If you start out kicking the ground and taking full advantage of the "law of action and reaction*", the same amount of force with which you kicked the ground will propel you forward, making you run faster.

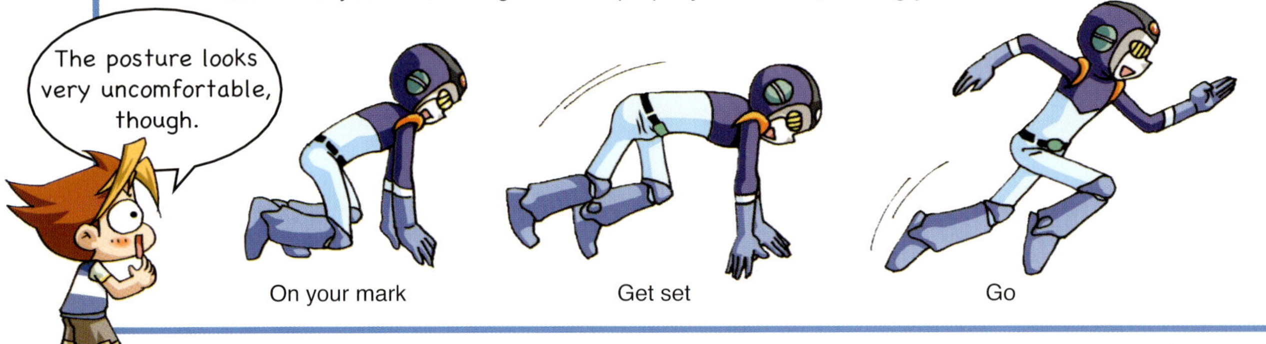

*The Law of Action and Reaction: When an object with mass pushes at something, it is pushed back by the same amount of force. The two forces are the same in size but opposite in direction.

The starting block is a means to increase starting speed, making the most out of the law of action and reaction.
The arms are easy to control because they're light. Swinging the arms faster makes your legs move faster, too. In addition, effective arm movement can help maintain the balance of the body.
And you can run faster if you swing your arms vigorously.

He seems to know something. Let's get him!
Whoosh

Now, let's run!
Zoom

Like this!
Who are those guys?
Yikes!
Ouch!
Yikes Ouch!

The Science in Long Distance Running

When running long distances, you must inhale through the nose and exhale through the mouth to avoid straining the throat.

Inhale through the nose.

Exhale through the mouth.

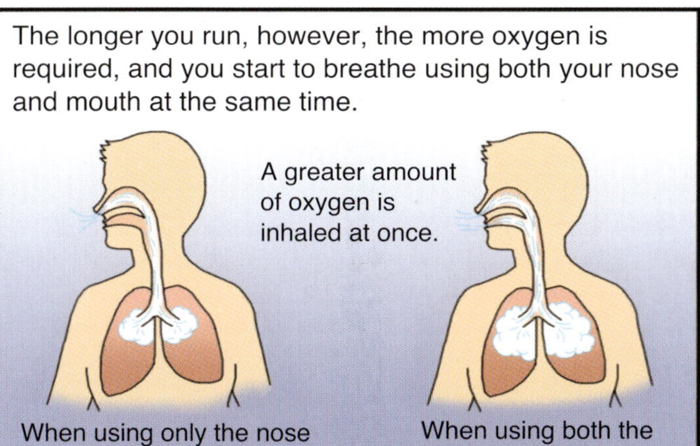

The longer you run, however, the more oxygen is required, and you start to breathe using both your nose and mouth at the same time.

Types of Respiration

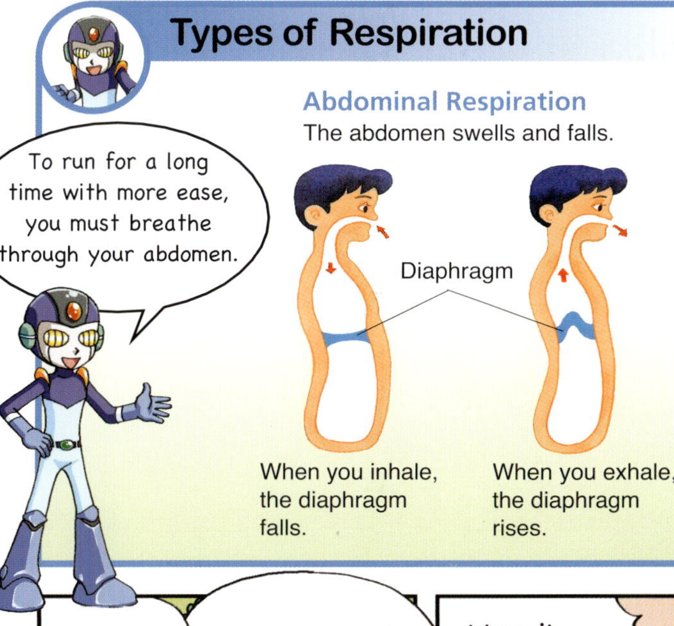

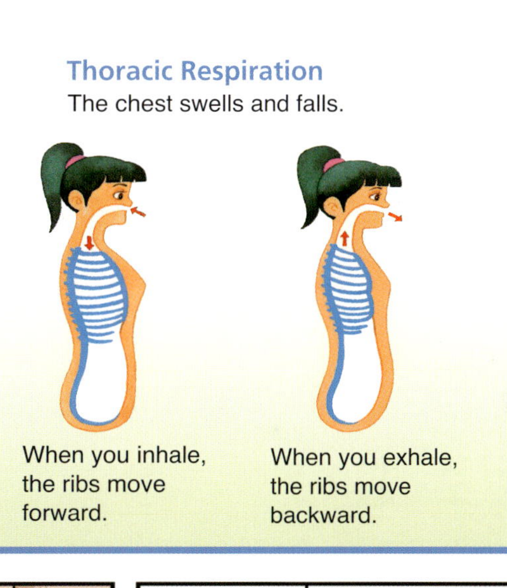

The Science in the Long Jump

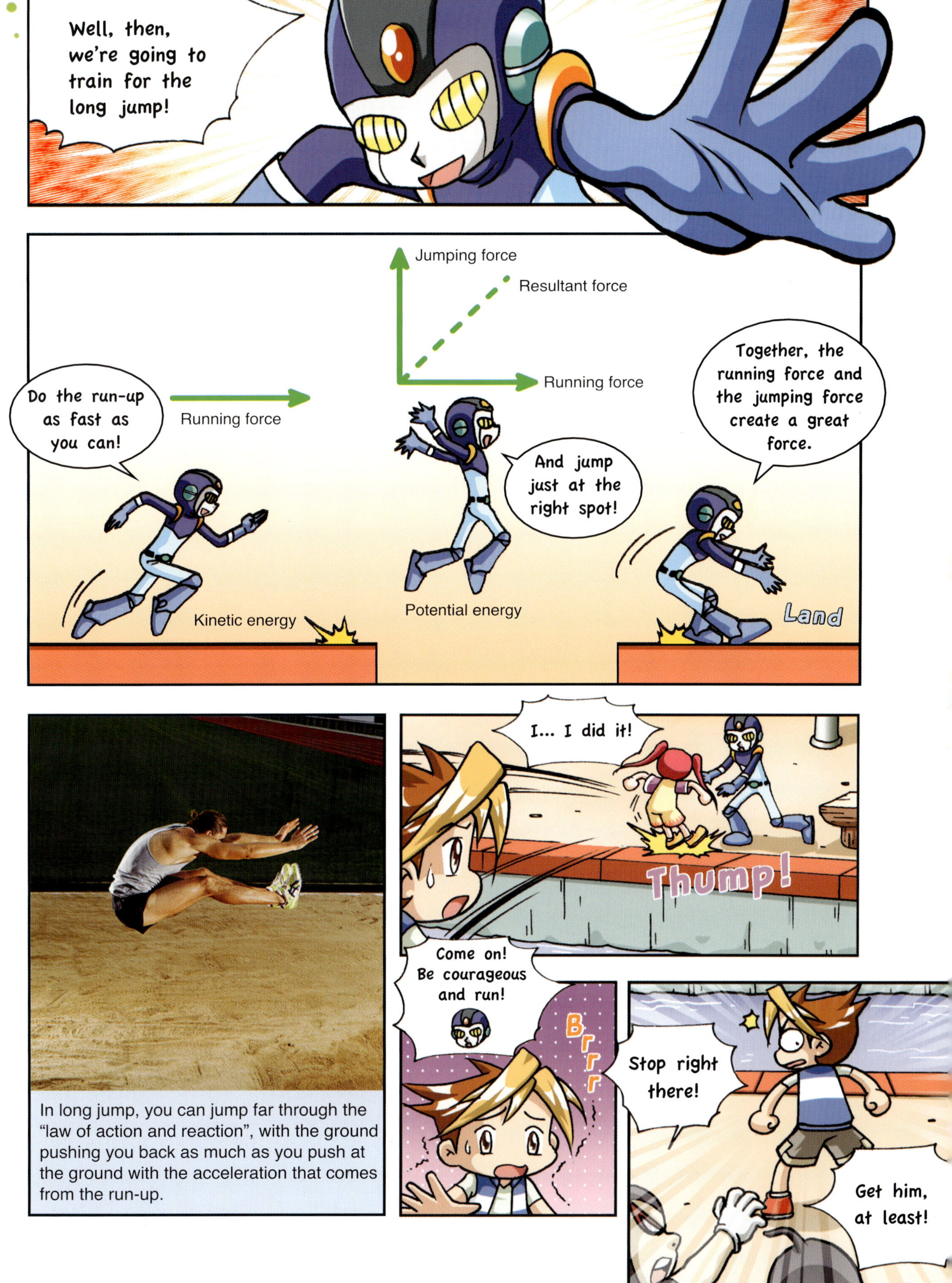

In long jump, you can jump far through the "law of action and reaction", with the ground pushing you back as much as you push at the ground with the acceleration that comes from the run-up.

The Science in Throwing

The greater the force and the lesser the mass, the greater the acceleration. The javelin, which is relatively light at 800 g, can gain great acceleration through a run-up. Also, the javelin, being long and lightweight, causes great air resistance, so it must be thrown with the direction of the wind in mind.

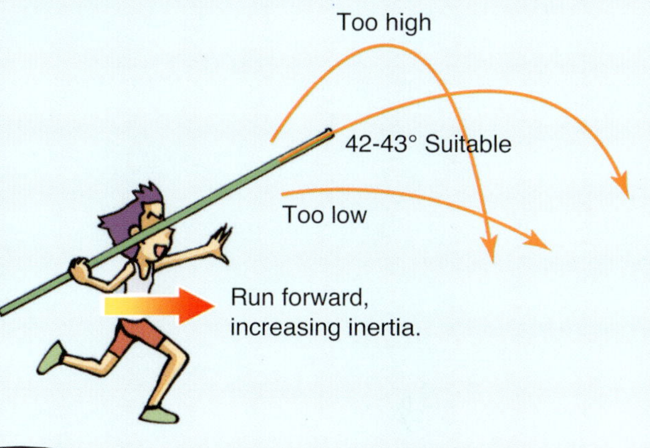

The Javelin
The run-up and the angle at which the javelin is thrown are critical.

In shot put, discus, and hammer throw the athlete spins around in place to gain centrifugal force.

The greater the mass, the faster the spin, and the bigger the radius of rotation, the greater the centrifugal force.

The Discus Throw
Rotary motion and timing of the throw are critical.

*Centrifugal Force: The tendency of an object in circular motion to move outwards.

The Science in the Pole Vault

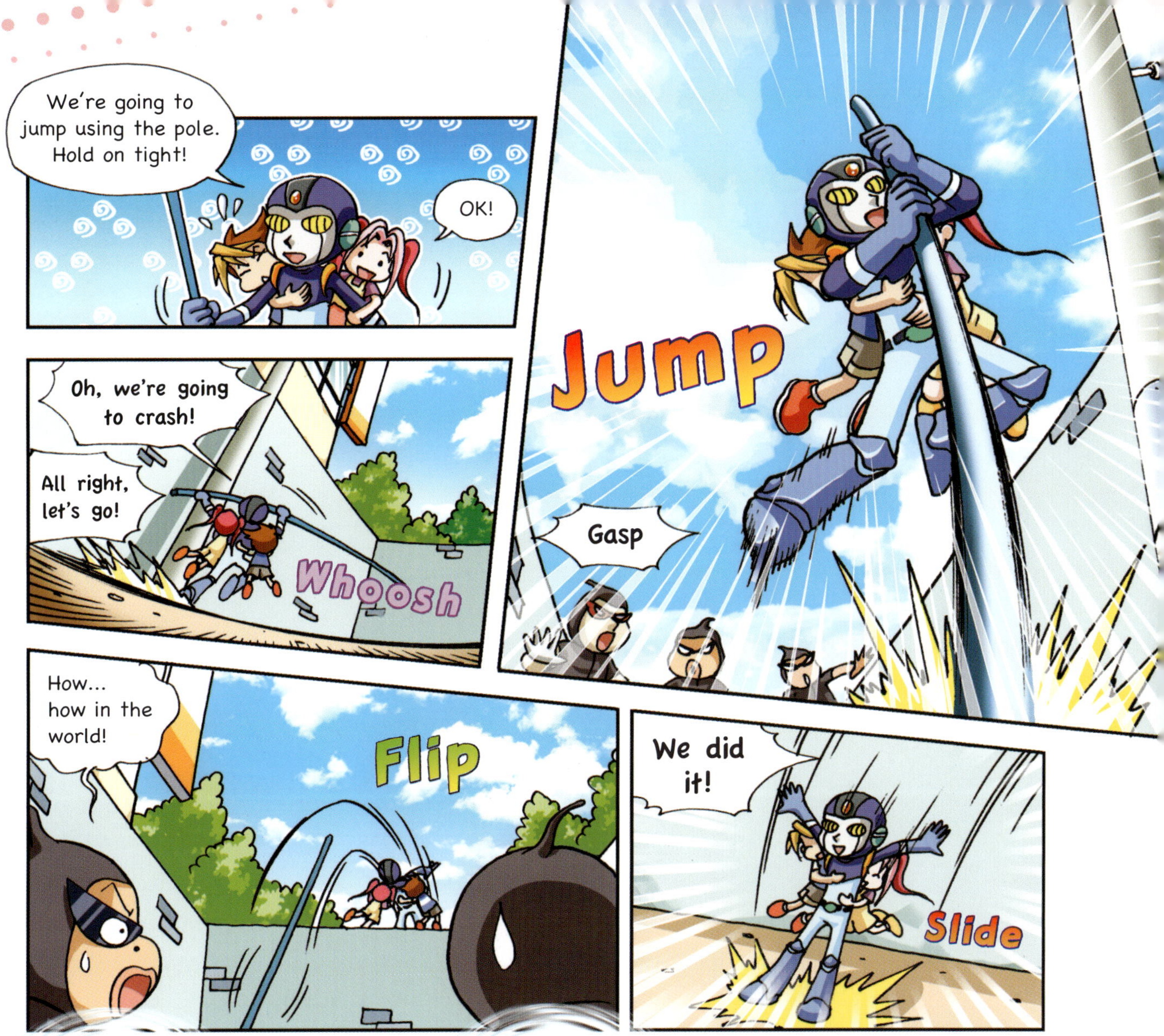

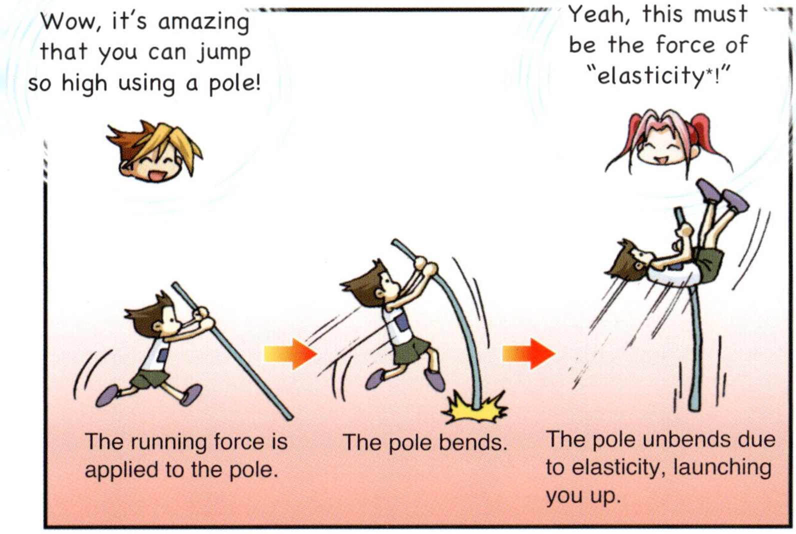

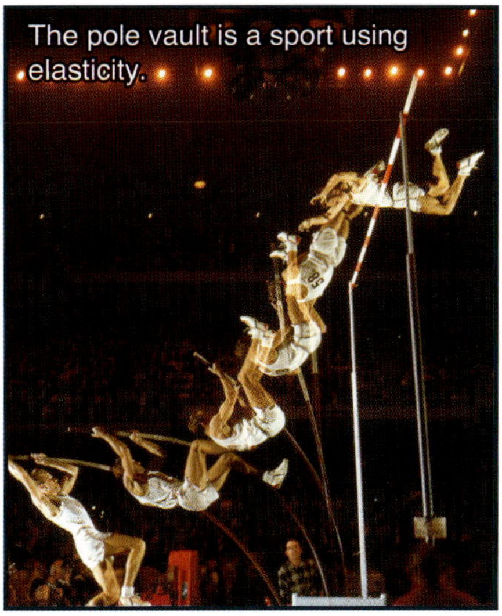

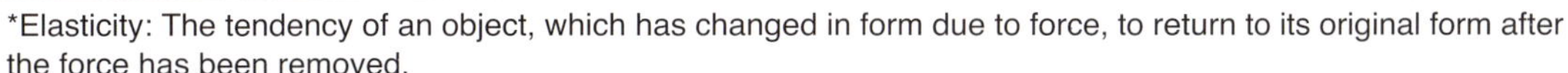

*Elasticity: The tendency of an object, which has changed in form due to force, to return to its original form after the force has been removed.

The Science in Swimming

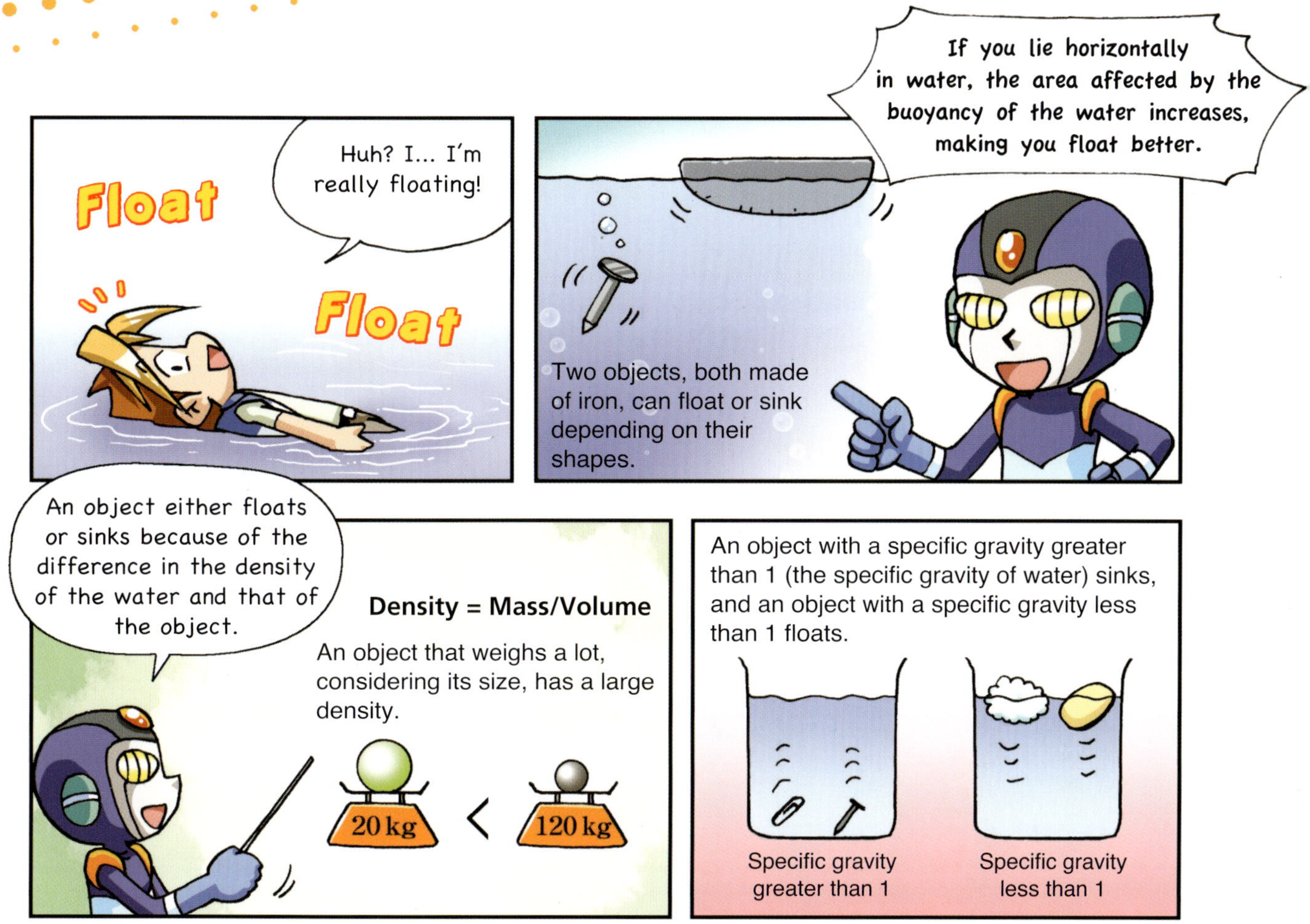

Density = Mass/Volume

An object that weighs a lot, considering its size, has a large density.

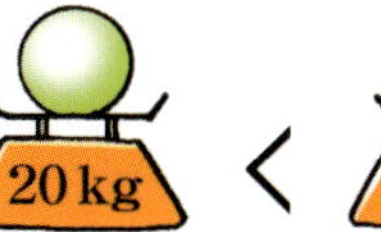 

An object with a specific gravity greater than 1 (the specific gravity of water) sinks, and an object with a specific gravity less than 1 floats.

The Specific Gravity of Body Parts

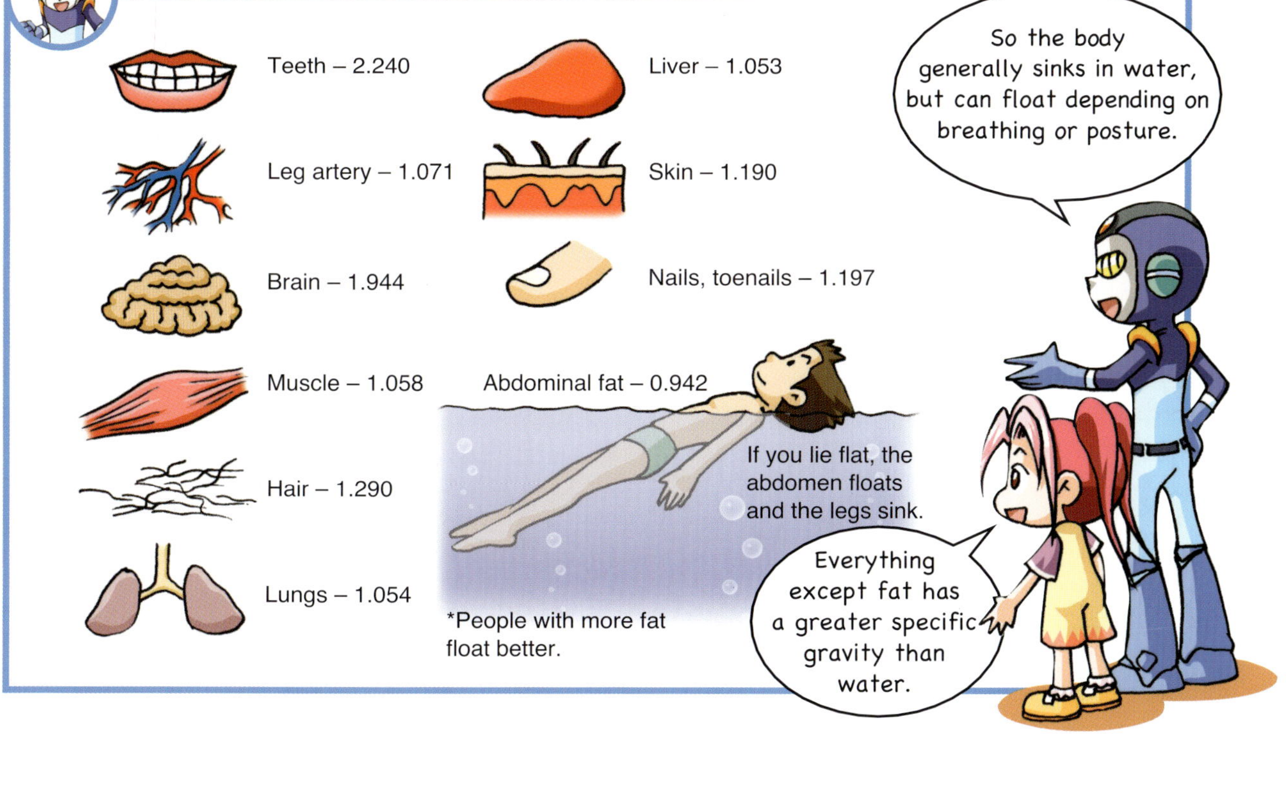

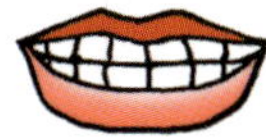 Teeth – 2.240

 Leg artery – 1.071

 Brain – 1.944

 Muscle – 1.058

 Hair – 1.290

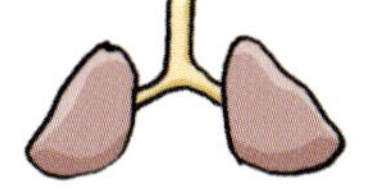 Lungs – 1.054

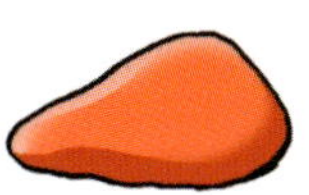 Liver – 1.053

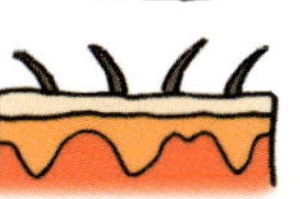 Skin – 1.190

 Nails, toenails – 1.197

Abdominal fat – 0.942

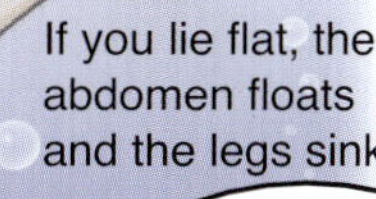
If you lie flat, the abdomen floats and the legs sink.

*People with more fat float better.

Come on, you can do better than that! Go jump in the water!

I can't swim...
I feel sick, just looking at the water...
Hurry, get them!

Oh...
Nyah!

Let's use the boat, then!
Oh, no!
Whoosh
Oh, we're in trouble!

Kick at the water, as though kicking at the ground, and it'll propel you forward. Come on, hurry!
But water is different from the ground!

When you kick at the ground, the ground pushes you back in the opposite direction. The force propels you forward.
The force with which you push the ground
Action
The force with which the ground pushes you
Reaction

There's nothing to kick at!
Flounder
Flounder
Thus, in outer space, which is almost a vacuum, you can't move forward, no matter how much you struggle.

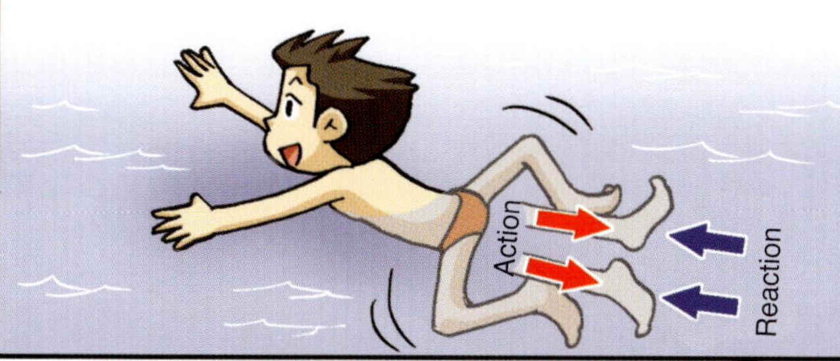

An object that has density, like water, is pushed back by the same amount of force with which it pushes. This is called "the law of action and reaction". The two forces, same in intensity, are opposite in direction.

Action
Reaction

So if you push the water using your arms and legs, you're propelled forward.

Swoosh

I can't move forward easily, though.

Splash
Splash

Don't flail around blindly. Take on a pose in which you can push back as much water as possible.

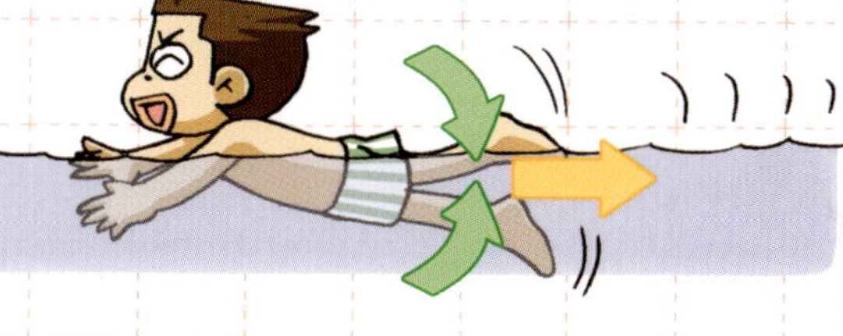

You have to move your arms and legs purposefully so that you can push back as much water as possible.

Wow! I really am moving forward!

Splash
Splash

What kind of a swimming style is that? My specialty is breaststroke.

Spot, can you tell me about different swimming styles?

Yes, there are pros and cons to each style.

Various Swimming Styles

Freestyle

Freestyle is an unregulated swimming form used in swimming competitions. The front crawl is used the most often because it is the fastest. Respiratory control is very important in the front crawl because the face goes in and out of the water.

Backstroke

The backstroke is a swimming style in which you lie straight on your back with your face above the water, enabling you to breathe at all times. The arms make alternate strokes, and the feet, stretched out in a straight line, move up and down in the water.

Breaststroke

The breaststroke is divided into two styles, one in which you swim a relatively long distance with your head above the water, and one in which you submerge your head below the water, coming up only to take a breath. You contract and expand your arms like a frog to move forward, so it's important to keep the arm movement, leg movement, and breathing in harmony.

Butterfly

The butterfly is a swimming style in which both arms and legs are used all at once to move the body forward like a wave. The motion in which the two arms stretch forward, pulling the water down, is compared to that of a butterfly.

Sharks can swim fast because the v-shaped scales, called denticles, on their skin reduce the friction resistance. Full body swimsuits are designed with a surface that mimics the rough shark denticles. They help increase speed.

Full body swimsuits help increase speed by pushing back the whirlpool created through the contact between the water and the body and reducing friction. They also firm up thigh muscles so that they can exert greater force.

Shark denticles

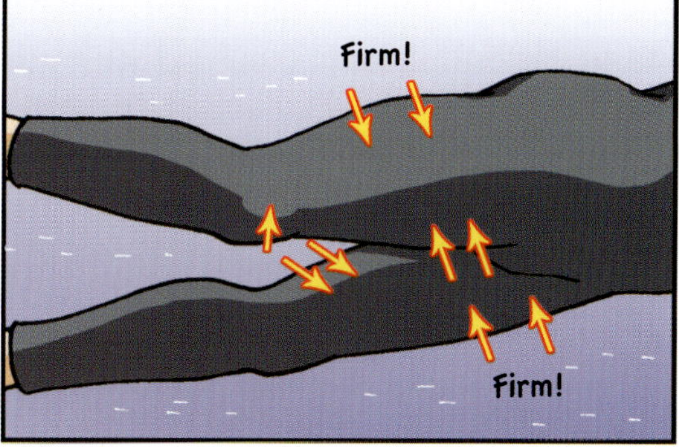

Ian Thorpe in a full body swimsuit

Ian Thorpe, a world-renowned swimmer, swam in a full body swimsuit in the 2000 Sydney Olympics and won three gold medals. FINA, the world governing body of swimming, issued the regulations banning the full body swimsuit in Jan. 1, 2010 after much controversy.

Tae-Hwan Park in half-body swimsuit

Tae-Hwan Park at the 2007 FINA World Aquatics Championships in half-body swimsuit which was 15% lighter than ordinary swimsuits and had 20% less resistance.

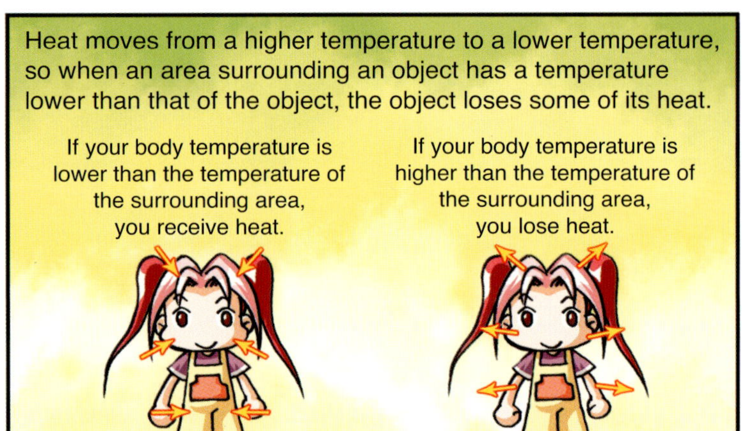
Heat moves from a higher temperature to a lower temperature, so when an area surrounding an object has a temperature lower than that of the object, the object loses some of its heat.

Hypothermia

Hypothermia occurs when the body temperature drops below 35°C, usually after a person falls into cold water or is exposed to cold air, snow, or ice over a long period of time. Symptoms include chill, reduced muscle activity, and disturbance of consciousness.

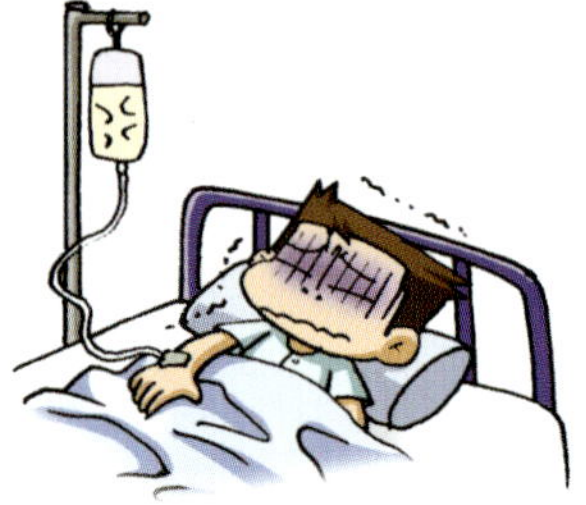

Temperature below 35°C
Major organs, such as the heart, brain, and lungs, start to function poorly.

Temperature below 27°C
The pulse becomes unstable.

Temperature below 25°C
The heart stops.

If a person shows symptoms of hypothermia and is still conscious, his body must be wiped down and wrapped in a blanket, and he must be given something warm to drink to increase his body temperature.

The Science in Shooting

*In actual paintball games, protective gear must be worn at all times and care must be taken against injury in short-distance shooting. Some of the contents in this book have been modified for a cartoon-like style.

Over there!
Be careful.
They have guns!

Don't come close!
We're going to shoot
if you do!
A paintball gun

Ha ha, you can't
hit us with a lousy
gun like that!
Flit

F... fire!
Ping
Ping

Ha ha,
what are you
trying to shoot?
We don't
even need to
dodge...
Whiz

Ow!
Thwack

You can't hit
the target shooting
like that! There's
science in shooting,
too!
Is there
anything you're
good at?
Oh, my head!

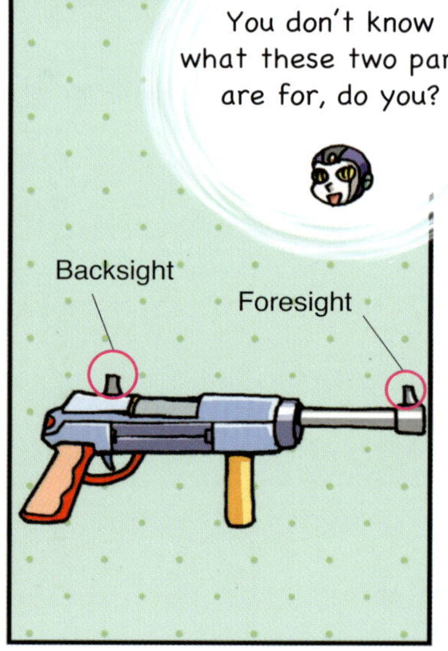
You don't know
what these two parts
are for, do you?
Backsight
Foresight

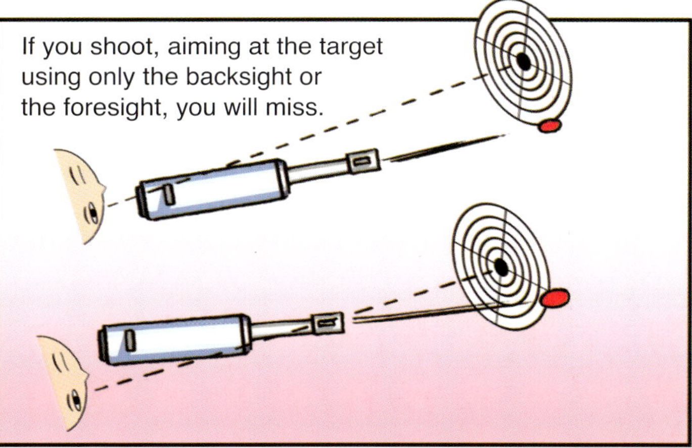

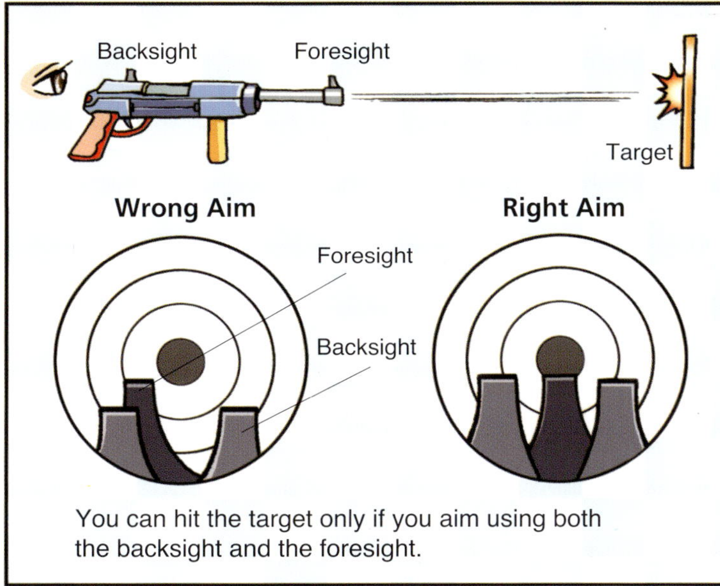

You can hit the target only if you aim using both the backsight and the foresight.

The aim is right when the eye, the backsight, the foresight, and the target are aligned in a straight line.

Ha ha, serves you right!

Gasp!
Ping
Ping

This is for you!
Ping
Ping

I can't hit them, they're too far away...

Ouch!
Thwack

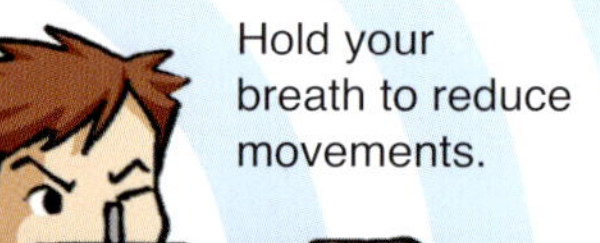

Huh? Spot hit the villain.
He must be using a better gun...
Ping

It's not the gun, it's the posture. Even if you're aiming right, you can't hit the target if your posture isn't stable.
Hold your breath to reduce movements.
Keep your shoulders close to prevent the gun from moving.

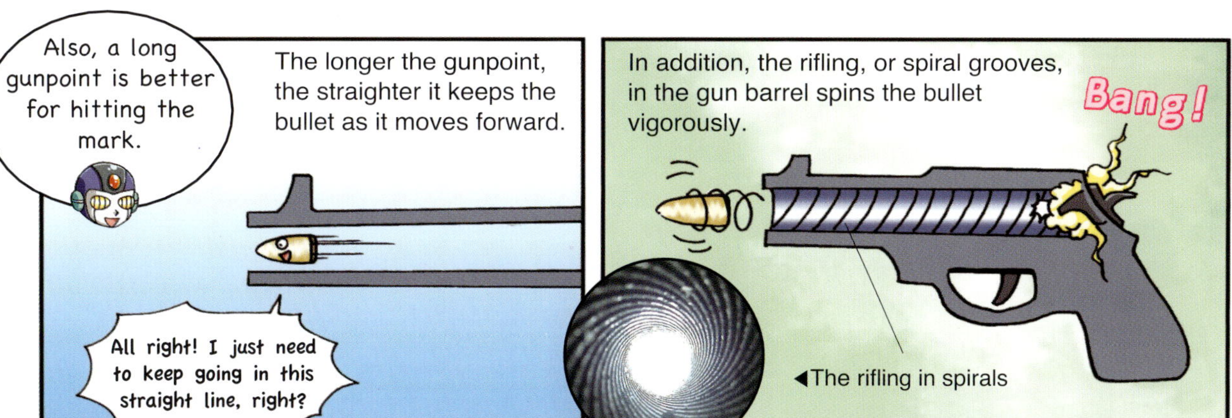

The Difference Between an Air Gun and a Rifle

Air Gun

An air gun fires bullets by means of compressed air or other gas. There are three types of air guns. Spring-piston guns operate by means of a coiled steel spring loaded piston. Gas spring guns use pressurized air or nitrogen held in a chamber built into the piston. Pneumatic air guns utilize pre-compressed air as the source of energy to propel the projectile. An air gun has a shorter range* than a rifle.

Rifle

A rifle is a weapon that launches one, or many, bullets at high velocity through burning of a propellant which pushes the bullet forward. A rifle, though it has a longer range than an air pistol, is noisy and the barrel vibrates more after shooting.

*Range: The maximum distance a bullet can reach.

The Science in Archery

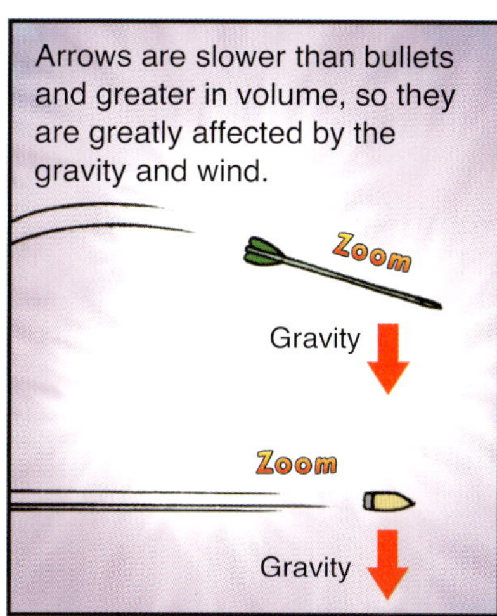

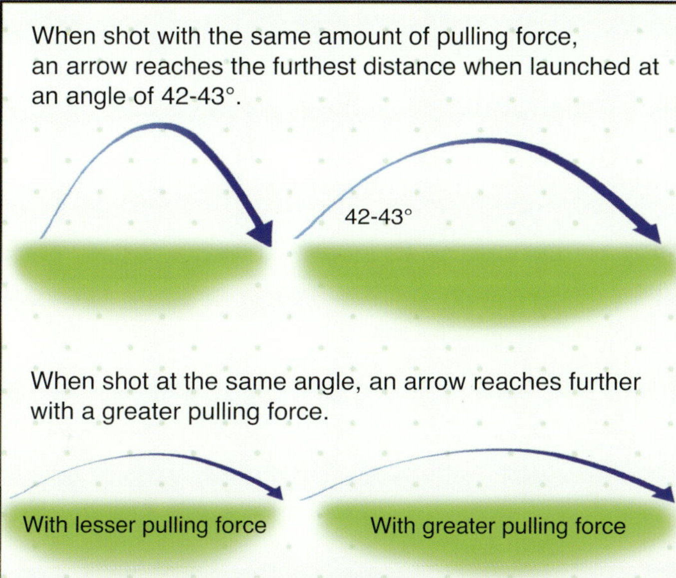

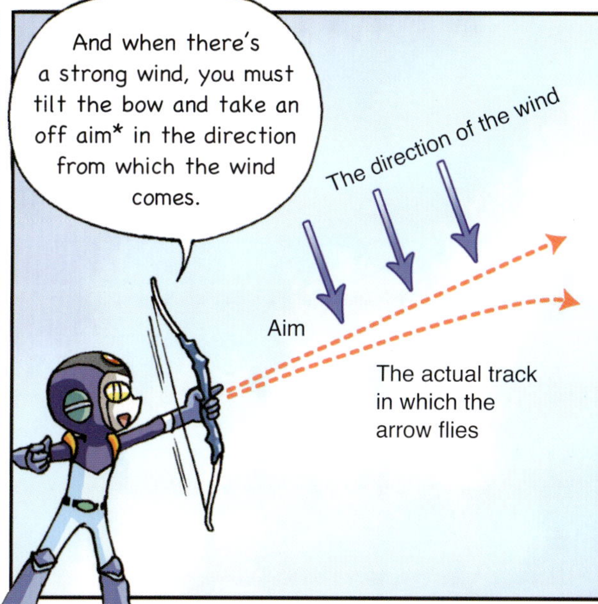

*Off aim: An aim in a direction different from that of the target

The fletching increases the stability of the flight by reducing the shaking of the arrow.

If the size of the fletching is inconsistent, or if it is damaged, the arrow can go in a wrong direction.

How Bulletproof Clothing Works

Bulletproof clothing is made with densely compressed glass fiber woven into a web. When a spinning bullet touches the clothing, the glass fiber, with its strength and elasticity, stops the bullet by wrapping itself around the bullet and absorbing the bullet's kinetic energy. In addition, the resistance of the clothing crushes the front of the bullet, increasing the surface area of the bullet which helps the bullet to come to a stop by rapidly reducing its force.

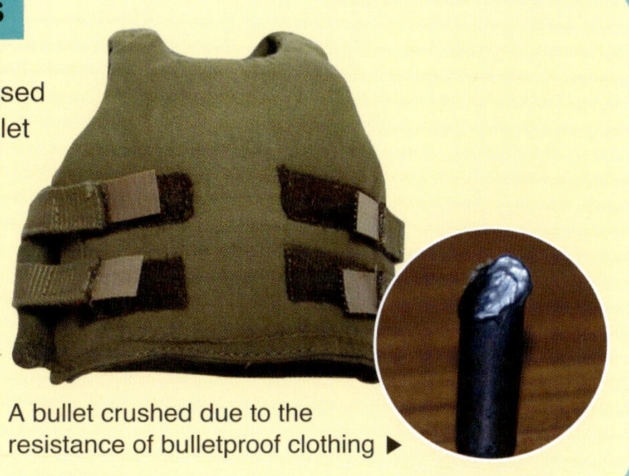

A bullet crushed due to the resistance of bulletproof clothing ▶

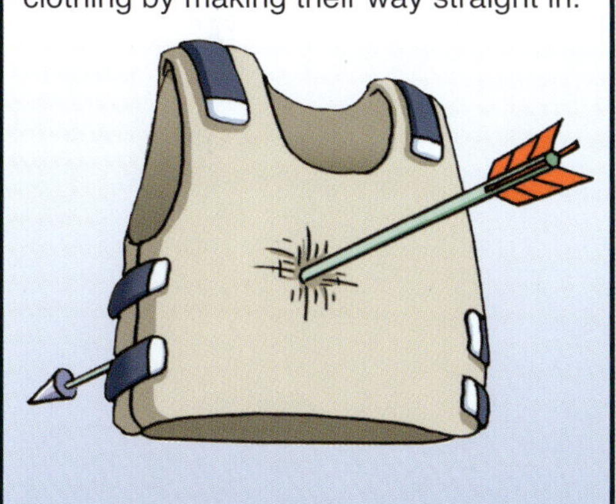

Because arrows are sharp and do not spin, they can penetrate bulletproof clothing by making their way straight in.

The Science in Cycling

The Principle of a Wheel and Axle

Using the principle of a wheel and axle, a bicycle can produce greater force with lesser force.

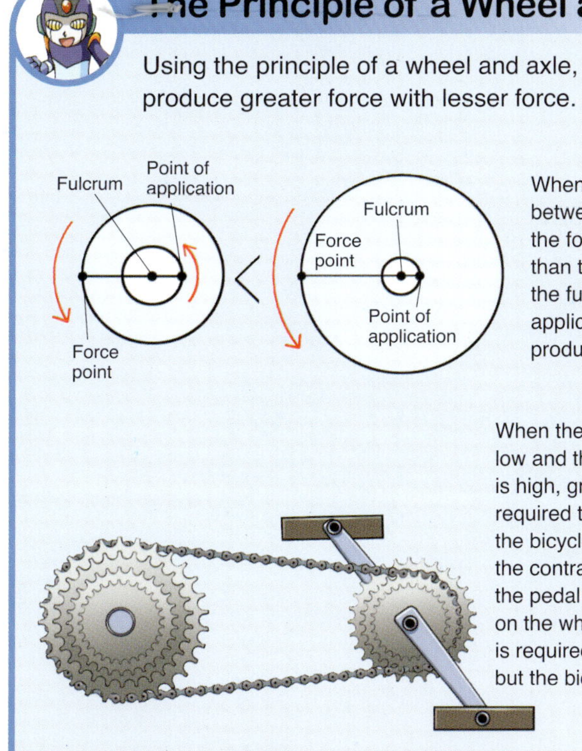

When the distance between the fulcrum and the force point is greater than the distance between the fulcrum and the point of application, greater force is produced.

When the gear on the pedal is low and the gear on the wheel is high, greater power is required to push the pedals but the bicycle moves slowly. On the contrary, when the gear on the pedal is high and the gear on the wheel is low, less power is required to push the pedal but the bicycle moves fast.

When you're starting out or going uphill, lower the pedal gear so that you may ride with less exertion.

When you're speeding up or going downhill, raise the pedal gear, since not as much exertion is required due to inertia.

A track bicycle is made so that the wind passes by without causing much friction.

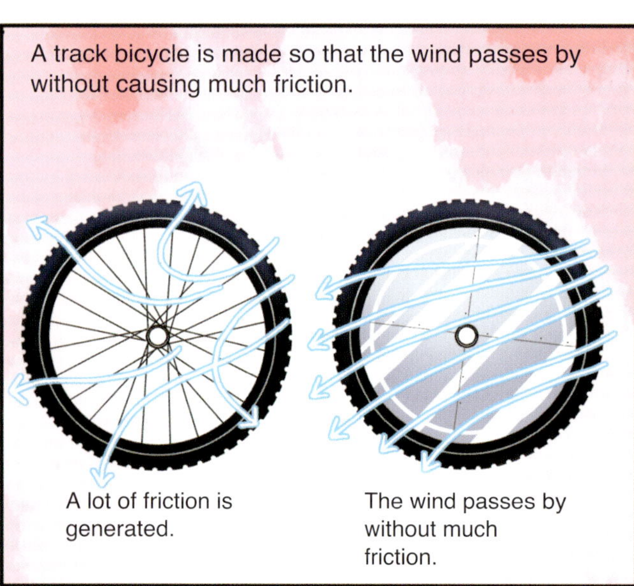

Velodrome

A velodrome is an arena with steeply banked oval tracks for track cycling.

When looking at a short track or cycling helmet, you can notice that the front of the helmet is round while the back is pointy. Such a shape is used to reduce friction with the air to increase speed.

Regular helmet

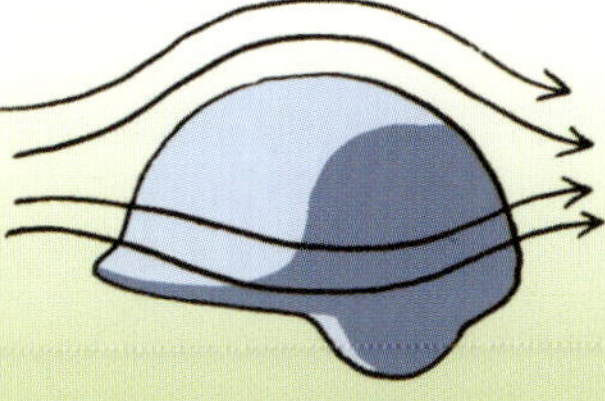

Speed decreases due to the air that pulls back the helmet.

Special helmet

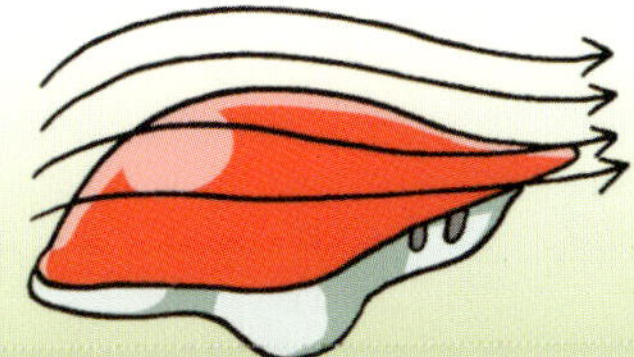

The air in the back glides by smoothly.

Sports Helmets for Safety

Cycling helmet

Short track helmet

Inline helmet

The Science in Skating

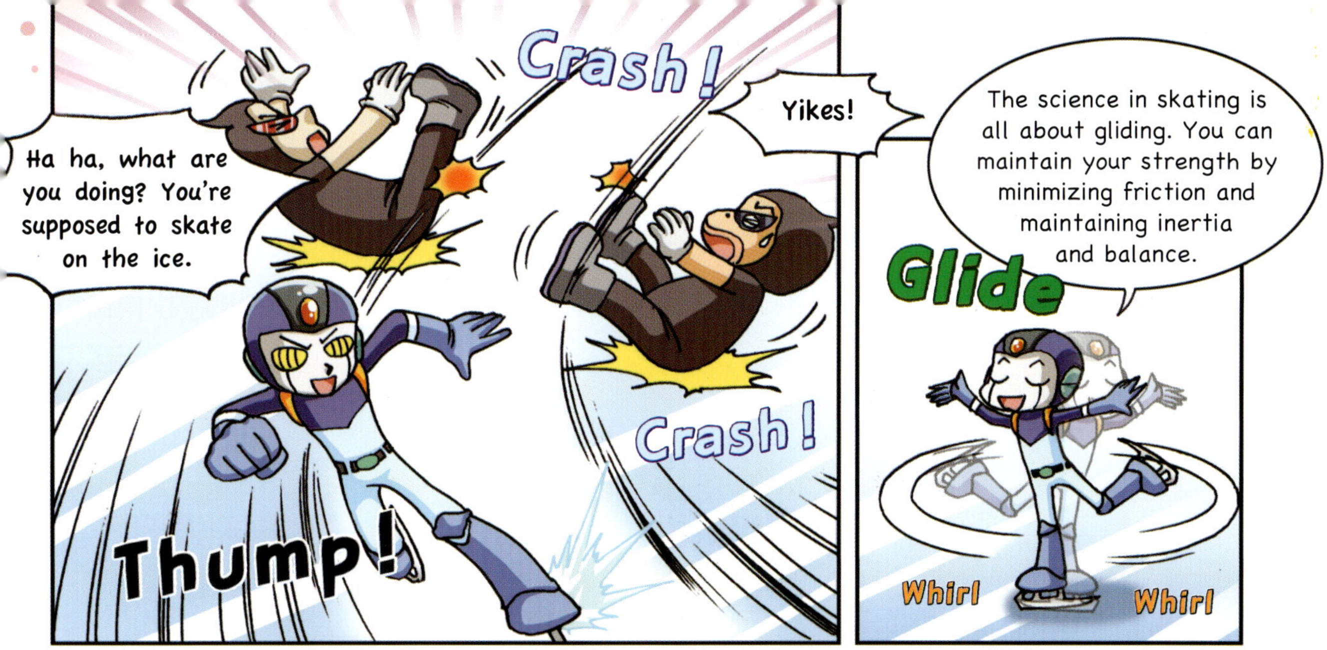

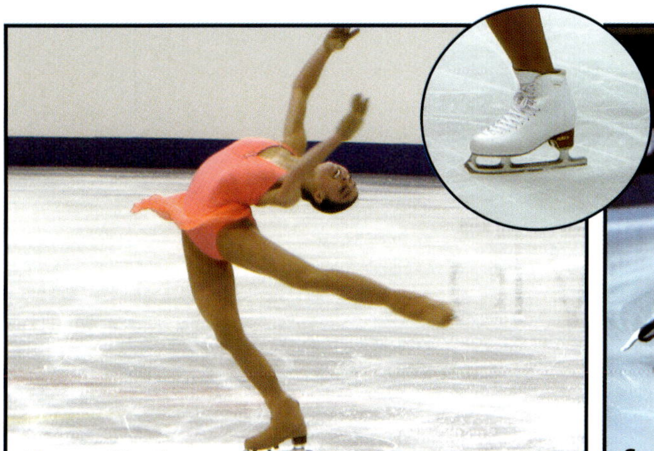

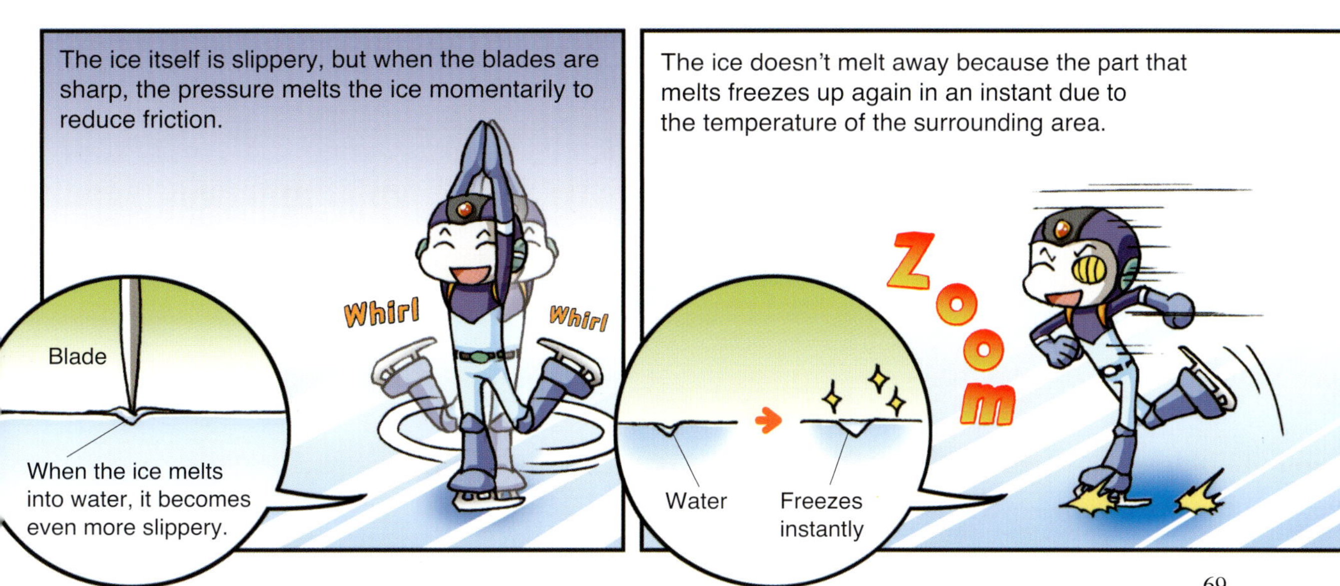

Figure Skating
The blades are short and thick, because various movements are required.

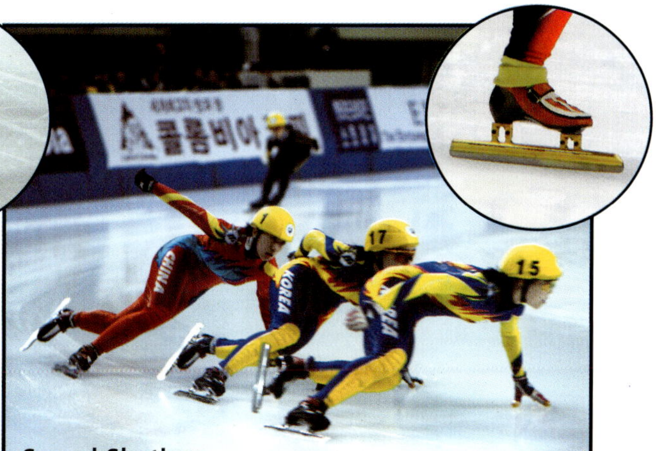

Speed Skating
The blades are long and thin, to minimize friction and keep the skater from veering off.

The ice itself is slippery, but when the blades are sharp, the pressure melts the ice momentarily to reduce friction.

The ice doesn't melt away because the part that melts freezes up again in an instant due to the temperature of the surrounding area.

Skid
Finished!
Wow!
Clap
Clap
It is a sports robot, after all... But that can't stop us!
We can just pour sand on the ice!
Then we'll have the advantage!
Swoosh
Swoosh
Hold on to me, everyone!
They're getting away again! Get them!
Whoosh
Swoosh
Rush
Wow, it's full of snow in here and it's not even winter yet!
It's so bright!
Swing

The Science in Skiing

Artificial snow is made by forcing water and pressurized gas through a snow machine. When the water and pressurized gas are mixed, the gas becomes low in pressure and takes heat away from the water droplets, causing the water droplets to freeze.

The gas suddenly expands and takes heat from its environment.

The water droplets lose their heat momentarily and crystallize to form snow.

Now, don't be scared and bend your body keeping your legs straight.

The lower you bend, the easier it becomes to find your balance because the center of gravity becomes lower.

When you go from a straight line to a curved line, the kinetic energy is reduced due to the friction with the snow and speed is reduced as well.

When you move in a curve, you must bend inward to create centripetal force*, to keep yourself from being pushed outward due to the centrifugal force*.

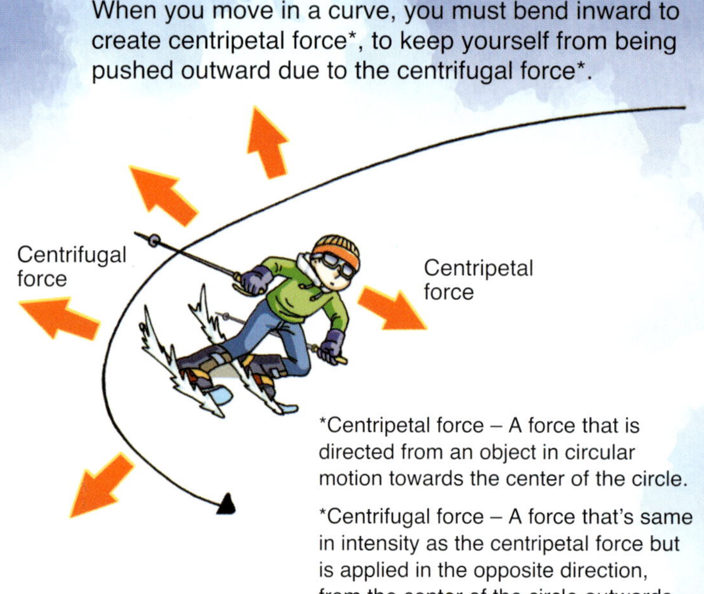

*Centripetal force – A force that is directed from an object in circular motion towards the center of the circle.

*Centrifugal force – A force that's same in intensity as the centripetal force but is applied in the opposite direction, from the center of the circle outwards.

How Skis Stay on the Snow

When you walk on snow, your feet sink into the snow. Why don't they sink in when you're wearing skis?
Your feet sink into the snow because of gravity. But when you're wearing skis, the pressure that was concentrated on the soles of your feet becomes dispersed, reducing the pressure in a given area and allowing you to stay on the snow.

The Science in Basketball

But if you don't pass the tests, the training continues!
What? Tests?
The first test is to shoot this basketball through the hoop.
You need to make three baskets standing on this spot.
Flick
Slap
Slam
That's easy! If I throw the ball ten times, it should go through the hoop at least once.
You pass the test only if you make three consecutive baskets.
Gasp
Wow, it went through! One!
Slap
Oh, the second one didn't.
Slam
Start over!

The Chance of Scoring a Basket

The chance of scoring a basket increases when the ball draws an arc and falls from right above the basket, and decreases when the ball goes in from the side.

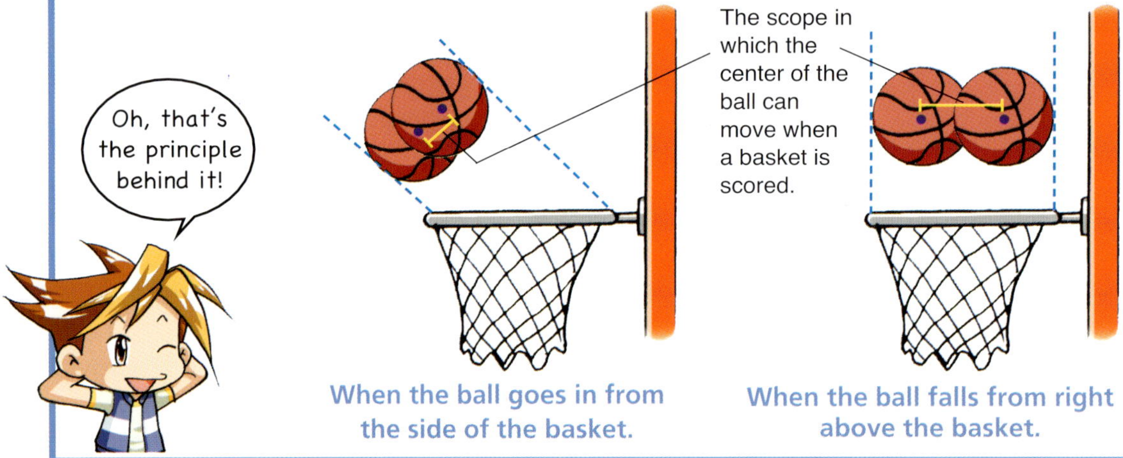

Tips for a Jump Shot

When you jump up and reach the maximum point, stretch out your arm and shoot, pushing the ball with a snap of the wrist. You can make a stable shot only when you maintain your balance in the air, so make a jump the moment you come to a stop. Bend your knees sufficiently and jump as high as possible; the more you bend your legs, the higher you can soar, but if you crouch down too low, your leg muscles will stretch out and you won't be able to make as great an exertion.

Jump shot

Why Do Basketballs Have Little Bumps?

The little bumps on a basketball increase friction with hands so that the ball doesn't slip away easily. The little bumps also help the basketball spin. The surface of a new ball is too rough, reducing the accuracy of passes and shots, and an old ball slips away too easily from hands, so in a basketball game a ball that has been tamed enough is used.

A basketball can be spun to change its direction, and the little bumps on the surface help the ball spin.

The Science in Soccer

It wouldn't be a test to score a goal in this big goalpost without any obstacles, would it?
Well, but...
How can you kick the ball when the goalpost is all blocked!
Well, let me show you!
Zip
Slam
Whirr
Slap
Wow, Spot!
Wow, the ball bent like a banana and went right in!
Ha ha, that's why they call it a banana kick when the ball draws a curve like this.
Spot, the secret's in the shoes, isn't it?
What are you talking about? The secret's in the spinning ball!

The upper surfaces of airplane wings are curved and the lower surfaces are flat, which allows air to flow faster on the upper surfaces than on the lower surfaces. This reduces the pressure on the upper side and increases the pressure on the lower side. Because air flows from an area with higher pressure to an area with lower pressure, the plane takes off due to the lifting force that pushes the wings up from below.

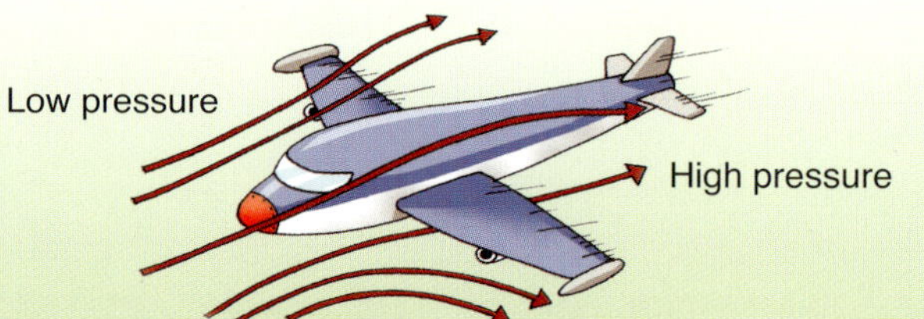

The Magnus Effect of a Soccer Ball

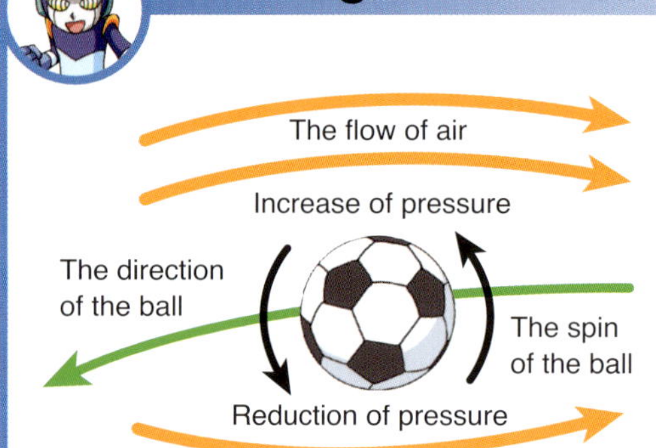

The air travels faster relative to the center of the ball where the periphery of the ball is moving in the same direction as the airflow, which reduces the pressure. The opposite effect happens on the other side of the ball, where the air travels slower relative to the center of the ball, which increases the pressure. As air travels from an area with higher pressure to an area with lower pressure, the ball bends and moves from an area with higher pressure to an area with lower pressure. This phenomenon in which a spinning object bends due to difference in pressure is called the "Magnus effect".

When you kick the ball with an inward spin, it bends inward.

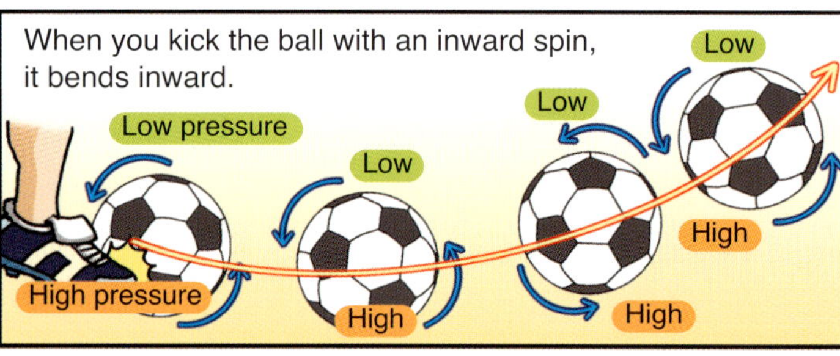

When you kick the ball with an outward spin, it bends in the opposite direction.

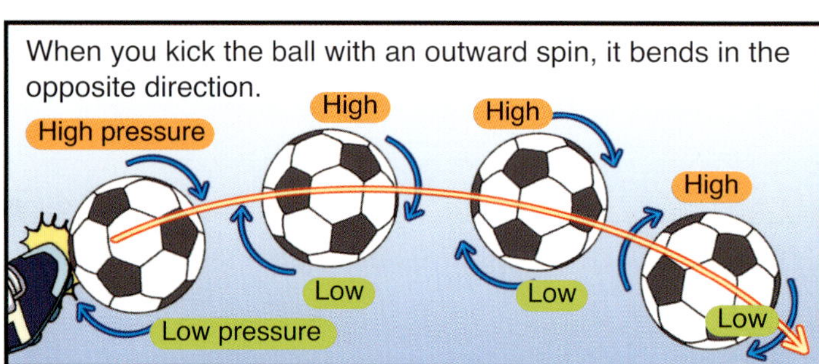

Now, I'm going to show you a real magic kick!
Zip
Shoot
Why are you kicking it that way?
Slap
Huh? The ball is bending all of a sudden!
Swoosh
How did the ball that was flying in a straight line suddenly go into the goalpost?
It couldn't have taken on a spin all of a sudden...

Was the secret in the shoes, after all?

It wasn't spinning when it was flying in a straight line?
Yes, it was spinning when it was flying in a straight line.

So why didn't it bend at first?
Because the secret's in the shoes...

That's because in the moment the ball is kicked, it's going too fast to be affected by the change in the pressure.

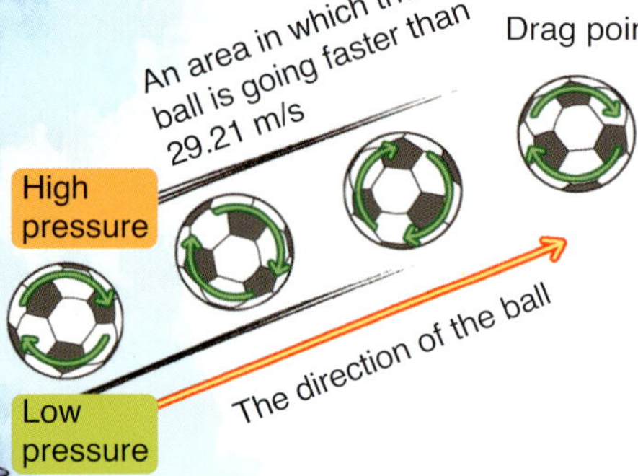

When the ball is going faster than 29.21 m/s (Drag point = Reynolds number*), it isn't affected by the change in the pressure, but when it slows down and the speed drops below the Reynolds number, it bends due to the spinning.

An area in which the ball is going faster than 29.21 m/s
Drag point
High pressure
Low pressure
The direction of the ball

*Reynolds number: The value of the boundary condition between turbulent flow and laminar flow when an object is placed in a moving fluid.

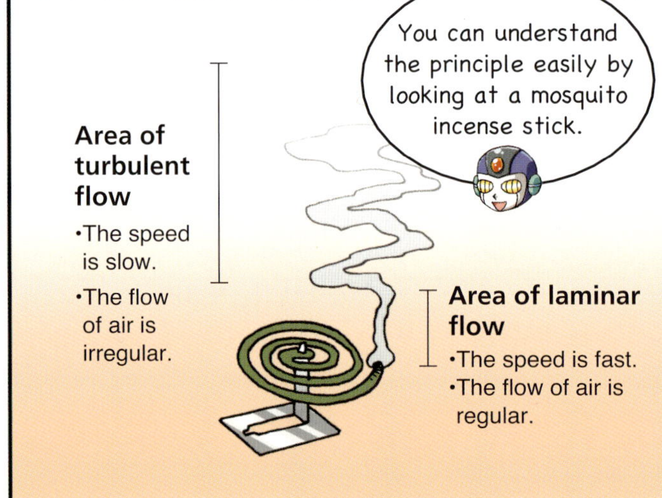

You can understand the principle easily by looking at a mosquito incense stick.

Area of turbulent flow
•The speed is slow.
•The flow of air is irregular.

Area of laminar flow
•The speed is fast.
•The flow of air is regular.

Carlos, who is famous for kicking the ball at a speed above the Reynolds number

Wow, I did it, too!
Slap

You don't think you passed the test, just by scoring a goal in a goalpost without a goalkeeper, do you?

I'll be the goalkeeper this time, so give it a try.
You can stand a lot closer and there aren't any obstacles.

All right! From this distance, it doesn't matter if there's a goalkeeper!
Wham

Thump

Again!
Wham

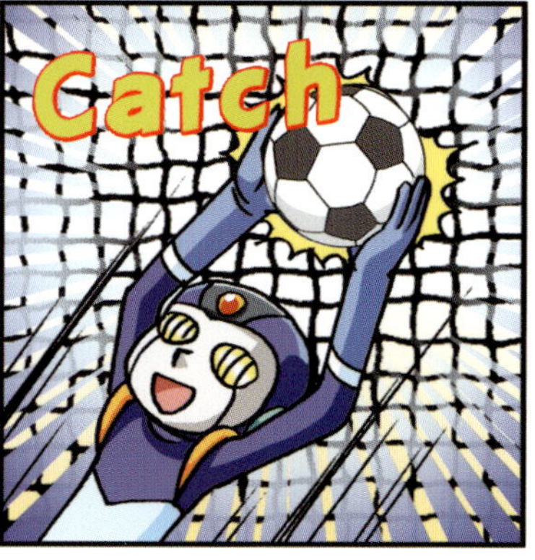

Catch

I'm going to go up closer and then kick the ball!
Zip

Oh!
Zip

Catch

The goalkeeper was out of the goal and you still didn't score?
You try scoring! It's hard to shoot the ball when the goalkeeper is near you.

The goalkeeper runs out when the opponent runs towards the goal with the ball, to reduce the shooting angle.

Plenty of space exists for shooting the ball.

The space is reduced.

If you make a pass as in the picture, the space in front becomes unoccupied, so the goalkeeper comes out only at critical moments.

Passes that Facilitate the Flow of a Game

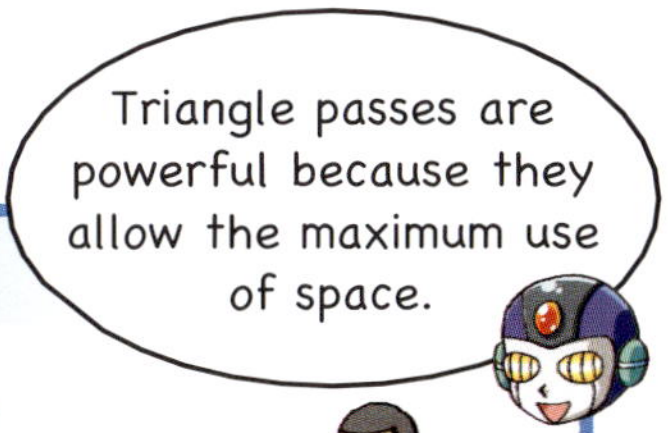

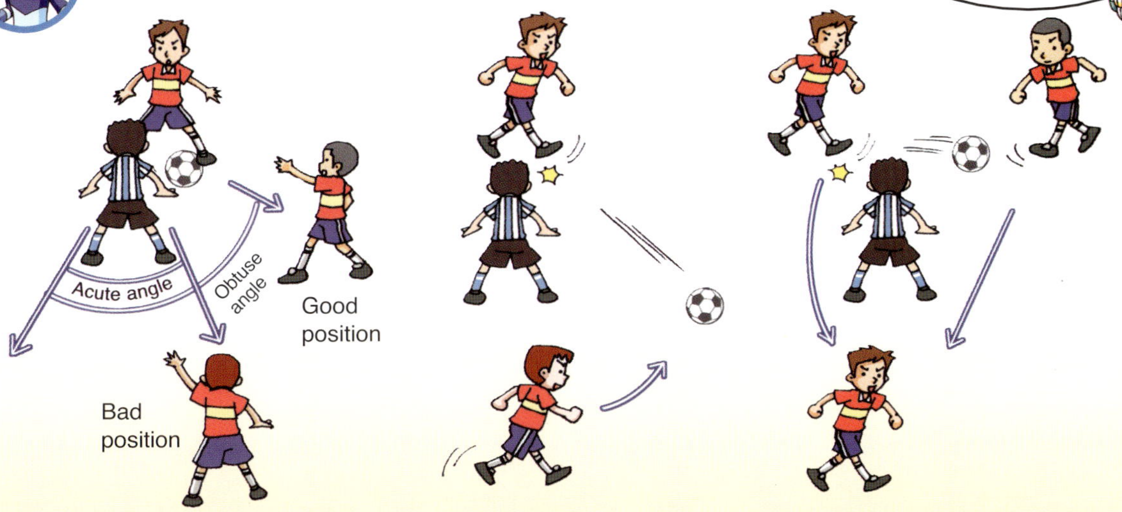

Obtuse Angle Pass

When you're at a position with an acute angle, the defense can take the ball away from you.

Space Pass

Pass the ball into an area where a player on your team can take it.

Triangle Pass

Pass the ball past the defense to a teammate around you.

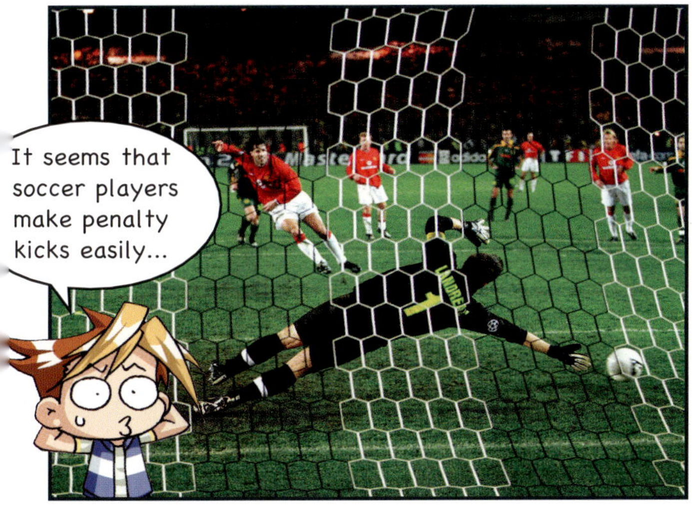

A penalty kick is made 11 m away from the goal line. The distance has been determined according to the speed of the ball and the speed of the goalkeeper's reaction. If the distance is more than 11 m, a good goalkeeper can catch the ball.

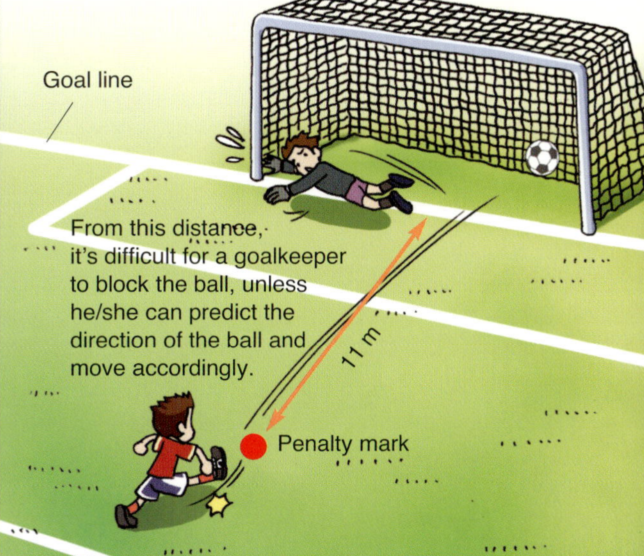

But the thing is, you can't make as strong a shot as soccer players do!
Oh, I forget how the offense shoots ...
Oh! I remember!
Oh, you're coming up close again?
OK, so first I kick the ball lightly.
Tap
And now, shoot!
Swoosh
No way!
He he, I tricked you!
Oh!
Tap
Oh! I missed!
Kick
Duh, how can you miss when the goal is empty?
Thunk

An offense can deceive an opponent through using feints. When using a feint, the center of gravity is focused on the next movement.

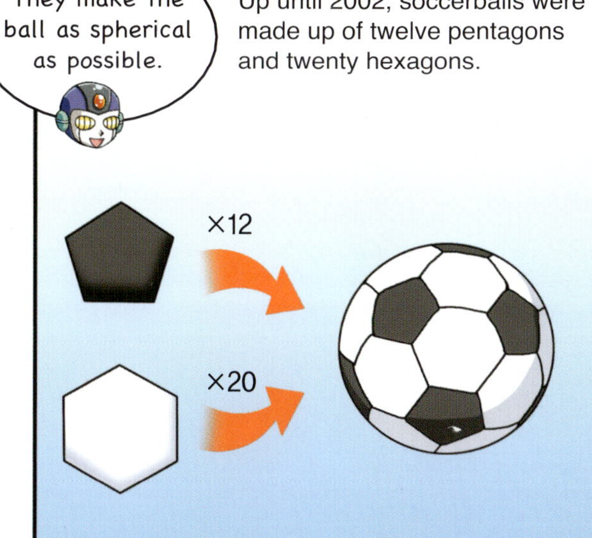

Up until 2002, soccerballs were made up of twelve pentagons and twenty hexagons.

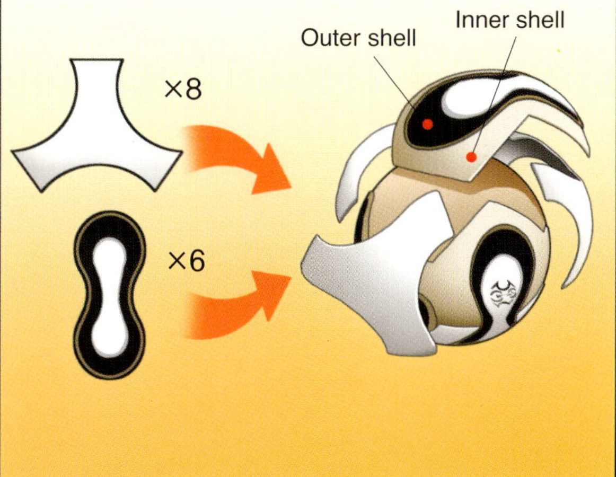

The Teamgeist, developed in 2006, is even more spherical with 14 separate pieces, and more stable with less joints. It has great elasticity and turning effect.

The Science in Volleyball

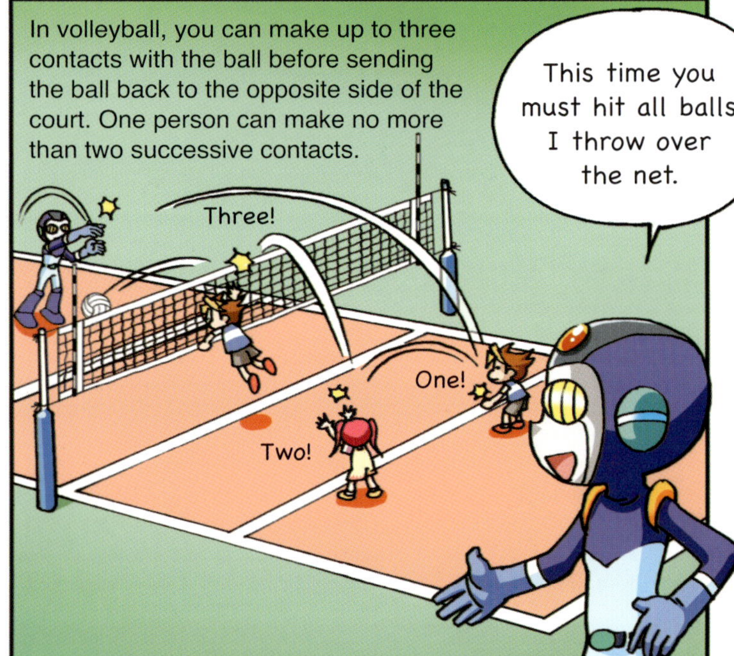

*Inertia of Rest: The tendency of an object at rest to stay at rest

I can hit that easily!
Whop

Yikes! I hit it too hard.
Thunk

Tap
Whop
I got it! Hit!

Oh! Great pass!
Swoosh
Wow, I saved it!

And Gomji's amazing jump!
Hop

Yikes!

You wasted my awesome pass!
That's weird... I was looking right at the ball when I jumped, but the ball suddenly dropped.
Hmm...

You can't just jump without thinking. First, you must observe the movement of the ball!

The ball that soars up into the air moves in an arc. The speed is the slowest at the top, and becomes faster as the ball drops.
Peak (The speed is the slowest.)
The speed accelerates.

Volleyball players calculate this curve quickly to plan their jumps accordingly.
Wilson
Wilson
Wilson
Wilson
Wilson
UCLA
1

That might be a little difficult for you, I imagine.
Let's do it over! I can do it! Even in computer games, I never make the same mistake twice!
Yeah, let's do it over!

All right, I like the attitude!
Slam

You said you don't make the same mistake twice!
Oh, I missed again!
Thump
Zip

Thump
Oh!
Wham

Great job, Omji!
Twirl
Here it comes!

All right! Let's calculate the ball's falling speed, my running speed, and the timing when I made the mistake before...

OK! Now!
Zip

Hmm... This time, I need to block it!
Swing
Hup!

Tap
Oh!

Thump

Did you see it? I did it!
Calm down... That was just a coincidence.
Hop
Hop
Hop

Different Types of Attacks

The different types of attacks include the "time lag attack", in which 2-3 attackers feint and the last attacker makes an attack in safety, "the shifting position attack", in which players move from their spots and attack as they shift with their eyes on the ball, the "back attack", in which the ball is tossed* to a player in the back so that an attack can be made in the back, and the "A, B, C quick attacks", in which the timing of the opponent's defense is disturbed so that they can't hit the ball easily.

A Quick Attack
An attacker quickly hits the ball tossed by the setter* (to a player nearby within 1 m)

B Quick Attack
The ball is tossed to an attacker further away than the one in A quick attack (to a player within 2-3 m)

C Quick Attack
The ball is tossed to an attacker further away than the one in B quick attack (to a player within 4-5 m)

*Toss: The act of throwing the ball lightly up into the air so that it's easy for the attacker to make an attack.
*Setter: The player that tosses the ball so that it's easy for the attacker to make an attack.

The Science in Baseball

Helmets for amateurs are equipped with ear protection on both sides.

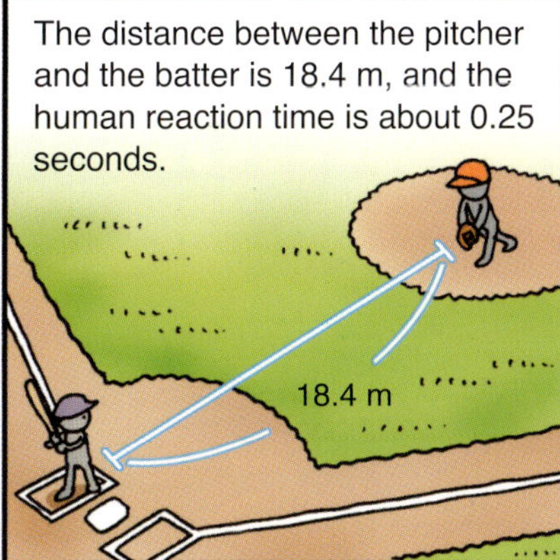

If the pitcher throws a ball at the speed of 150 km/h, the ball arrives at the catcher's glove in about 0.4 seconds.

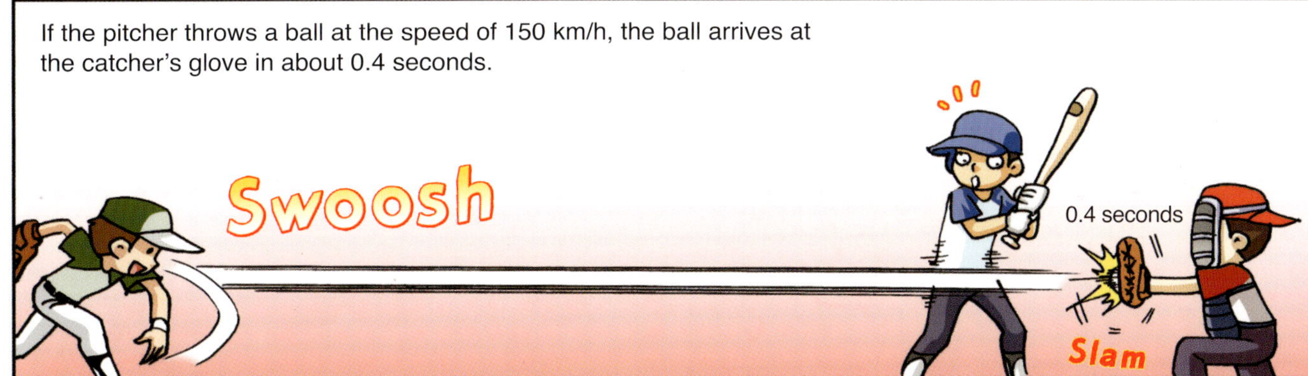

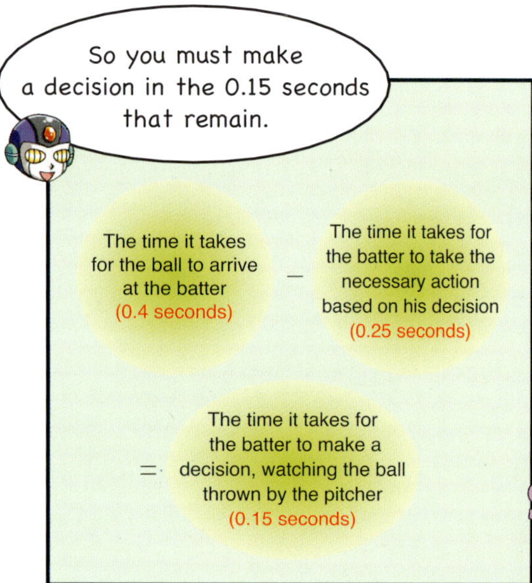

So you must make a decision in the 0.15 seconds that remain.
The time it takes for the ball to arrive at the batter (0.4 seconds)
The time it takes for the batter to take the necessary action based on his decision (0.25 seconds)
The time it takes for the batter to make a decision, watching the ball thrown by the pitcher (0.15 seconds)

In other words, when the batter starts to swing the bat after seeing the ball making its way towards him, it's already too late to hit the ball.
Swing
Slam

So batters swing the bat based on the pitcher's characteristics, his pose, and how the ball looks the moment it leaves his hand.
Now!
Swoosh

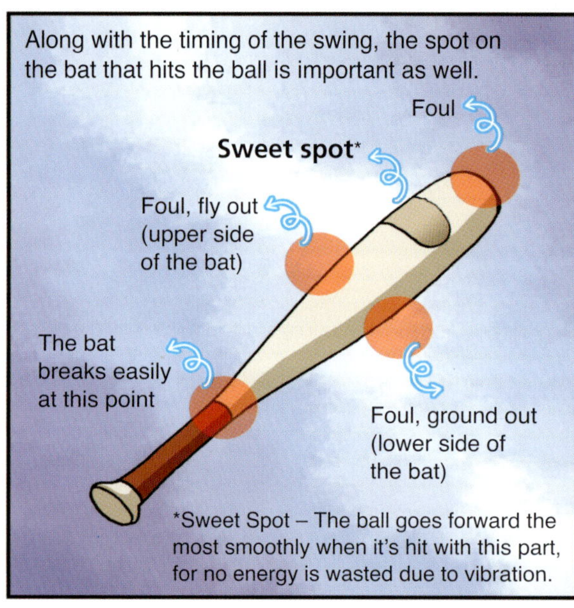

Along with the timing of the swing, the spot on the bat that hits the ball is important as well.
Foul
Sweet spot*
Foul, fly out (upper side of the bat)
The bat breaks easily at this point
Foul, ground out (lower side of the bat)
*Sweet Spot – The ball goes forward the most smoothly when it's hit with this part, for no energy is wasted due to vibration.

VOLVO
Homerun batters strike out easily because the wider they swing the bat, the harder it becomes for them to hit accurately.

So this time, don't throw so hard!
All right, I'll throw more slowly this time.
Swing

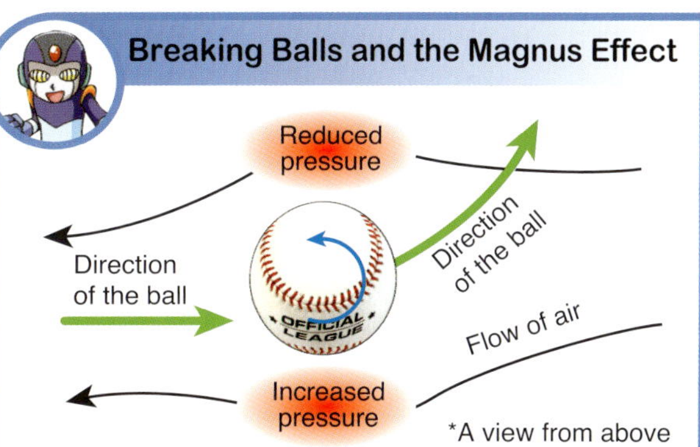

When the ball flies forward as it spins, the flow of air in the direction in which the ball spins speeds up and pressure is reduced, and where the flow of air is in the opposite direction, it slows down and pressure increases. The air flows from an area with greater pressure to an area with lesser pressure, so the ball bends as in the diagram.

The Characteristics of a Baseball

Baseballs are made by wrapping threads around a core made of cork or rubber, then sewing together two pieces of horsehide or cowhide with thick threads. The 108 stitches that form in the process help the ball fly faster and further.

When the ball flies fast, a pulling force is created behind the ball, and the stitches in the ball help reduce the whirlpool behind the ball to make it fly better.

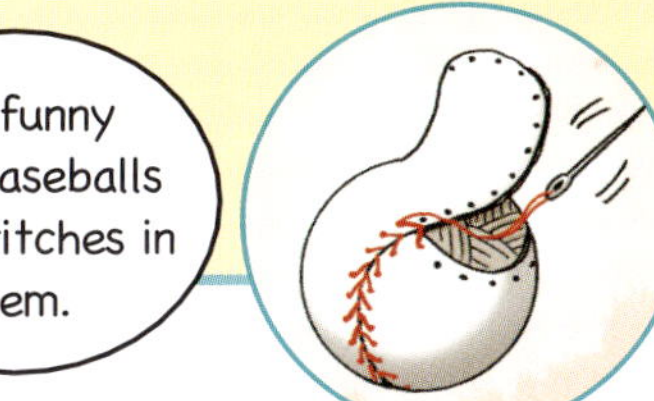

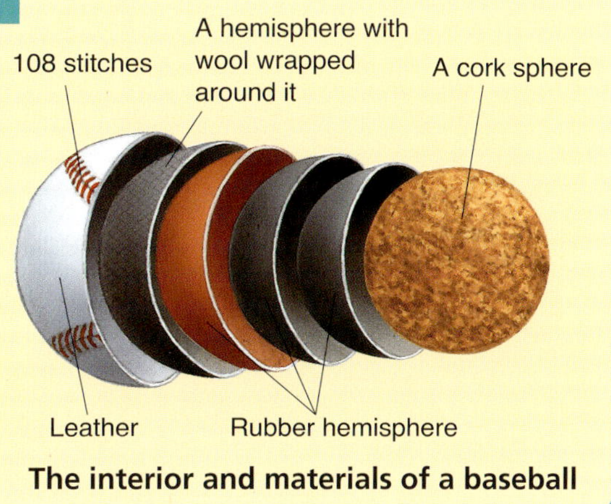

The interior and materials of a baseball

Different Pitches According to Grip

Baseball pitches differ depending on how the pitcher grips the ball.

Fast ball

The ball is fast with less of a bend. A skilled pitcher can make the ball float or sink.

Curve ball

Batters don't like curve balls, which look like fast balls but drop to the ground before the plate.

Slider

Sliders look like fast balls up to 60 cm away from the batter's box, then bend outwards of a right-handed batter.

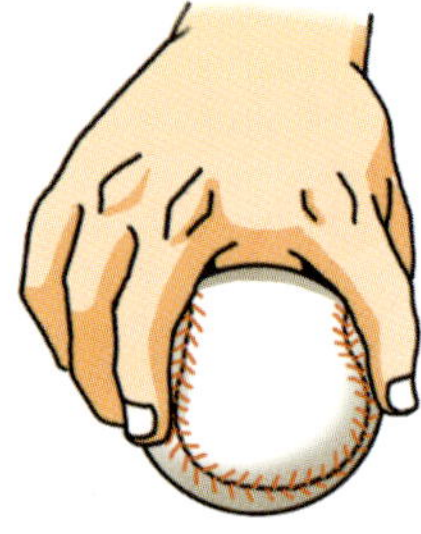

Fork ball

Fork balls are slow, because the diverging fingers disperse the force, but they suddenly drop in front of the batter.

How to Throw a Strong Pass

For a strong pass or swing, stand firmly on both legs, and if you're right-handed, place your weight on your right foot, then transfer it to your left foot.

To add speed to the ball, place your weight on your right foot and twist your arm and waist.

Stand at an angle, facing the target.

Move your left foot forward and transfer your weight onto it.

A batter lifts his leg before swinging the bat to make a powerful swing using his weight.

Yay! I got it this time!
Oh, pretty good!
Flop

But you can't say you got it with just one hit.
Swoosh

Slam

Wow, you learned pretty quickly.
He he.

I studied all your throws so far, and I saw a pattern. So I could predict what your next throw would be like.
1st throw
4th throw
3rd throw
2nd throw
5th throw

Yes, that's it. Batters need to study the pitcher's characteristics. As long as you can make a good prediction, you'll have no problem hitting the ball.

Pitchers also analyze the propensities of the batter, and decide on what kind of a pitch to throw next after signaling with the catcher.

The Science in Golf

So when a ball with a smooth surface flies, the air flows to create a force that pulls the ball back.

If there are dimples on the surface of the ball, however, the air crashes into the dimples, which decreases the pulling force and the ball can fly far.

In the days when golf balls were smooth, people often used old balls with nicks and scratches.

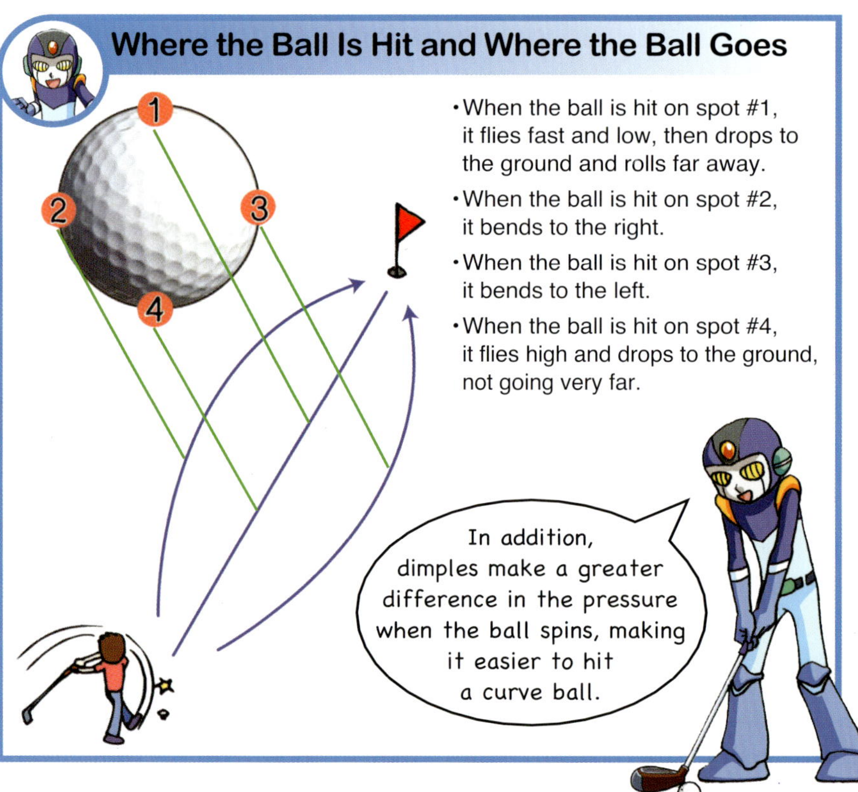

Where the Ball Is Hit and Where the Ball Goes

- When the ball is hit on spot #1, it flies fast and low, then drops to the ground and rolls far away.
- When the ball is hit on spot #2, it bends to the right.
- When the ball is hit on spot #3, it bends to the left.
- When the ball is hit on spot #4, it flies high and drops to the ground, not going very far.

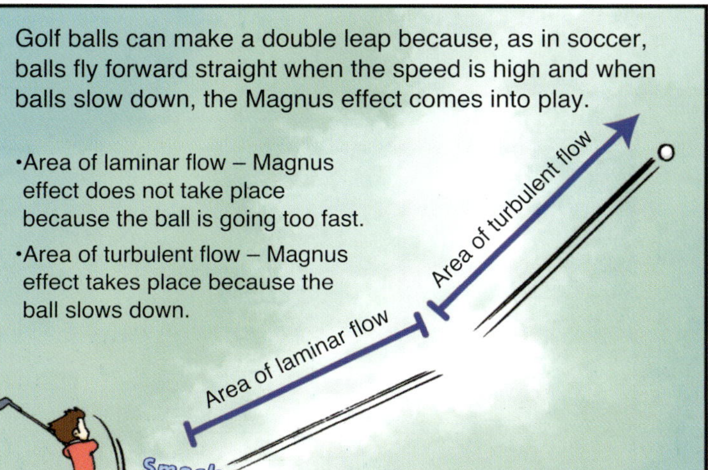
Golf balls can make a double leap because, as in soccer, balls fly forward straight when the speed is high and when balls slow down, the Magnus effect comes into play.

- Area of laminar flow – Magnus effect does not take place because the ball is going too fast.
- Area of turbulent flow – Magnus effect takes place because the ball slows down.

To hit a ball that makes a double leap, the ball must be fast, so to make a powerful swing use centrifugal force, making a big, fast swing.

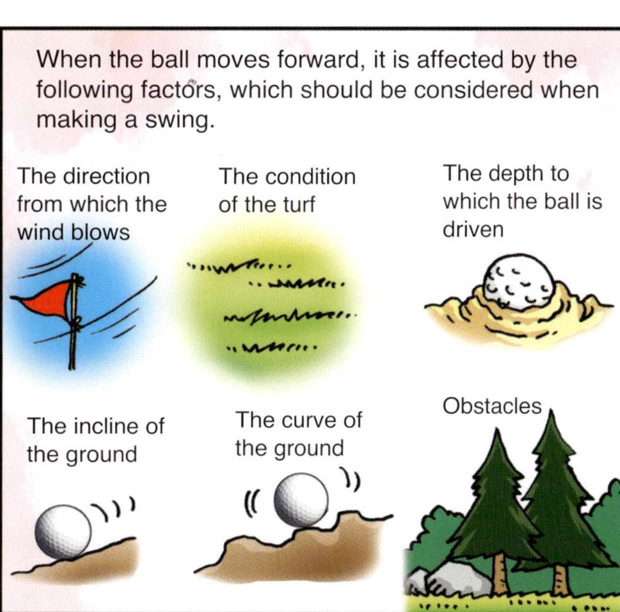

When the ball moves forward, it is affected by the following factors, which should be considered when making a swing.

This won't be an easy task, either.
All right, watch me make a hole in one.
Tap
Oh, just a little more!
Stop
All right... one more time!
Thwack
Oh, did I hit too hard this time?
Roll
Why is it bending now?
Move aside! Let me give it a try.
Come on, what are you doing?
Hold on!
The ball can roll off in a different direction because of the curve of the ground, so I want to take a careful look.

If the hole is up high, use more force, and if it's down low, use less force. (If the ground is slanted, choose the side with high incline).

Professional golfers calculate various factors, such as the distance, carefully even if the hole is close.

The Science in Bowling

But can't you knock down more pins with a heavier ball?
Not always.

If you use a ball that's too heavy for you, you can hurt your muscles, and you won't be able to throw the ball quickly with accuracy.
You can produce more force with heavier balls, but even if you use a light ball, you can hit a strike with no problem.

Oh, how embarrassing! The ball rolled off to the side!
That was weird. Let me try again!
Swoosh
Oh, look at your pose...
Oh, I came too close.
Your steps are all wrong. You need to be in a stable position to exert your energy towards the pins.
Crash
Yikes!
Slip
Tsk, tsk!

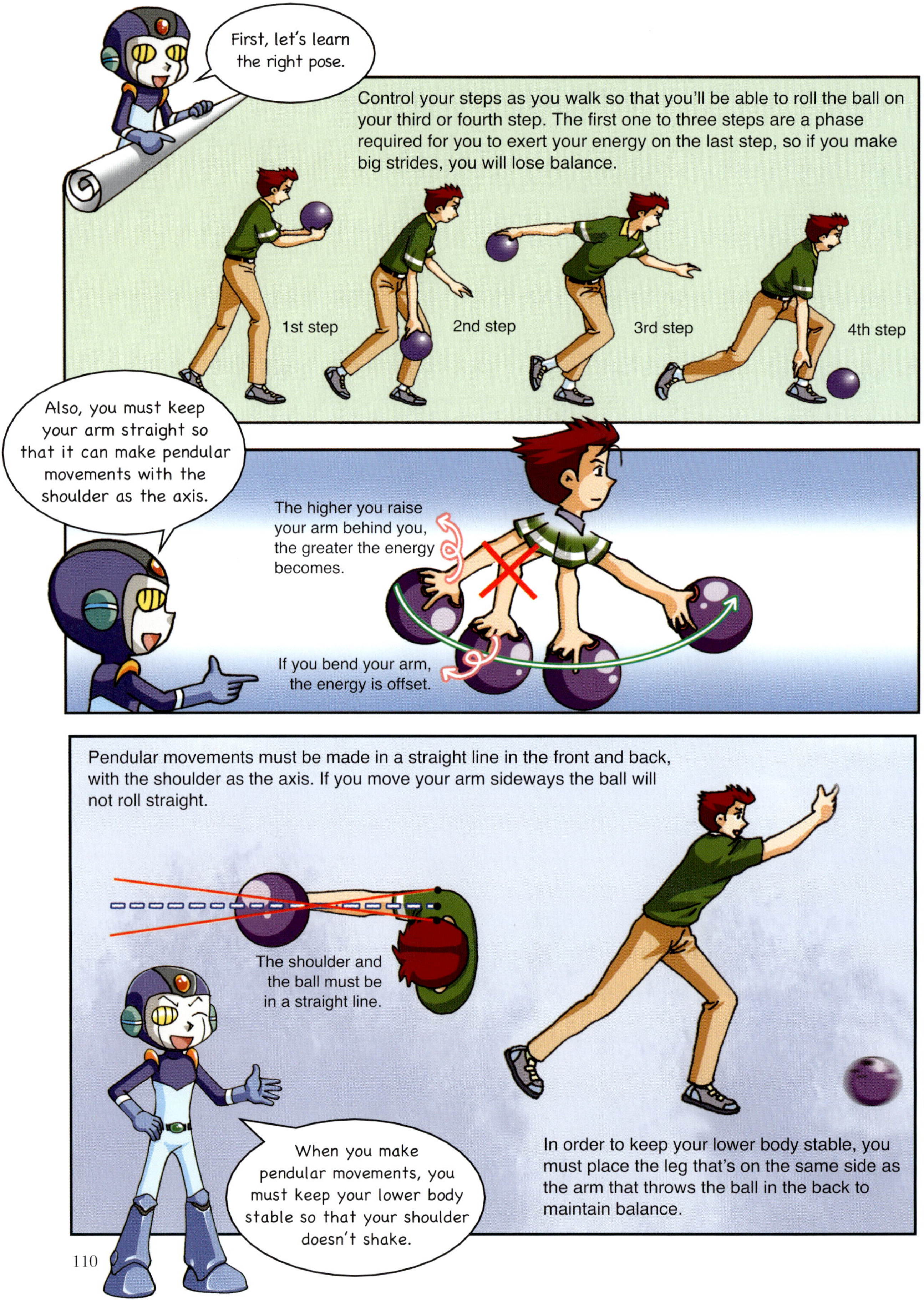

Control your steps as you walk so that you'll be able to roll the ball on your third or fourth step. The first one to three steps are a phase required for you to exert your energy on the last step, so if you make big strides, you will lose balance.

The higher you raise your arm behind you, the greater the energy becomes.

If you bend your arm, the energy is offset.

Pendular movements must be made in a straight line in the front and back, with the shoulder as the axis. If you move your arm sideways the ball will not roll straight.

The shoulder and the ball must be in a straight line.

In order to keep your lower body stable, you must place the leg that's on the same side as the arm that throws the ball in the back to maintain balance.

110

Wow, there's science even to bowling... Sports really are science!

All right! My turn now!
Zip

Wow! It's going straight to the center!
Oh, oh...

Hey! Why is the ball bending all or a sudden?
Oh, it went into the gutter.
That's because of wrist movement.

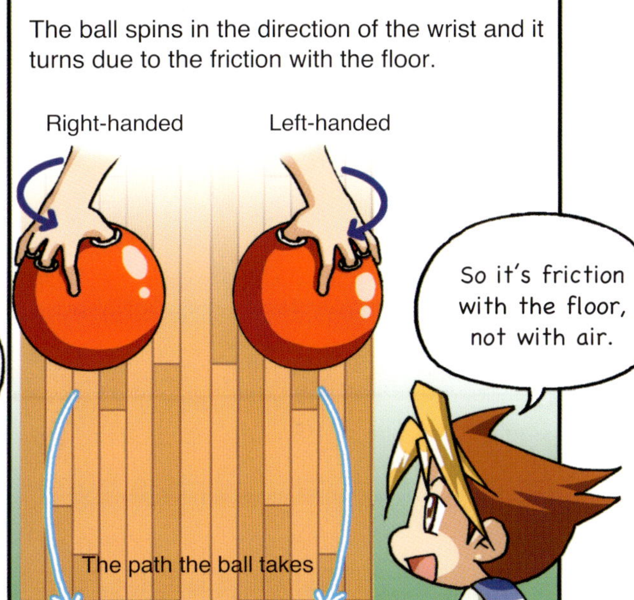
The ball spins in the direction of the wrist and it turns due to the friction with the floor.
Right-handed
Left-handed
The path the ball takes
So it's friction with the floor, not with air.

So when it bends all of a sudden, is it based on the same principle you told us about during soccer?

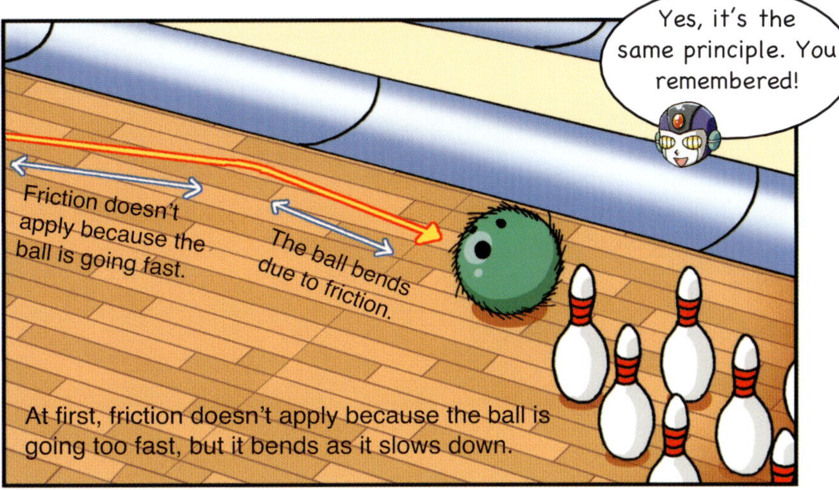
Yes, it's the same principle. You remembered!
Friction doesn't apply because the ball is going fast.
The ball bends due to friction.
At first, friction doesn't apply because the ball is going too fast, but it bends as it slows down.

111

Various Kinds of Split

When the #1 pin is left, it isn't called a split.

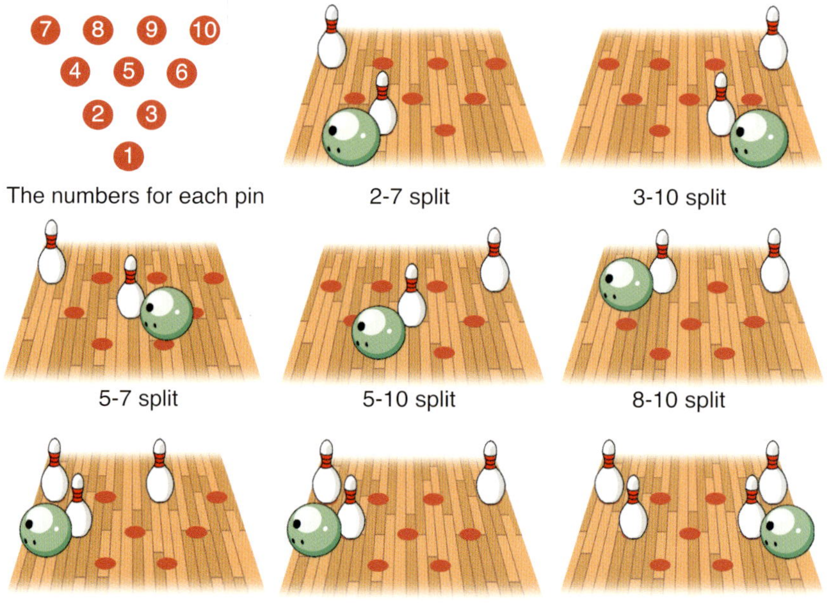

The numbers for each pin

2-7 split

3-10 split

5-7 split

5-10 split

8-10 split

4-7-9 split

4-7-10 split

4-6-7-10 split

*Kickback: A wooden wall on which a pin can bounce and hit another pin, knocking it down.

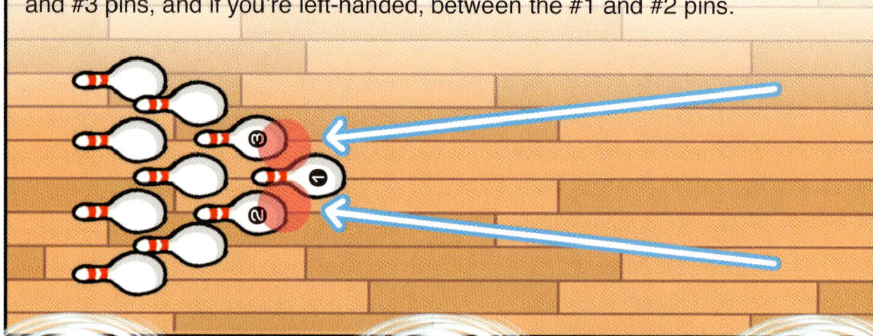
You have a greater chance of hitting a strike if you aim at the left or right side of the #1 pin than if you roll the ball towards the center. If you're right-handed, you have a greater chance of getting a strike if the ball goes in between the #1 and #3 pins, and if you're left-handed, between the #1 and #2 pins.

The Science in Tennis

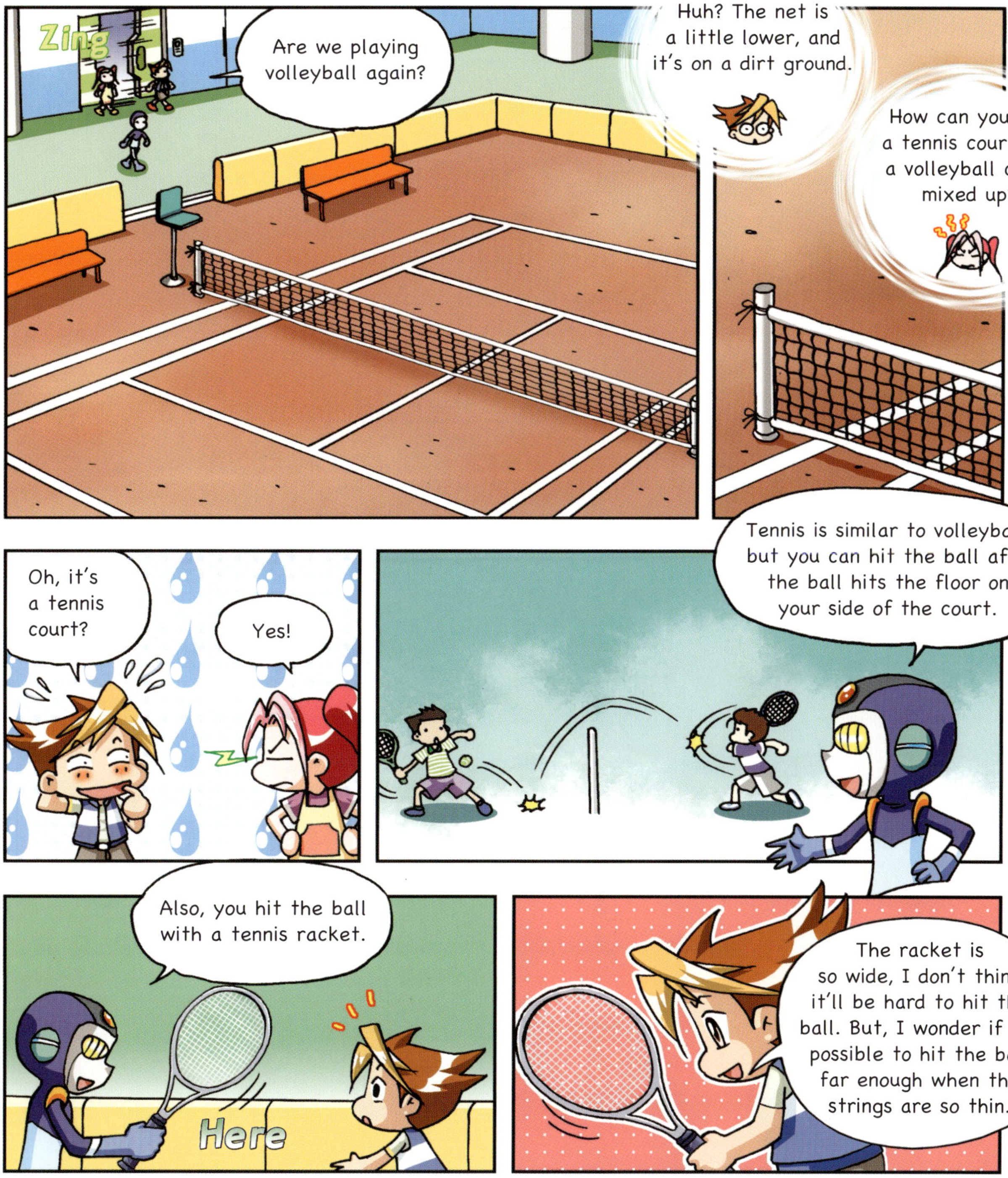

Of course! The elasticity of these strings, together with the elasticity of the ball, enables you to hit the ball far with little force.
Here, I'll make a serve, and you hit it!
Slam
OK! You said I could hit the ball after it hits the ground, right?
Swoosh

Oh!
Thump

Tennis balls are quite fast, so it's hard to hit the ball directly as it flies over. In most cases, it's better to hit the ball after it hits the ground, observing the force and angle of the ball and approaching it from behind.
All right!
Thump

The ball bounces pretty well, even on a dirt ground.
Bounce
Bounce

The dirt here is harder and more moist than ordinary dirt, isn't it? That's because salt is scattered over the court.
Salt?

So the ground becomes hard when you mix salt in it? That's interesting.

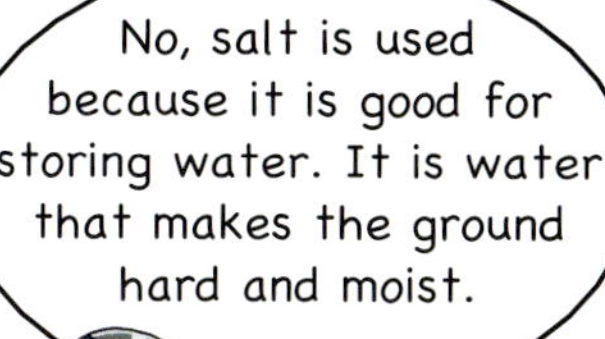

No, salt is used because it is good for storing water. It is water that makes the ground hard and moist.

You can't leave me out!
Salt
Water

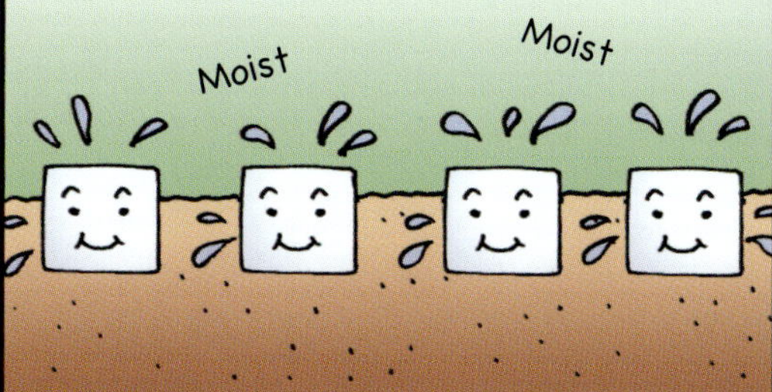

The ground cracks when it is dry. If you sprinkle water on ground with salt, the salt absorbs water and stores it for a long time, so the ground doesn't crack or become dry and dusty.
Moist
Moist

In addition, salt lowers the freezing point of water, so the ground doesn't freeze easily even in cold weather. You didn't know that there was this much science hidden in a tennis court, did you?
Wow!

The dirt on the ground of a tennis court

I'm an iceberg! I fell off ice on the mainland and am floating on the sea.
Seawater doesn't freeze easily due to its salinity. Salt is sprinkled on the ground of a tennis court for the same reason.

Wow, salt is amazing!
Yeah, and it gives flavor to food.

When you make something with clay, you can mix in some salt so that it doesn't break easily.
Oh, that's a good idea, Gomji.

The Science in Table Tennis

In tennis, you have an advantage if you're tall, but height doesn't matter very much in ping-pong. When you make a serve in tennis, you pass the ball right to the opponent's court, but in ping-pong you must first make the ball hit your side of the court so that it is possible for the opponent to hit it.

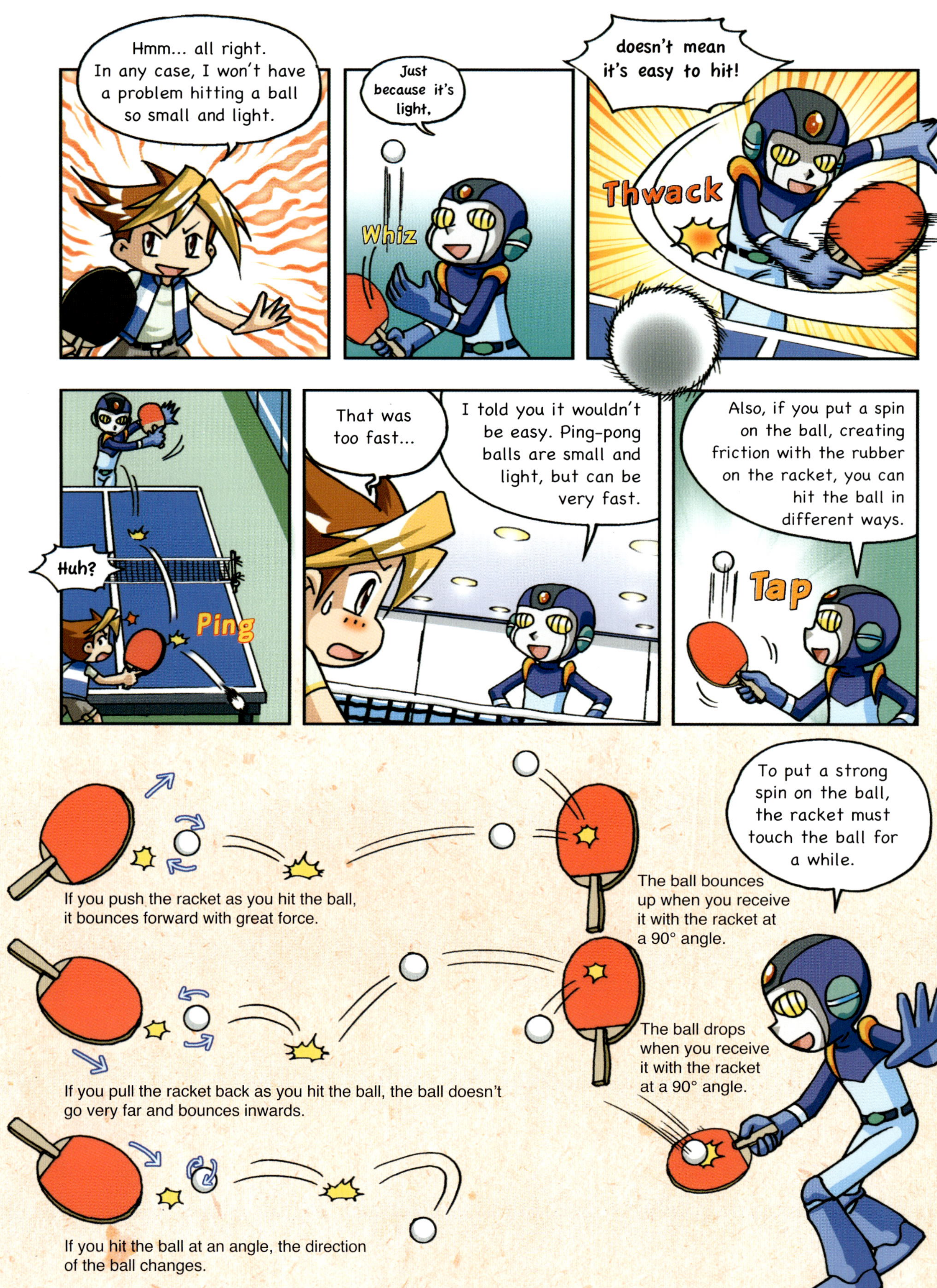

Hmm... all right. In any case, I won't have a problem hitting a ball so small and light.
Just because it's light,
doesn't mean it's easy to hit!
Whiz
Thwack
Huh?
Ping
That was too fast...
I told you it wouldn't be easy. Ping-pong balls are small and light, but can be very fast.
Also, if you put a spin on the ball, creating friction with the rubber on the racket, you can hit the ball in different ways.
Tap
If you push the racket as you hit the ball, it bounces forward with great force.
If you pull the racket back as you hit the ball, the ball doesn't go very far and bounces inwards.
If you hit the ball at an angle, the direction of the ball changes.
To put a strong spin on the ball, the racket must touch the ball for a while.
The ball bounces up when you receive it with the racket at a 90° angle.
The ball drops when you receive it with the racket at a 90° angle.

The higher up an object, the greater energy it has. When you hit a ball that falls from higher up, its potential energy and the horizontal energy combine together to make the ball move with greater force.

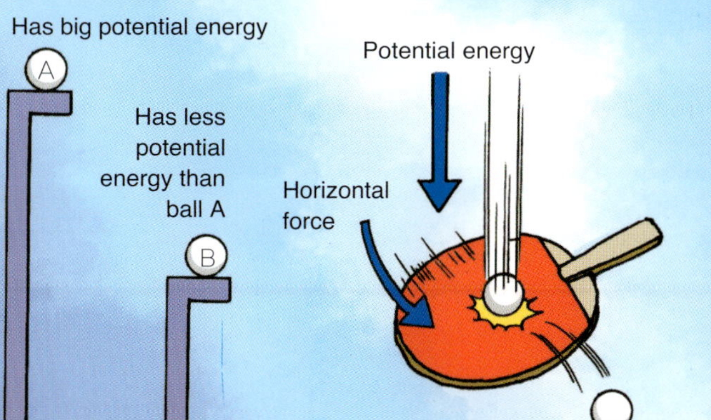

The Change in Volume of Objects Due to Heat

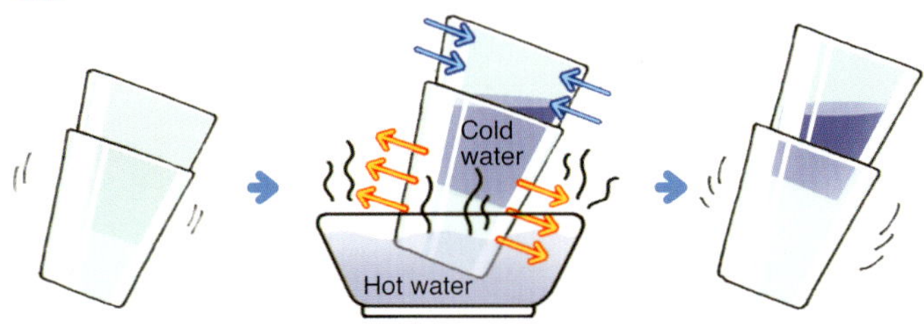

When it's hard to separate cups that are stacked together, place the cups in a tub of hot water, and pour cold water in the inner cup. The cup on the outside will expand due to heat and the cups will separate. This demonstrates how volume expands due to heat.

When air is heated, the molecules that make up the air move actively, increasing the volume. A crushed up ping-pong ball can thus be straightened out when placed in hot water.

The Science in Badminton

*Edge: When a ping-pong ball hits the corner of the table

The Instantaneous Velocity* of Balls Used in Various Sports Games

*The Instantaneous Velocity: The speed of the ball after it hits the racket, hand, or foot.

Hey, but it's fast only at the beginning, and slow when it falls.

Yes, that's the charm of the shuttlecock.

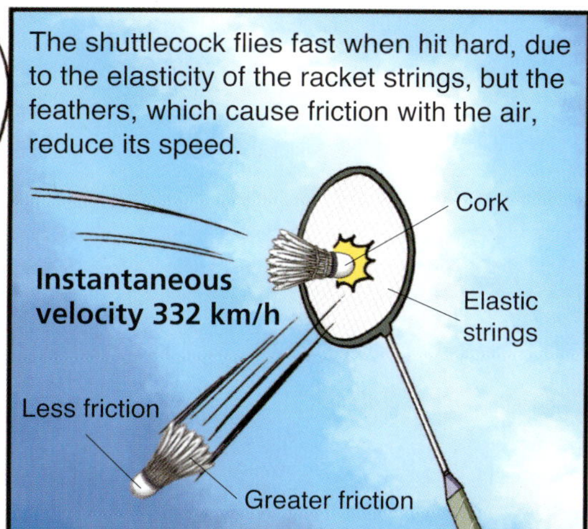

The shuttlecock flies fast when hit hard, due to the elasticity of the racket strings, but the feathers, which cause friction with the air, reduce its speed.
Cork
Instantaneous velocity 332 km/h
Elastic strings
Less friction
Greater friction

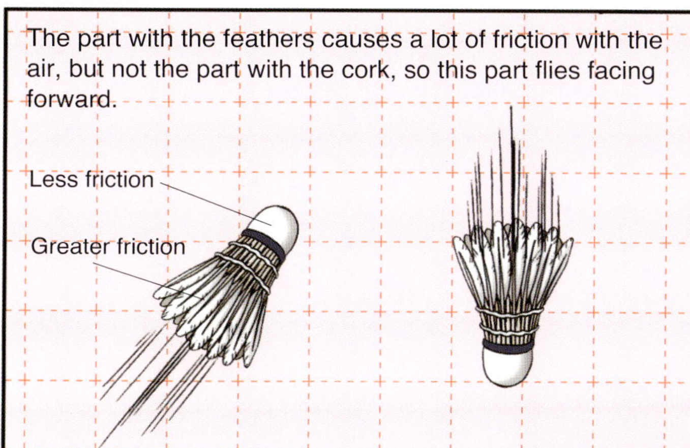

The part with the feathers causes a lot of friction with the air, but not the part with the cork, so this part flies facing forward.
Less friction
Greater friction

This time, the two of you try receiving my smash.
No problem, because the speed will drop as the shuttlecock falls...

Hey, it's still fast!

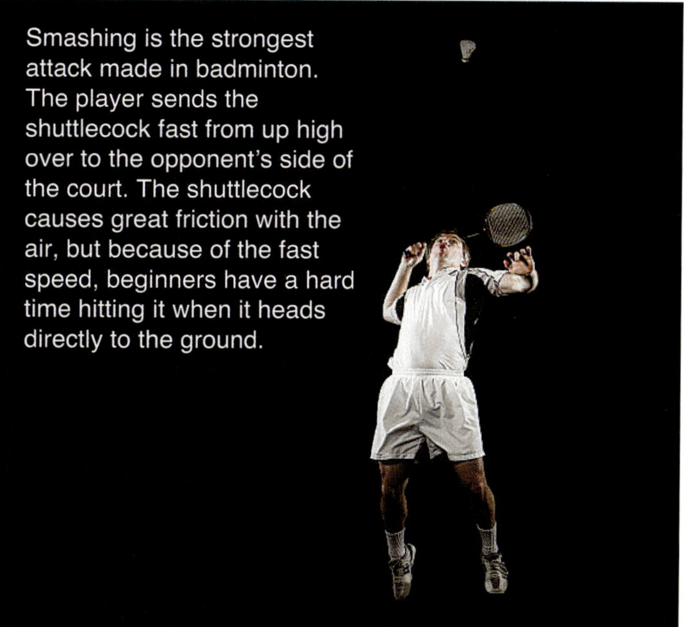

Smashing is the strongest attack made in badminton. The player sends the shuttlecock fast from up high over to the opponent's side of the court. The shuttlecock causes great friction with the air, but because of the fast speed, beginners have a hard time hitting it when it heads directly to the ground.

Lower your position, and place the center of gravity at the front so that you can always run forward.

If you lower your position, reducing the inertia of rest, you can react quickly to the ball that comes flying fast.

The Science in Gliding

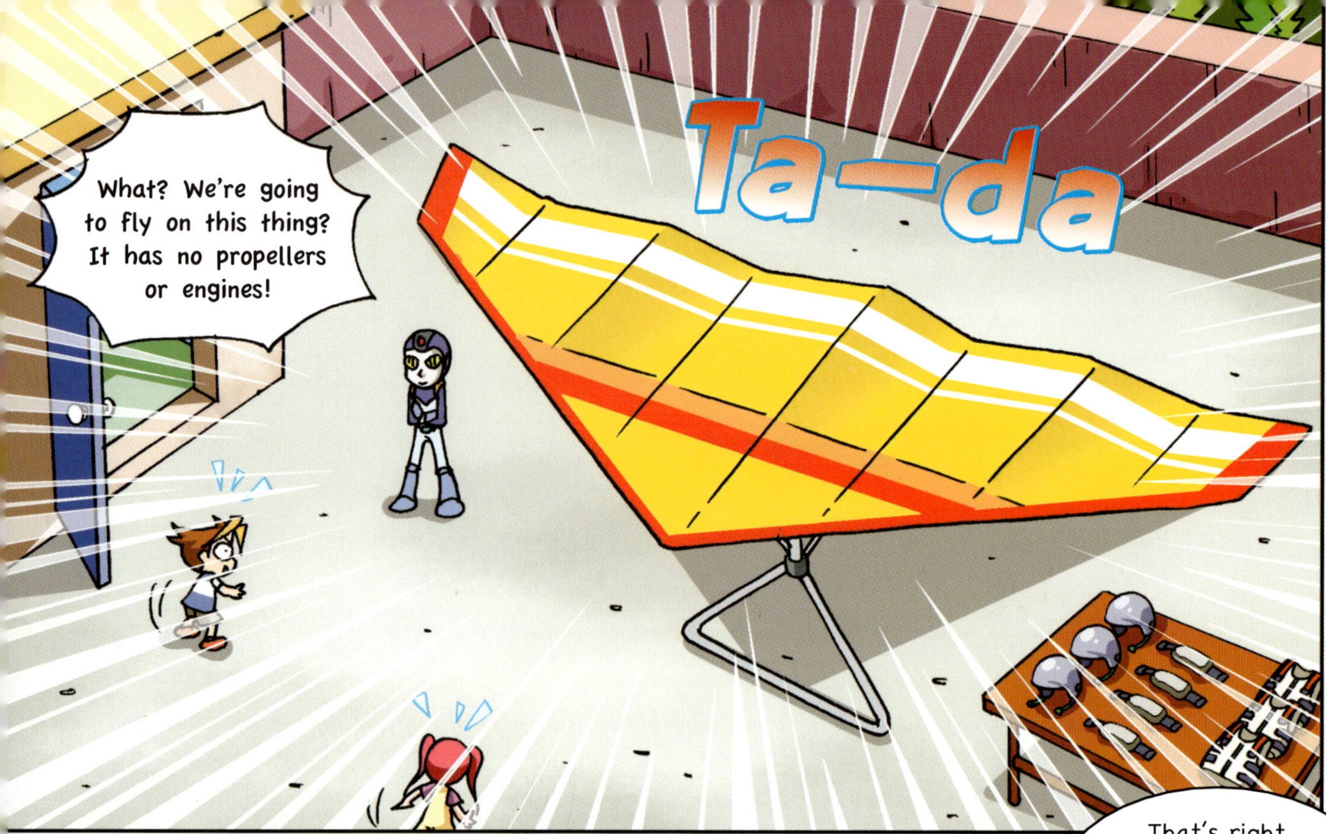

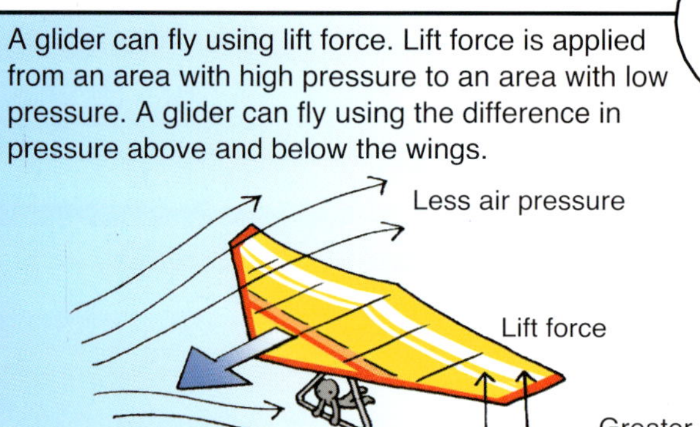

Hang Glider A hang glider flies using the lift force of the air. It requires no electric power at all, and can soar 50-60 m higher than its initial altitude. It flies at 40-120 km/h.

Paraglider A paraglider also flies using the lift force of the air. The strings, which move the wings, are used to control the speed and direction. It is slower than a hang glider, moving at 20-30 km/h.

Now, let me tell you something while we're at it. The weather is very important in gliding, because it's a sport that relies on the air current (the flow of air).

When the sunlight is intense, the ground is heated, causing an updraft, so it's better for beginners to avoid such weather and fly early in the morning, when the wind is mild and the air current starts to move.

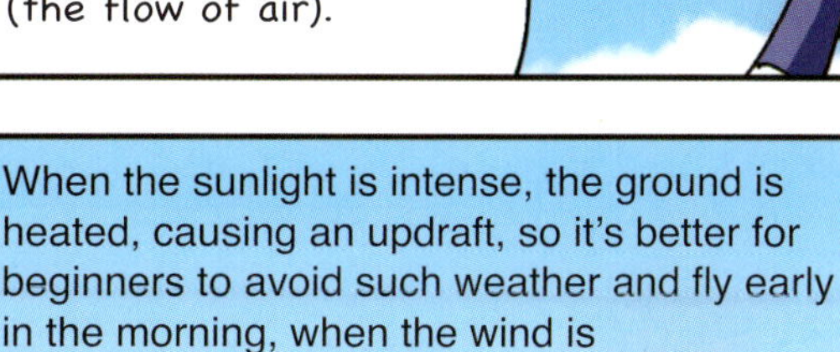

You should avoid the back of mountains or valleys because the air current is irregular when the wind blows.

The Science in Judo

Yawn
Gasp!

Hey! What are you guys doing here?
Oh, no! We can't even run because the path is too narrow!

What do you mean run? It's better that the path is narrow, since I can take him one on one!
Spot, he looks a lot bigger and stronger than you. Are you sure you can beat him?

Ha ha, if you knew the principles of force, you could beat him easily!

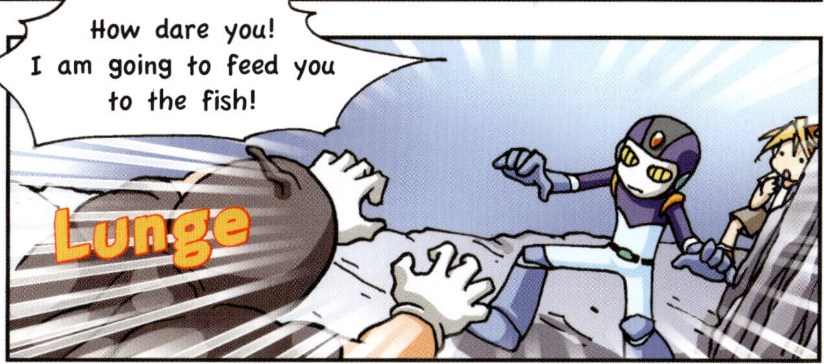

How dare you! I am going to feed you to the fish!
Lunge

Grab

Yikes!
Whoosh

This is a technique used in judo. You use the other guy's strength as well as your own.

It's difficult to throw over someone who's standing still.

But when someone runs at you blindly like that, his center is unstable.

So if you use his strength on top of your own, you can exert greater force.

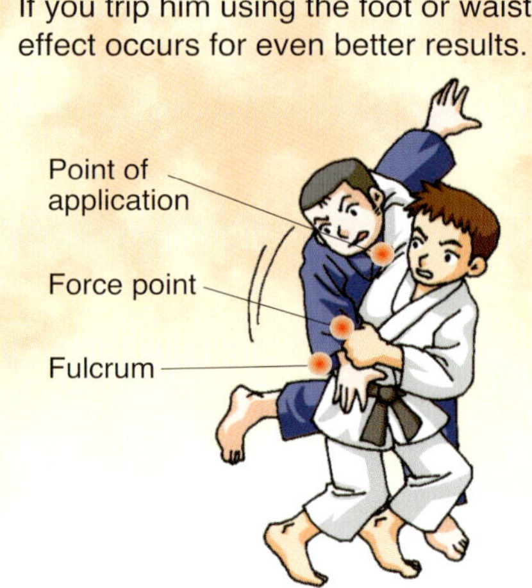
If you trip him using the foot or waist, the leverage effect occurs for even better results.

- Point of application – the point where force is applied to the object
- Fulcrum – the part where the lever is supported
- Force point – the point where the person applies his strength

Hand technique

Leg technique

Waist technique

If you destabilize the opponent, it becomes easier to use your techniques.
Pulling the opponent using the arms is a technique used to throw off his center.

Grab the opponent for a more advantageous position for using your techniques.

Hey, Spot! They're coming from behind me, too!

You take him! You can do it!
Slap

How... how can I?
You're going to get it, now!
Rush

Thunk
Oh, I don't know!
Slip
Swoosh
Ugh!
Huh?
Oh, that was a great throw*!

He he, did you see? Did you see my prowess?
Yes, yes, I'm so proud of you!

Whoa
Whoa
What's that?

Hurry, this way!
Get them!
You're not going anywhere this time!
Rush

To stand, you must rise head first, so it's difficult to stand when someone pushes down on your forehead with a finger.

*Throw: The technique used in judo with which you throw or knock down the opponent.

When you pin someone down, you should suppress his upper body so that he can't get up, roll over, or counterattack.

A twist is a technique used to twist or wring the opponent's joints, making him surrender due to pain.

The Joints in the Body and Their Movements

Pivot joint (neck bone)
The neck bone is joined together like a millstone and can be turned around.

Synchondrosis Joint (the spine)
The bones that make up the spine are connected through cartilage, like the support of a desk lamp, and can move forward and backward.

Hinge joint (elbow bone)
The elbow bone can move only in one direction like a hinge (a component that helps open and close doors, furniture, and such).

Ball-and-socket joint (wrist bone and others)
The wrist bone can move in diverse directions, like a pen holder.

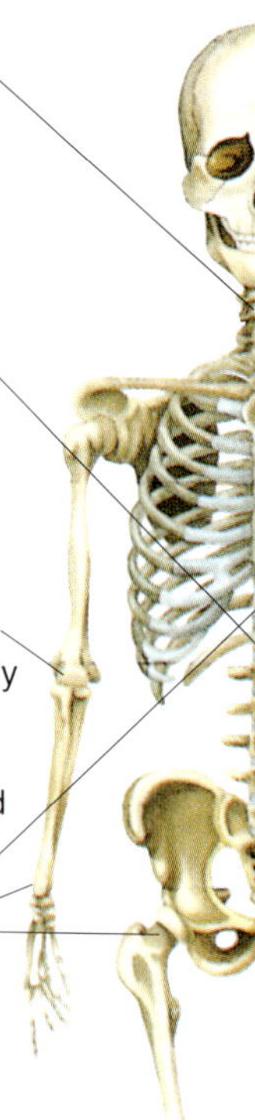

I... I'll tell you. The doctor is across the hall, three doors down!

Let's go!
Groan
Groan
Rush

Swoosh

It's this one right here!

Whirr

Doctor!
Grandpa!
Oh! How did you...

It... it's dangerous here! Run!
No, I can't do that!

The Science in a Taekwondo Smash

You need to learn the principles of smashing. First, the direction and point of application of the force!

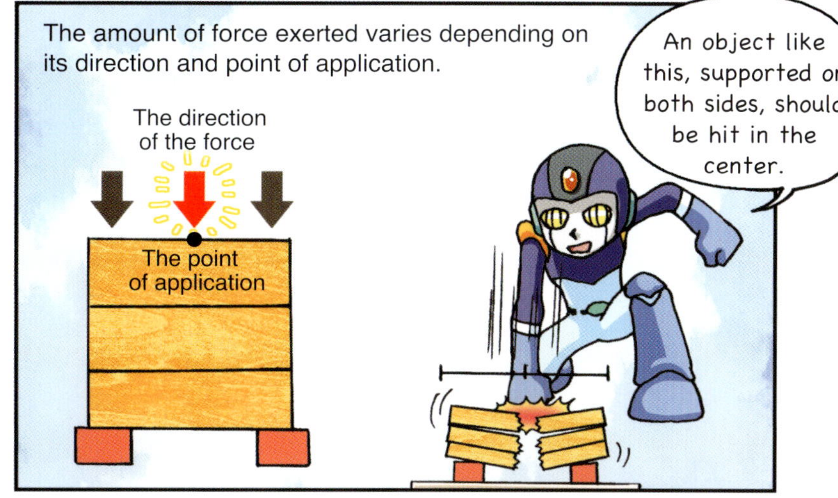

The amount of force exerted varies depending on its direction and point of application.
The direction of the force
The point of application
An object like this, supported on both sides, should be hit in the center.

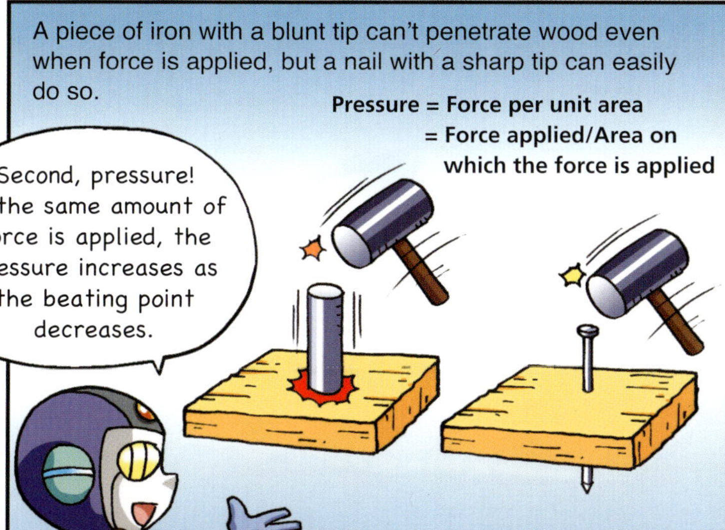

A piece of iron with a blunt tip can't penetrate wood even when force is applied, but a nail with a sharp tip can easily do so.
Pressure = Force per unit area
= Force applied/Area on which the force is applied
Second, pressure! If the same amount of force is applied, the pressure increases as the beating point decreases.

When smashing bricks, use the blade of your hand to reduce the beating point.

Third, speed!
Flash
Momentum = Mass x Speed

When the mass is the same, momentum increases with speed, and the momentum brings great shock to the object.
Slow
Fast
Bam
Thwack

If your arm isn't stretched straight out, the shock is buffered and less force is applied.

The object for smashing must be placed on hard ground to reduce the buffer effect.

If the object isn't fixed firmly, the shock will be buffered and the force will not be properly applied.

More force can be exerted when you hit with a sledgehammer instead of a hammer.

When you place your weight in your arm, you can exert greater strength.

All right, we're going to hit all at once! Ready!
One!
Two!
Three!
Bang
Crack
Crack
Wow! We did it!
Crash
Doctor!
Rush
Good job! I'm so proud of you!
Grandpa!
Hmm...

The Science in Boxing

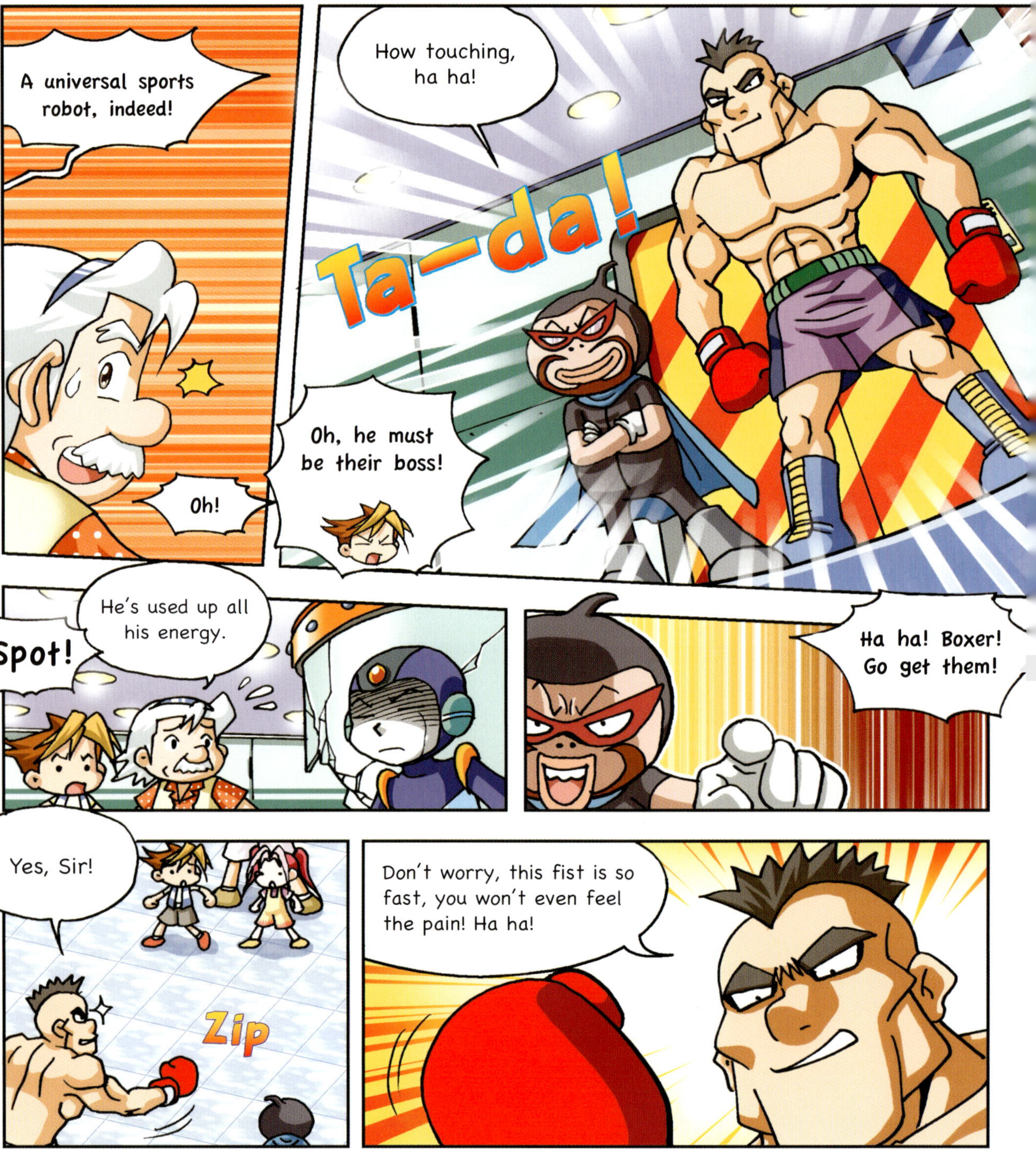

Here it goes!
No!
Swoosh
Stop!
What? He still had energy left?

He's using his emergency energy. It's not going to last long.

Ha ha, a robot is no match for me! Come on!
Bam
Bam
Just a little longer...

Flicker
Flicker

Ha ha! Are you kidding me?
Zip
Whip

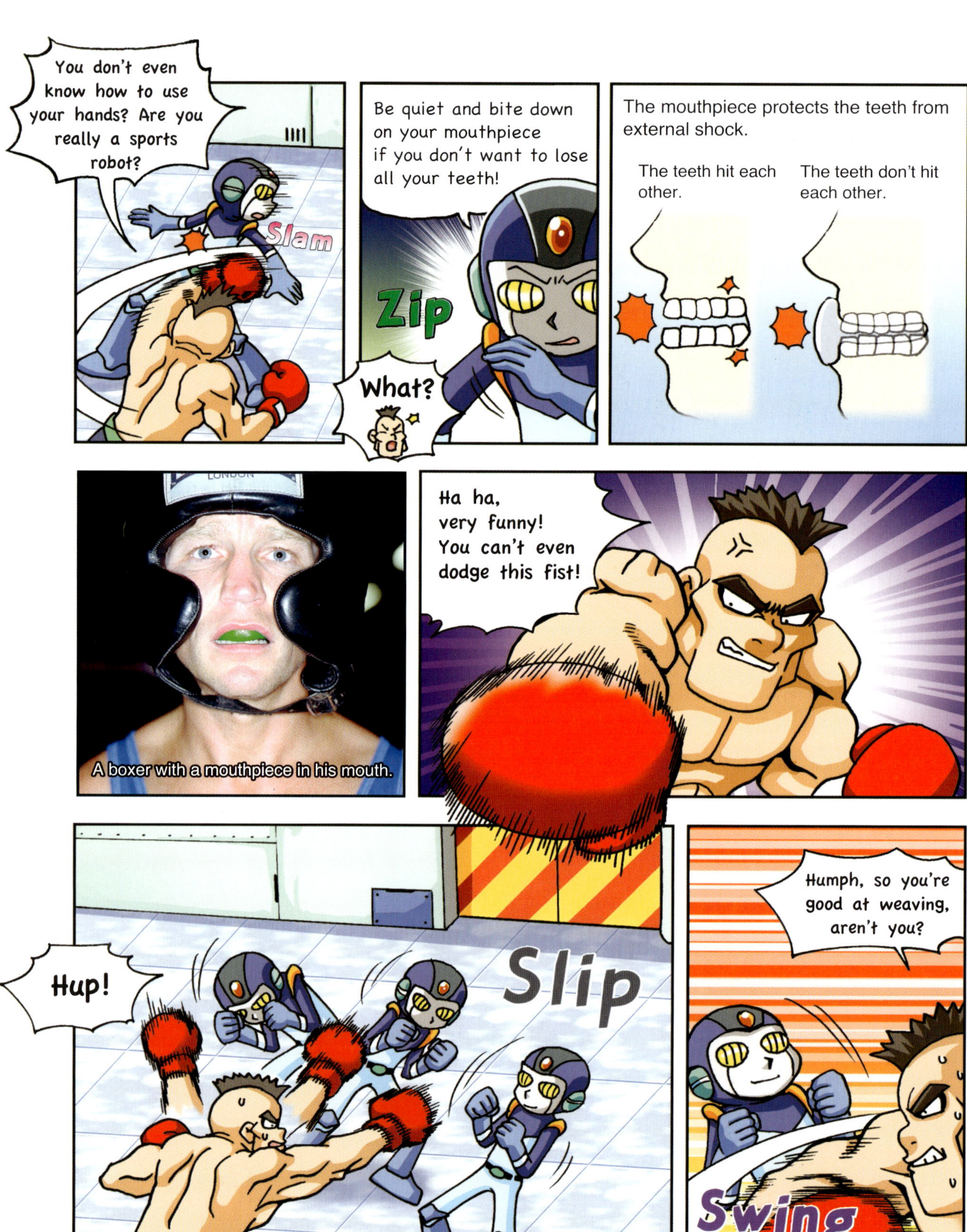

You don't even know how to use your hands? Are you really a sports robot?
Slam
Be quiet and bite down on your mouthpiece if you don't want to lose all your teeth!
Zip
What?
The mouthpiece protects the teeth from external shock.
The teeth hit each other.
The teeth don't hit each other.
A boxer with a mouthpiece in his mouth.
Ha ha, very funny! You can't even dodge this fist!
Hup!
Slip
Humph, so you're good at weaving, aren't you?
Swing

Weaving is a technique in which you can throw off your opponent by moving and can dodge your opponent's fists. You can throw off your opponent and move so that you're not strongly impacted by the opponent's blows.

When the chin is hit, the neck bone acts as a lever and shakes up the brain. Because of the shock, the cerebellum can't carry out its functions and the body doesn't move properly.

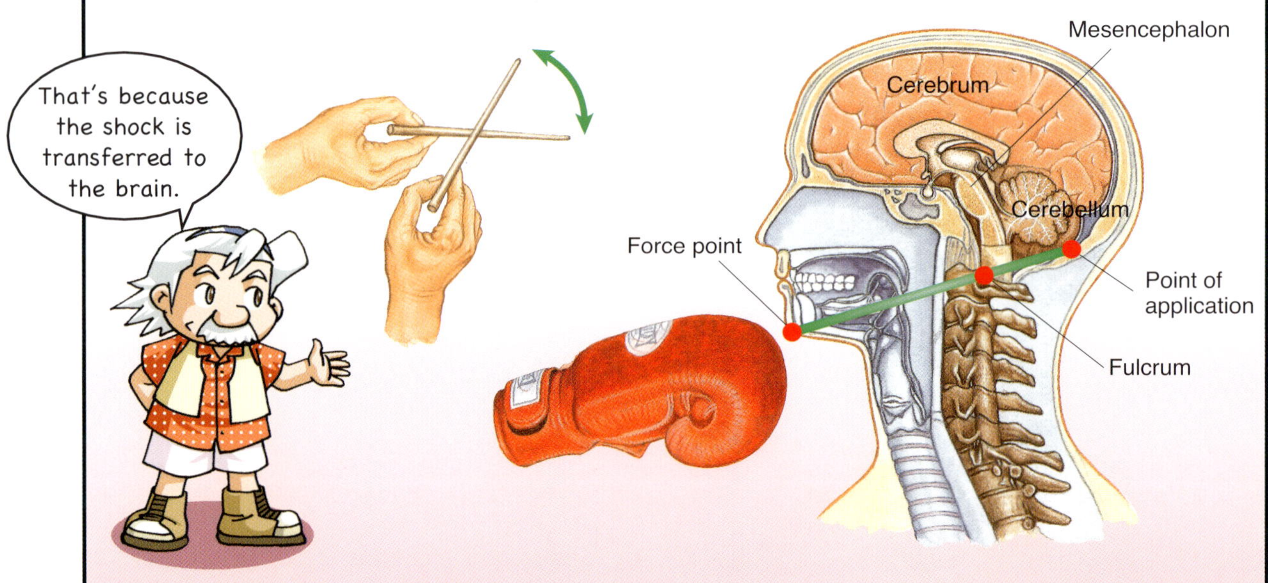

A boxer who has lost his balance due to the shock transferred from the chin to the brain

Sports and Safety (Injury)

Types of Injuries

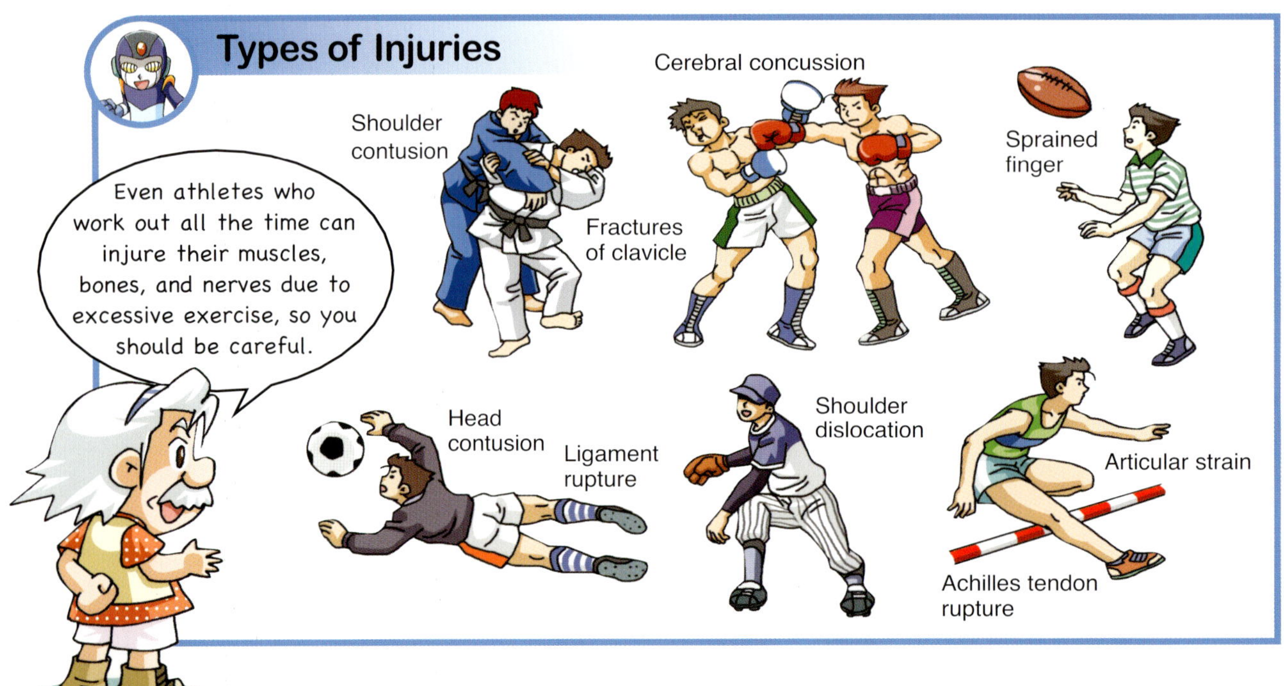

But if you take just a little care, you can prevent most accidents.

Check the equipment before working out to make sure it's safe.
Hmm... nothing unusual here.

Warm up sufficiently so that your body isn't strained.

Adhere to the safety instructions.
Please dismount after the machine has come to a complete stop.
Aha!

Ouch! What's a dumbbell doing here?
Trip

That's why you should put away the equipment after you're done.
Oh...
Gomji never does...

First Aid

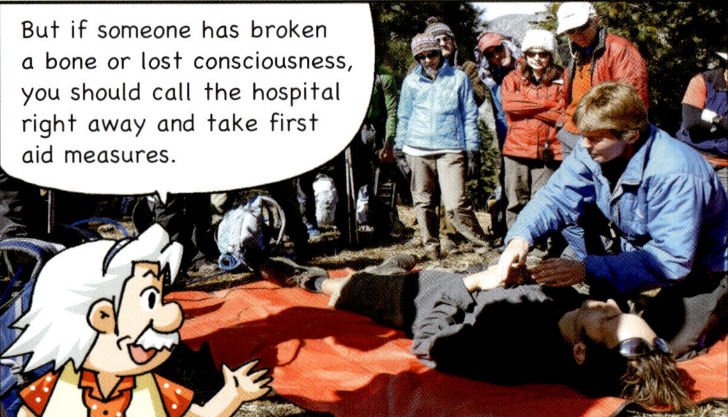

Various First Aid Measures

Broken Bones
Put a splint on the broken part and alternately apply an ice pack and a hot pack.

Dislocated Bones
Apply an ice pack, then put a splint on the dislocated part.

Food Poisoning
Drink a lot of saline solution and throw up, then take an enema or a purgative.

Concussion
Elevate the head and lie down, keeping the body warm.

Nosebleed
Bend the head forward, and pinch the part below the nasal bone with the thumb and the index finger. Wipe the blood with a clean towel.

Heatstroke
Lie down in a cool place with the head elevated and apply an ice pack on the head.

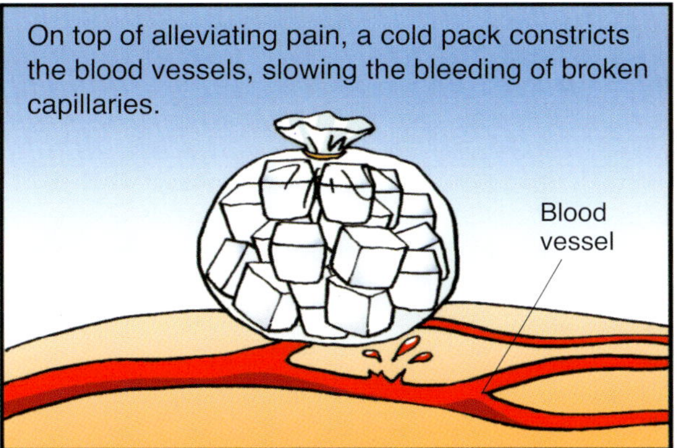
On top of alleviating pain, a cold pack constricts the blood vessels, slowing the bleeding of broken capillaries.

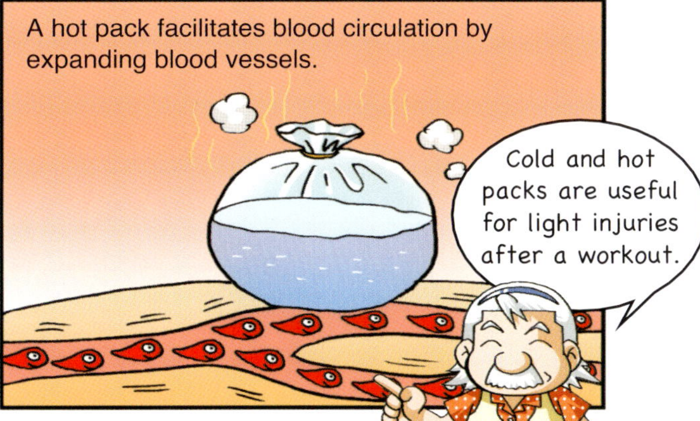
A hot pack facilitates blood circulation by expanding blood vessels.

Artificial Respiration

Artificial respiration is carried out to catalyze the gas exchange in lungs when breathing has stopped or when there isn't sufficient gas exchange. The air breathed in leads to a natural release of air due to the pressure, and helps the functioning of the lungs.

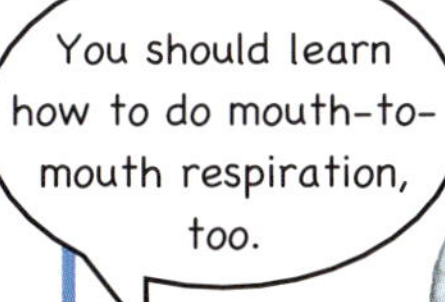

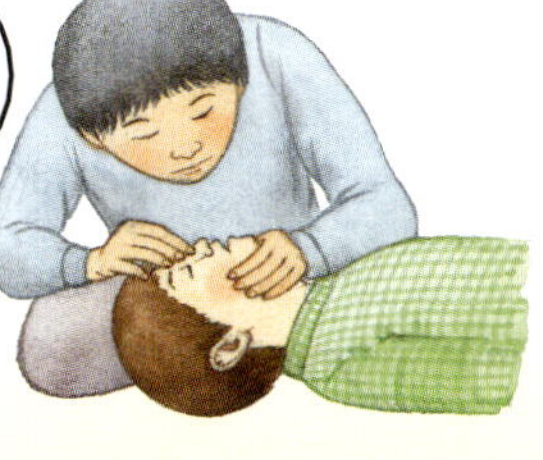

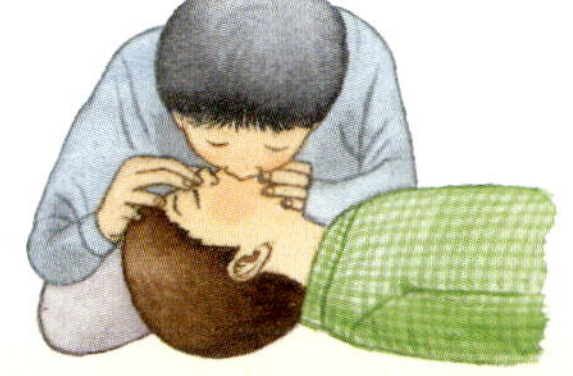

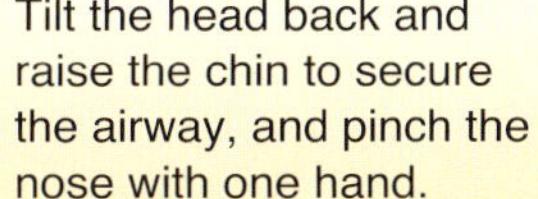

Tilt the head back and raise the chin to secure the airway, and pinch the nose with one hand.

Breathe forcibly into the mouth, breathing air into the lungs.

Check the chest to see if breathing has returned, and listen for the sound of breathing.

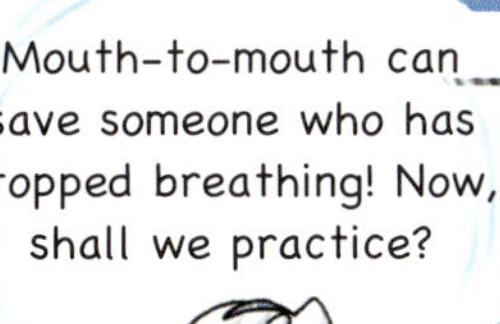

Sports and Eating (Nutrition)

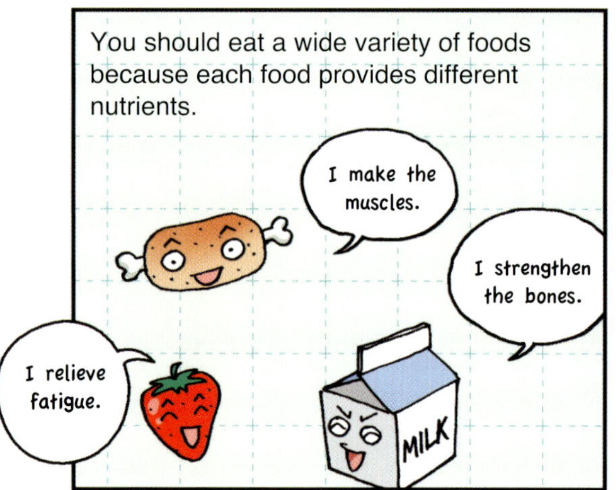

The food bicycle

The food bicycle shows a distribution of the six food groups, divided according to the amount of food in a way that makes it easy to see how much of which foods should be eaten at each meal. The illustration shows the importance of having balanced meals (back wheel) consisting of various kinds of food, as well as the importance of water intake (front wheel) and the prevention of obesity through proper exercise (the bicycle). An individual food intake schedule can be planned or evaluated based on the number of representative foods in each food group.

The Function of Each Nutrient

Carbohydrate

Main source of energy; develops good reflexes

Proteins

Main component of bodily tissues (muscles, hormones)

Fat

Main source of energy during long hours of exercise; helps maintain body temperature

Vitamins

Helps with the function of main nutrients; helps maintain physical functions

Minerals

Regulates osmotic pressure and body fluids

Water

Regulates temperature, transports nutrients, discharges waste

Sports and Mental Health

When you're healthy, you feel more confident because you can use your body the way you want, and you can also have better relationships with people.
Who can jump over this?
I can!

In addition, if you relieve your stress through exercising, you can control yourself better in stressful situations.
Nyah!
Coward!
Peace!
Serenity!

Yeah, I don't even care anymore when Omji teases me, he he.
Hmm...
Ha ha

But whenever I think about Spot...

He taught me to enjoy sports, but I left him behind...

Huh? What do you mean? I brought him back.
What?

Spot's Rebirth

Just as the brain is what matters the most in the human body, the program is what matters the most in a robot.

Huh? He looks different!
Wow, so pretty!

So pretty, I love it!
It's only a robot!

Good to see you again, Spot!

Good to see you again, too! Now, shall we start training again?
Grab

Start warming up!
It is Spot! I'm still happy, though. He he.
One, two!
One, two!
Tap
Tap

So if you switched programs, what happened to the original Spot?

I installed a program that will do them a whole lot of good. I'm sure it's helping them out a lot, about now.
Ha ha

In the meantime, at the villains' headquarters
We're back, Boss!

Did you deliver the message I sent?
Of course!

These are all for you, from the children at the orphanage. Aren't there a lot? He he.
Children?

Dear Sir,
Thank you for playing with us and giving us gifts.
Dear Sir,
I love you.
Dear Sir,
Hello! I want to be good, just like you.
Dear Boss, I love you! I want to be like you when I grow up!
From Hyeonseong

And this is from the people in the town, a token of gratitude.
Oh, they shouldn't have...

Boss, we need to get to class, so...
Hurry, we're late!
Rush   Rush
Hmm... they sure have changed.

On your feet, everyone! Mr. Spot's here!

Today's topic is "love".
LOVE
When you treat people with love, they'll open the door to their hearts.
LOVE
The door you can't open even with guns and hammers, right?
Say "I love you" with sincerity to the person standing next to you.
Oh, that's... that's so...
Repeat after me, everyone!
"I love you!"
Bark
I... I... No, I can't!
It looks like we need to do it, too.
No, something's not right... this isn't right...
I love you...
I... I love you ...
I love you
I love you
Me... me too...
I love you
I... I love you ...
Good, everyone! Very good!

Why? Science Edu Comic

감수자| **목진실**(Jinsil Mock)

미국 어바나 샴페인 일리노이대학교에서 초등 교육을 전공하고 일리노이 주 중학교에서 과학, 수학 교사로 근무하였다.
하버드대학교에서 교육 교수법 석사 과정을 마쳤으며 현재 테네시 주 내시빌 소재, 밴더빌트 대학교에서 교육학 박사 과정을
이수 중이다.

편집장| **스콧 리히텐스타인**(Scott Lichtenstein)

미국 캘리포니아에서 태어나 하버드대학교에서 화학을 전공하였다. 하버드대학교 재학 시절 의회 토론 회의 회장을
역임하였으며, 졸업 후 교육 출판사 데미덱에서 근무하였다. 2007년 임페리얼 출판사를 설립하여 현재 CEO로 활동 중이다.

편집자| **데이비드 빈선트 키멀**(David Vincent Kimel)

이스라엘에서 태어나 스콧 리히텐스타인과 같은 시기에 하버드대학교에서 전통 문학을 전공하였다. 현재 예일대학교에서
토론 수업을 가르치는 동시에 임페리얼 출판사의 편집자로 다양한 교육 컨텐츠를 개발하는 일을 맡고 있다.

2013년 2월 28일 1판 1쇄 발행

회장 | 나춘호
펴낸이 | 나성훈   펴낸곳 | (주)예림당
등록 | 제4-161호   주소 | 서울특별시 강남구 삼성동 153
구매 문의 전화 | 예림M&B 561-9007   팩스 | 567-9660
책 내용 문의 전화 | 3404-8459   홈쇼핑 문의 전화 | 3404-9286
http://www.yearim.co.kr
ISBN 978-89-302-1357-8 18690
ⓒ 2013 예림당

| STAFF |

편집 상무 | 유인화   편집 이사 | 백광균
영어 판 편집 | 고은정/한민혜 장민경   한국어 판 편집 | 연양흠/장효순 박효정 이나영 이연옥 최혜원 김승현 최은송 박인의 박소현 김현경
사진 | 김창윤/이건무   디자인 | 정수현   홍보마케팅 | 박일성/채청용   제작 | 정병문/신상덕 곽종수 이기성   마케팅 | 예림M&B

| Photo CREDITS |

14p 체지방 측정계 ⓒ 자원메디칼 / **21p** 웨이트 트레이닝 ⓒ The U.S Navy / **23p** 마라톤 ⓒ hojusaram / **39p** 스타팅 블록 ⓒ Miaow Miaow / **45p** 원반던지기 ⓒ AdamKR / **52p** 자유형 ⓒ Jim Bahn, 배영 ⓒ Greg L. photos / **66p** 벨로드롬용 자전거 ⓒ bikeride, 벨로드롬 ⓒ Salim Virji / **67p** 바퀴살 자전거 ⓒ cobber cpd, 사이클 헬멧 ⓒ thefsb, 쇼트트랙 헬멧 ⓒ Emiel Ketelaar, 인라인 헬멧 ⓒ Miles Cave / **69p** 피겨 스케이트 ⓒ Kcr / **93p** 배구 ⓒ JMR_Photography / **117p** 빙산 ⓒ 극지연구소 / **121p** 스카이 서브 ⓒ enviziondotnet / **133p** 다리 기술 ⓒ Fotos Gov Ba, 잡기 싸움 ⓒ Fotos Gov Ba / **136p** 꺾기 ⓒ West Point Public Affairs / **140p** 격파 ⓒ David Reber's Hammer

그 외 ⓒ 유로크레온, 타임스페이스, 이미지클릭, 멀티비츠, 연합뉴스, 예림당

Why?

Sports Science

Workbook

정명숙 지음

McGraw Hill   YeaRimDang

Why? 이제 영어로 읽는다!

Why? Sports Science는 꼭 알아야 할 중요 단어를 체크하고
Why? 영어판의 내용을 제대로 이해했는지 확인할 수 있도록 구성했습니다.
워크북의 각 단원(Unit)을 공부하기 전에 오디오 CD를 들으며 영어판의 해당 단원을 다시 읽어 보세요.
꾸준히 반복하면 어려운 과학 용어를 익히고 실생활에 꼭 필요한 영어 회화도 배울 수 있어요.
Why? 이제 영어로 재미있게 읽어 보세요!

I. Vocabulary

주어진 단어의 뜻을 파악하고 정리한 다음 순서에 맞게 나열하여 문장을 완성해 보세요.
어휘와 작문 실력을 한꺼번에 키울 수 있어요.

II. Reading Comprehension

주제 찾기, 추론, 사실 여부 확인, 내용 파악, 숙어와 대명사의 이해, 글쓴이의 의도 파악, 지문의 순서 확인 등 다양한 유형의 문제가 골고루 실려 있어요. 본문의 내용을 잘 이해했는지 확인하면서 독해력을 길러 보세요.

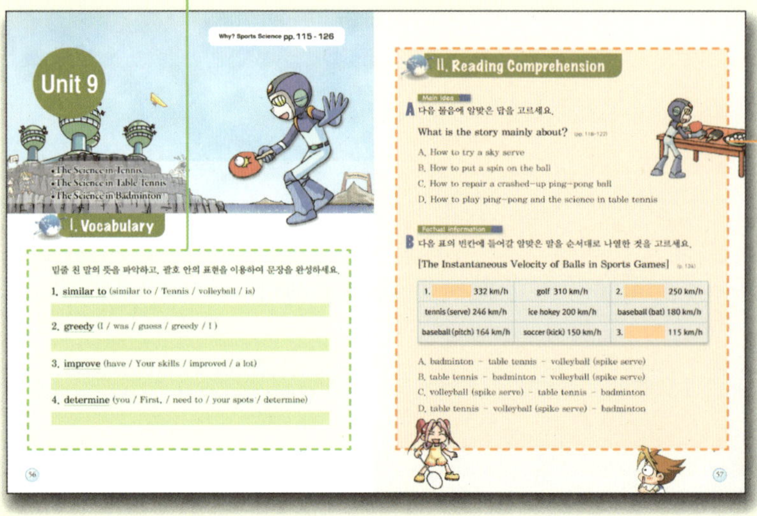

III. Summary

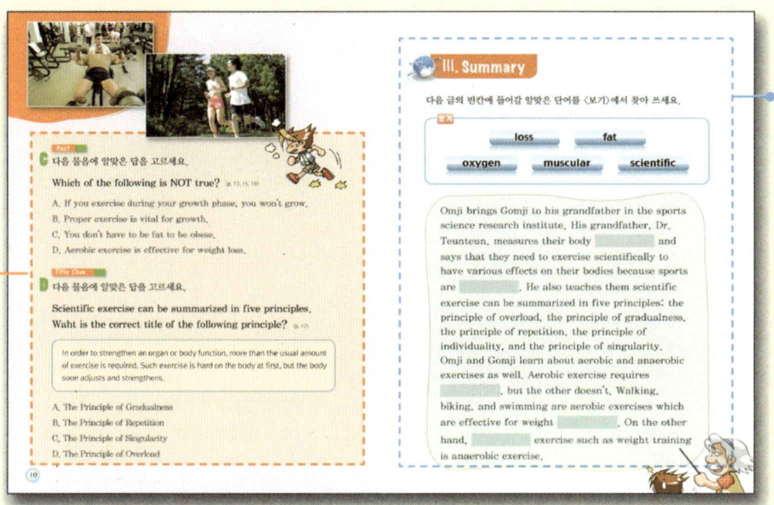

본문 내용을 간단하게 정리한 지문을 읽고, 〈보기〉에서 제시한 단어를 이용해 문장을 완성해 보세요.

IV. Speaking

A. 본문의 대화 내용을 떠올리며 바르게 대답해 보세요.

B. 〈보기〉에서 제시한 단어를 이용해 문장을 완성해 보세요. 실생활에 필요한 짧은 대화문을 익힐 수 있어요.

V. Puzzle

뜻풀이에 맞는 단어를 〈보기〉에서 찾아 다양한 퍼즐을 완성하세요. 퍼즐 게임을 하다 보면 단어도 외우고 영어에 대한 흥미도 키울 수 있어요.

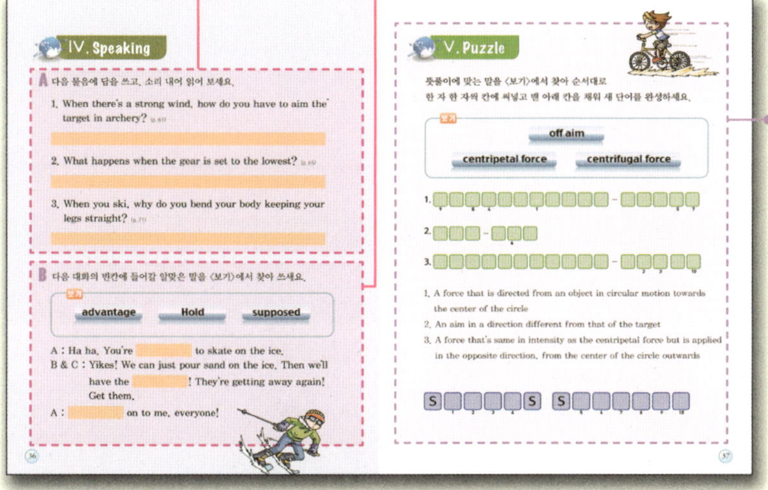

정답 및 해설

정답 및 해설을 통해 자신이 푼 문제를 꼼꼼히 확인해 보세요. 틀린 문제는 다시 확인하면서 실력을 키워 나가세요.

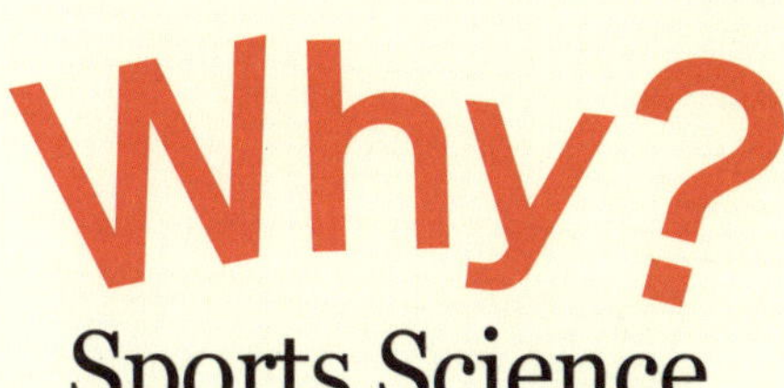

Why? Sports Science

Workbook

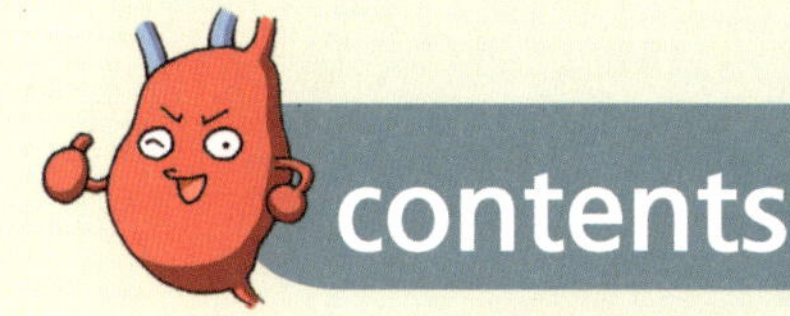

contents

Unit 1

I. Sports is a Science
- Gomji's Evaluation
- Exercising Scientifically
- Aerobic and Anaerobic Exercises

I. Vocabulary

밑줄 친 말의 뜻을 파악하고, 괄호 안의 표현을 이용하여 문장을 완성하세요.

1. <u>potbelly</u>
(first! / You / get rid of / should / your potbelly)

2. <u>stiff</u> (how / Look / you / stiff / are!)

3. <u>even if</u> (exercise / I'm / even if / healthy / I / don't)

4. <u>on a regular basis</u>
(to exercise / You / need / on a regular basis)

II. Reading Comprehension

A 다음 물음에 알맞은 답을 고르세요.

1. **What is the story mainly about?** (pp.17–18)

   A. The different reasons for exercising

   B. The different kinds of exercise

   C. Five principles of scientific exercise

   D. How to measure body fat

2. **What do scientists study in sports science?** (p. 12)

   A. Human organs and function

   B. Human body structure and function

   C. Human psychology and philosophy

   D. Human physiology and philosophy

B 다음 글의 빈칸에 들어갈 알맞은 말을 고르세요.

Jogging is the most typical   exercise. (p. 21)

A. aerobic   B. anaerobic

C. scientific   D. effective

C 다음 물음에 알맞은 답을 고르세요.

Which of the following is NOT true? (p. 13, 15, 19)

A. If you exercise during your growth phase, you won't grow.

B. Proper exercise is vital for growth.

C. You don't have to be fat to be obese.

D. Aerobic exercise is effective for weight loss.

D 다음 물음에 알맞은 답을 고르세요.

Scientific exercise can be summarized in five principles. What is the correct title of the following principle? (p. 17)

> In order to strengthen an organ or body function, more than the usual amount of exercise is required. Such exercise is hard on the body at first, but the body soon adjusts and strengthens.

A. The principle of gradualness

B. The principle of repetition

C. The principle of singularity

D. The principle of overload

III. Summary

다음 글의 빈칸에 들어갈 알맞은 단어를 〈보기〉에서 찾아 쓰세요.

보기

loss　　　　fat

oxygen　　　muscular　　　scientific

Omji brings Gomji to his grandfather in the sports science research institute. His grandfather, Dr. Teunteun, measures their body ＿＿＿＿ and says that they need to exercise scientifically to have various effects on their bodies because sports are ＿＿＿＿. He also teaches them scientific exercise can be summarized in five principles: the principle of overload, the principle of gradualness, the principle of repetition, the principle of individuality, and the principle of singularity. Omji and Gomji learn about aerobic and anaerobic exercises as well. Aerobic exercise requires ＿＿＿＿, but anaerobic exercise doesn't. Walking, biking, and swimming are aerobic exercises which are effective for weight ＿＿＿＿. On the other hand, ＿＿＿＿ exercise such as weight training is the most typical anaerobic exercise.

IV. Speaking

A 다음 물음에 답을 쓰고, 소리 내어 읽어 보세요.

1. Why does Gomji look stiff? (p. 11)

2. What is body fat (percentage)? (p. 13)

3. How do people grow in height? (p. 15)

B 다음 대화의 빈칸에 들어갈 알맞은 말을 〈보기〉에서 찾아 쓰세요.

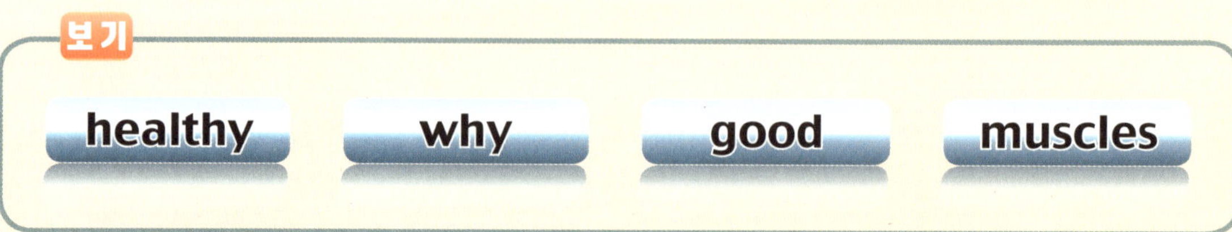

A : Do you know ___________ people exercise?

B : To build ___________, I guess.

C : It's fun to exercise, and it makes us ___________.

A : Yes, everyone has different reasons for exercising, but everyone knows that it is ___________ for you, right?

V. Puzzle

뜻풀이에 맞는 단어를 〈보기〉에서 찾아 퍼즐을 완성하세요.

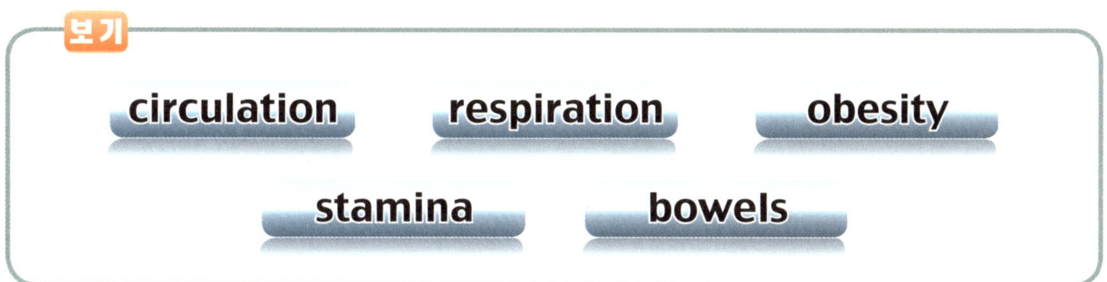

Across

3. the long tube in the body that helps digest food and carry solid waste out of the body

5. the movement of blood through the body that is caused by the pumping action of the heart

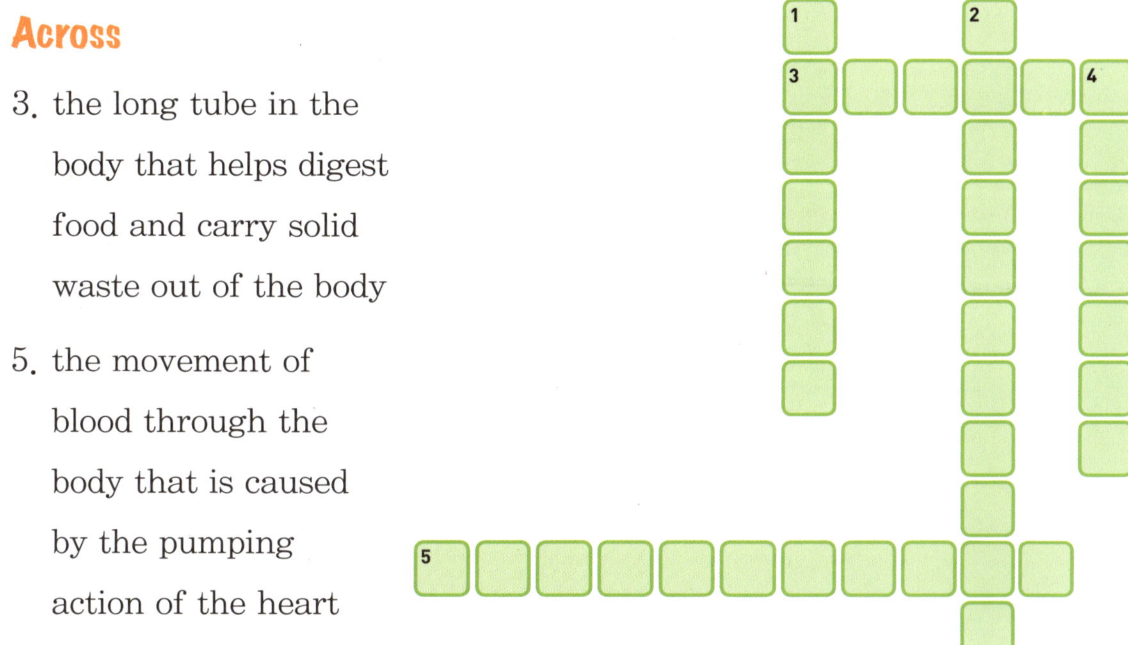

Down

1. more than average fatness

2. the act or process of breathing

4. the ability for the body to take in oxygen and continue with exercise

Unit 2

- Lactic Acids, the Cause of Muscle Fatigue
- Sports and the Heart
- Power Walking
- An Attack by Unidentified Assailants
- The First Encounter with Spot

I. Vocabulary

밑줄 친 말의 뜻을 파악하고, 괄호 안의 표현을 이용하여 문장을 완성하세요.

1. <u>trim</u> (all trim and fit / when / Don't fall / I'm / for me)

2. <u>resolve</u> (how long / I / your resolve / wonder / will last)

3. <u>scold</u>

(scolds him / Gomji / every day / needs / who / a strict instructor)

4. <u>be famous for</u> (is famous for / never growing / Ji−Sung Park / tired!)

II. Reading Comprehension

A 다음 물음에 알맞은 답을 고르세요.

1. **What is the story mainly about?** (pp. 22–23)

    A. Why athletes can run for a long time

    B. How aerobic exercise helps break down lactic acids quickly

    C. How to remove lactic acids, the cause of muscle fatigue

    D. Why taking a hot bath helps you get rid of fatigue

2. **What is required to break down lactic acids?** (p. 22)

    A. Chlorine   B. Oxygen

    C. Nitrogen   D. Hydrogen

B 다음 글의 빈칸에 들어갈 알맞은 말을 고르세요.

> The melting point for lactic acids is 25–26℃, so it breaks down quickly if you
> ___________ after exercise.   (p. 23)

A. take a cold shower   B. stretch yourself out

C. take a hot shower   D. take off your clothes right

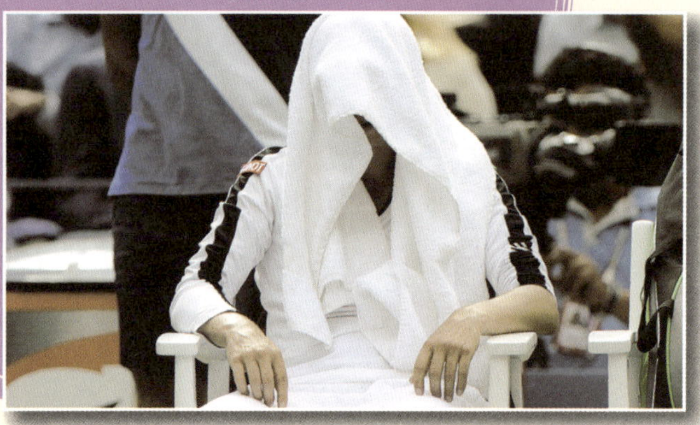

C 다음 물음에 알맞은 답을 고르세요.

Which of the following is NOT true about the basic posture for power walking? (p. 27)

A. You should walk between 6.4 to 8.9 km/h.

B. You should turn your waist excessively.

C. You should raise your arms high and swing them briskly.

D. You should keep your feet parallel.

D 다음 물음에 알맞은 답을 고르세요.

What can you infer from Gomji? (p. 22)

A. When lactic acids build up through exercise, muscles grow tired.

B. When lactic acids are removed, the muscle fatigue decreases.

C. During light aerobic exercise, lactic acids break down.

D. Regular aerobic exercise can help you recover quickly from fatigue.

III. Summary

다음 글의 빈칸에 들어갈 알맞은 단어를 〈보기〉에서 찾아 쓰세요.

heart	fatigue	abducted
oxygen	straight	warming

Dr. Teunteun explains the ways to remove lactic acids, the cause of muscle ____________. Light aerobic exercise and ____________ yourself up after exercise break down lactic acids quickly. Also, if you increase your ____________ consumption through regular aerobic exercise, you can recover quickly from fatigue. If your ____________ is strong, it can supply the body with a lot of oxygen in a short time. Then a lot of energy can be produced, and fatigue will go away quickly. The doctor adds that power walking will help maintain a ____________ figure, and muscular strength and cardiopulmonary function will improve. However, he is ____________ all of a sudden after saying that he has found an instructor for Gomji. Omji and Gomji find Dr. Teunteun's key to the laboratory. Soon, they encounter Spot who is programmed to train Gomji.

A 다음 물음에 답을 쓰고, 소리 내어 읽어 보세요.

1. Which heart beats slower per minute, an ordinary heart or an athletic heart? (p. 25)

2. How does oxygen enter our bodies? (p. 24)

3. How does the oxygen spread throughout the body? (p. 24)

B 다음 대화의 빈칸에 들어갈 알맞은 말을 〈보기〉에서 찾아 쓰세요.

> 보기
>
> longer   Power   fat   improvement

A : If you change just one habit, you'll see a dramatic ____________.

B : Really? Which habit?

A : The way you walk! ____________ walking is better than running for cutting down on body ____________, because it's easier and can be done for a ____________ amount of time.

V. Puzzle

뜻풀이에 맞는 단어를 〈보기〉에서 찾아 퍼즐을 완성하세요.

보기

laboratory　　fatigue　　function　　consumption

Across

2. a room or building with special equipment for doing scientific experiments and tests
3. the state of being very tired

Down

1. the act of eating or drinking something
3. the special purpose or activity for which a thing exists or is used

II. The Hidden Sports in Science
- Stretching and Physical Balance • The Science in Sprinting
- The Science in Long Distance Running • The Science in the Long Jump
- The Science in Throwing • The Science in the Pole Vault

I. Vocabulary

밑줄 친 말의 뜻을 파악하고, 괄호 안의 표현을 이용하여 문장을 완성하세요.

1. <u>cramp</u> (have / I / in / my leg / cramps)

2. <u>fool</u> (us / You / with / a wrestling dummy! / tried to fool)

3. <u>elastic</u> (elastic / like / are / Your arms / rubber bands!)

4. <u>be supposed to</u> (knock / is supposed to / out / you / It)

II. Reading Comprehension

A 다음 물음에 알맞은 답을 고르세요.

What is the story mainly about? (pp. 37–47)

A. The science in stretching

B. The science in physical balance

C. The science in arena events

D. The science in track and field events

B 다음 글의 빈칸에 들어갈 알맞은 말을 순서대로 나열한 것을 고르세요. (pp. 37–47)

1. In   , starting speed is crucial for setting the record.
2. When   , you must inhale through the nose and exhale through the mouth to avoid straining the throat.
3. In the   , do the run-up as fast as you can and jump just at the right spot!
4. In   , the athlete spins around in place to gain centrifugal force.
5. The   is a sport using elasticity.

A. running long distance − short distance running − long jump
− shot put, discus, hammer throw − pole vault

B. short distance running − running long distance − long jump
− shot put, discus, hammer throw − pole vault

C. long jump − short distance running − running long distance
− pole vault − shot put, discus, hammer throw

D. shot put, discus, hammer throw − short distance running
− long jump − running long distance − pole vault

C 다음 결과의 원인에 해당하는 답을 고르세요. (pp. 35-36)

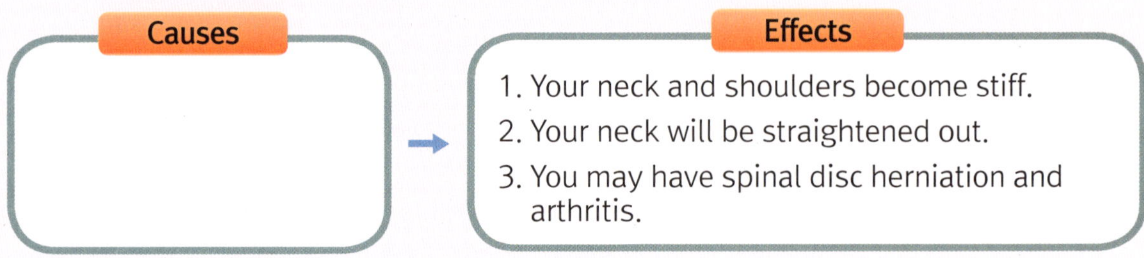

A. You keep your head bent for a long time.

B. You keep your head straight for a long time.

C. You sit in a chair for a long time.

D. You stand upright for a long time.

D 다음 물음에 알맞은 답을 고르세요.

In Gomji's speech bubble, we can see the underlined word 'file'. What is the word that we can use instead of it? (p. 37)

A. bind

B. smooth

C. computer data

D. submit

다음 글의 빈칸에 들어갈 알맞은 단어를 〈보기〉에서 찾아 쓰세요.

보기

short	long	
throwing	pole vault	long jump

Spot asks Gomji to warm up and do some stretching before starting training. Suddenly, assailants who abducted Dr. Teunteun appear and try to catch the kids. However, Spot begins training the kids by running with the starting posture in __________ distance running. Soon after, Spot tells them to touch the ground heel first and to breathe using both their noses and mouths at the same time as they run a __________ distance. When they reach a ditch, they are trapped by the assailants. To jump over the ditch, Spot trains for the __________. And then, Spot tells the kids why athletes do a run-up and spin around in __________ when throwing a stone at the assailants. The kids are trapped again at a dead end. Fortunately, it's Spot's plan to come this way to teach the kids the science in the __________.

Ⅳ. Speaking

A 다음 물음에 답을 쓰고, 소리 내어 읽어 보세요.

1. Why do athletes warm up before a race? (p. 35)

2. What is the law of action and reaction? (p. 38)

3. Why do javelin throwers do a run-up before throwing? (p. 45)

B 다음 대화의 빈칸에 들어갈 알맞은 말을 〈보기〉에서 찾아 쓰세요.

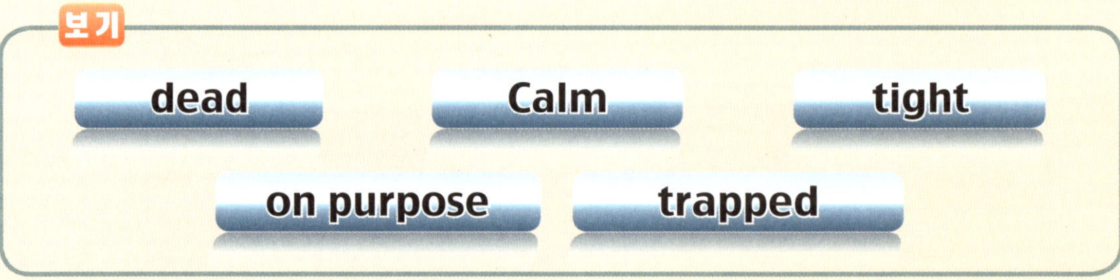

A : Uh-oh, it's a 　　　　　 end.
D : Ha ha, you're 　　　　　 for sure, now!
C : Don't worry. I came this way 　　　　　.
A : What? You got us trapped on purpose!
B : 　　　　　 down, I'm sure Spot has his reasons.
C : Of course I do. Look at this pole! We're going to jump
　　using the pole. Hold on 　　　　　!

사진에 해당하는 육상 경기 종목을 〈보기〉에서 찾아 퍼즐을 완성하세요.

보기

running   (the) javelin

(the) long jump   (the) discus throw   (the) pole vault

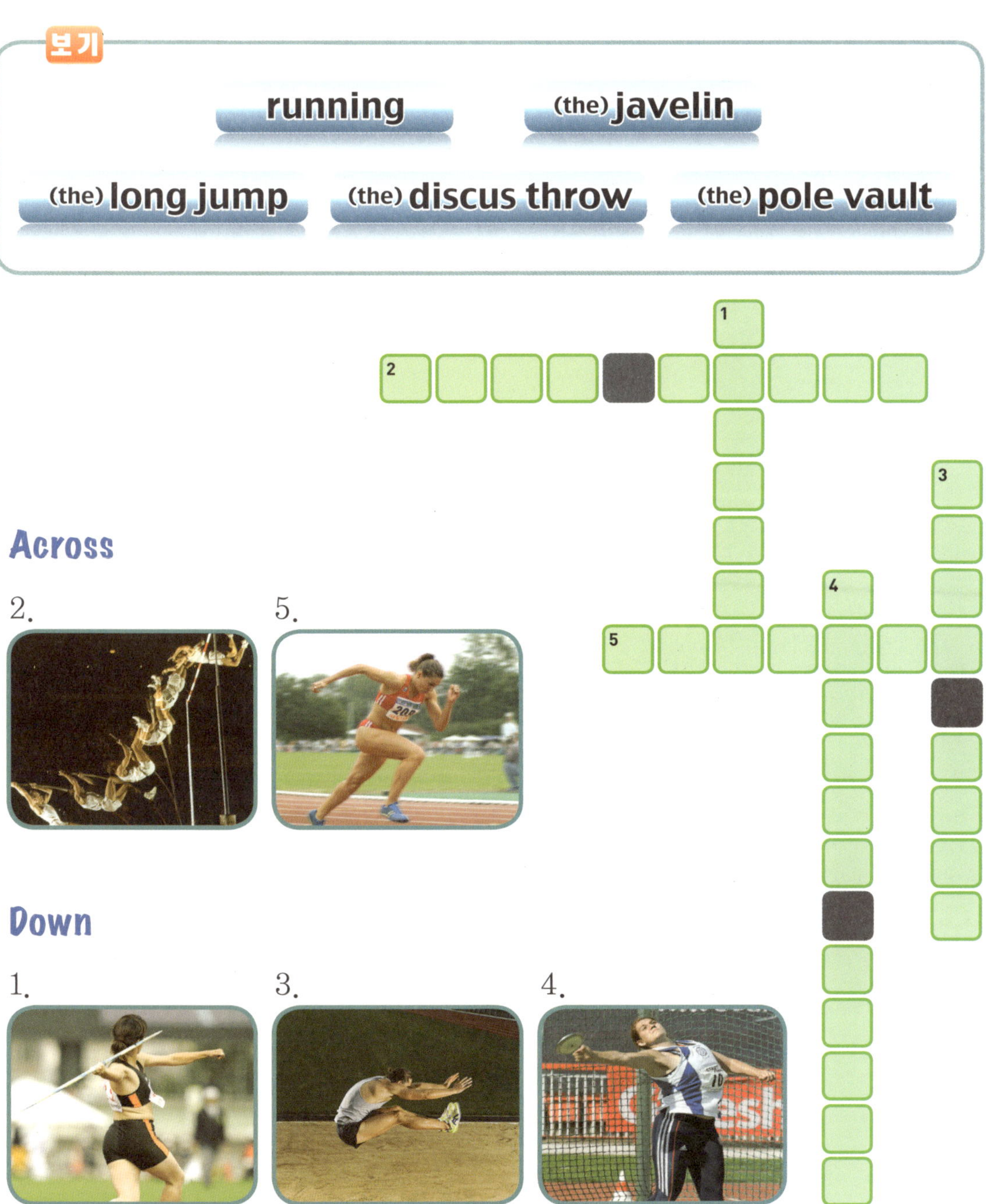

Across

2.

5.

Down

1.

3.

4.

Unit 4

I. Vocabulary

밑줄 친 말의 뜻을 파악하고, 괄호 안의 표현을 이용하여 문장을 완성하세요.

1. <u>rescue</u> (my grandfather! / rescue / have to / We)

2. <u>float</u> (People / better / more fat / with / float)

3. <u>different from</u> (is / Water / the ground! / different from)

4. <u>be good at</u> (are good at? / Is / anything / there / you)

II. Reading Comprehension

A 다음 물음에 알맞은 답을 고르세요.

What is the story mainly about? (pp. 50–51)

A. Why an object floats

B. How to move forward in water

C. Why a full body suit reduces friction

D. Why hypothermia occurs

B 다음 글의 빈칸에 공통으로 들어갈 알맞은 말을 고르세요.

> Some swimmers shave their heads to reduce ▇▇▇▇▇. Actually, full body swimsuits reduce ▇▇▇▇▇ because they are made with special material and technology. (p. 53)
>
> The spinning reduces ▇▇▇▇▇ with the air, allowing the bullet to go further in a straighter line. (p. 59)

A. density

B. temperature

C. friction

D. speed

C 다음 물음에 알맞은 답을 고르세요.

Which of the following is NOT true? (pp. 48–59)

A. If you lie horizontally in water, you can't float better.

B. Everything except fat has a greater specific gravity than water.

C. When you kick at the ground, the ground pushes you back in the opposite direction.

D. You can hit the target only if you aim using both the backsight and the foresight.

D 다음 표의 빈칸에 들어갈 알맞은 말을 〈보기〉에서 찾아 쓰세요. (p. 59)

〈보기〉

Rifle   **Air Gun**   **Paintball Gun**

1.	2.
It fires bullets by means of compressed air or other gas. It has a shorter range than a rifle.	It is a weapon that launches one, or many, bullets at high velocity through burning of a propellant which pushes the bullet forward. It is noisy and the barrel vibrates more after shooting.

다음 글의 빈칸에 들어갈 알맞은 단어를 〈보기〉에서 찾아 쓰세요.

보기

shoots fast covers

hypothermia running

Spot, Gomji, and Omji keep __________ to the water. Spot gets the kids to jump in the water and teaches them how to swim. He also tells them about various swimming styles and why swimmers in full body swimsuits can swim __________. After a while, they come out of water feeling cold. Spot dries the kids so they don't get __________. Meanwhile, the assailants still chase them in a boat. Spot brings the kids to Sports Island where Gomji __________ the assailants with a paintball gun. However, Gomji can't hit the target, so Spot teaches him science in shooting. Then he __________ for the kids so that they go out through the back where there is a hole.

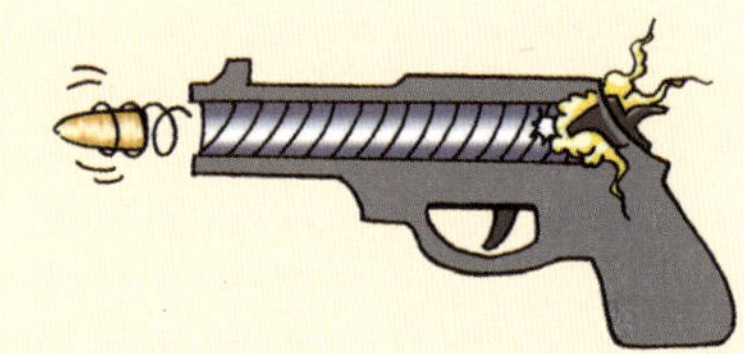

A 다음 물음에 답을 쓰고, 소리 내어 읽어 보세요.

1. What makes an object float or sink? (p. 49)

2. Why can't you move forward in outer space? (p. 50)

3. What are symptoms of hypothermia? (p. 54)

B 다음 대화의 빈칸에 들어갈 알맞은 말을 〈보기〉에서 찾아 쓰세요.

보기

breeze   heat   long   hypothermia

A : Were we in the water for too ____________? Come on!

B : Oh, it's cold!

A : If you stay in cold water for a long time, you can lose

____________ and come down with ____________.

B : Brrr!

A : Let me dry you up with a warm ____________! (Whoosh)

B : Wow, it's warm!

V. Puzzle

빈칸에 들어갈 알맞은 단어를 〈보기〉에서 찾아 퍼즐을 완성하세요.

> **보기**
>
> **freestyle**　　**breaststroke**　　**backstroke**　　**butterfly**

Across

3. The ____________ is a swimming style in which you contract and expand your arms and legs like a frog to move forward.

Down

1. The ____________ is a swimming style in which you lie straight on your back with your face above the water.

2. In ____________, respiratory control is very important in the front crawl because the face goes in and out of the water.

3. The ____________ is a swimming style in which both arms and legs are used all at once to move the body forward like a wave.

I. Vocabulary

밑줄 친 말의 뜻을 파악하고, 괄호 안의 표현을 이용하여 문장을 완성하세요.

1. <u>scarecrow</u> (I've / time / to have / set up / some scarecrows)

2. <u>equipment</u> (You / play / can't / the equipment! / with)

3. advantage
(We'll have / if we / the advantage / on the ice / pour sand)

4. <u>due to</u>
(the resistance / due to / crashes / of bulletproof clothing / A bullet)

II. Reading Comprehension

A 다음 물음에 알맞은 답을 고르세요.

What is the story mainly about? (pp. 60–63)

A. How to aim at the target

B. The role of the fletching on the arrow

C. How dangerous arrows are

D. All of the above

B 다음 표의 각 글을 읽고 맞으면 True, 틀리면 False에 동그라미 표시를 하세요. (pp. 60–73)

A	Archery is a sport which uses the elasticity of the bow.	True	False
B	When you're starting out or going uphill, you should raise the pedal gear so that you may ride with less exertion.	True	False
C	Cyclists bend forward to reduce the drag against the direction of the movement.	True	False
D	When the ice melts into water, it becomes even less slippery.	True	False
E	The pressure in a given area is reduced when the area contracts.	True	False

C 다음 물음에 알맞은 답을 고르세요.

Which of the following is NOT true? (pp. 60–73)

A. The arrow flies in an arc, so you must aim higher than the target.

B. A track bicycle is made so that a lot of friction against the wind is generated.

C. The science in skating is all about gliding.

D. Artificial snow is made by forcing water and pressurized gas through a snow machine.

D 다음 표의 내용을 읽고 피겨 스케이팅과 스피드 스케이팅의 각 특성을 해당하는 칸에 표시하세요.

[How are they similar? How are they different?] (p. 69)

Attribute	Figure Skating	Speed Skating
Skaters can maintain their strength by minimizing friction and maintaining inertia and balance.		
The blades are short and thick.		
The blades are long and thin.		
Various movements are required.		
The blades keep the skater from veering off.		

III. Summary

다음 글의 빈칸에 들어갈 알맞은 단어를 〈보기〉에서 찾아 쓰세요.

보기

| artificial | control | arrows |
| elasticity | bicycles | skating |

Spot takes Gomji and Omji to an archery field and teaches them about archery, which uses the ________ of the bow. He also tells them ________ can penetrate even a bulletproof vest. They soon find the assailants are hiding right behind them, and they start to get away riding ________. Spot tells them how to speed up using bicycles for racing and sports helmets for safety during the ride. The assailants chase them on motorcycles, but the kids follow Spot into an indoor ________ rink. Spot shows the kids how to skate and the differences between figure skating and speed skating. Then he brings the kids to the next door where it's full of ________ snow. There the kids ride skies down learning how to ________ the speed, and reach a locked door.

A 다음 물음에 답을 쓰고, 소리 내어 읽어 보세요.

1. When there's a strong wind, how do you have to aim at the target in archery? (p. 61)

2. What happens when the gear is set to the lowest? (p. 65)

3. When you ski, why do you bend your body keeping your legs straight? (p. 71)

B 다음 대화의 빈칸에 들어갈 알맞은 말을 〈보기〉에서 찾아 쓰세요.

A : Ha ha, you're __________ to skate on the ice.

B & C : Yikes! We can just pour sand on the ice. Then we'll have the __________! They're getting away again! Get them!

A : __________ on to me, everyone!

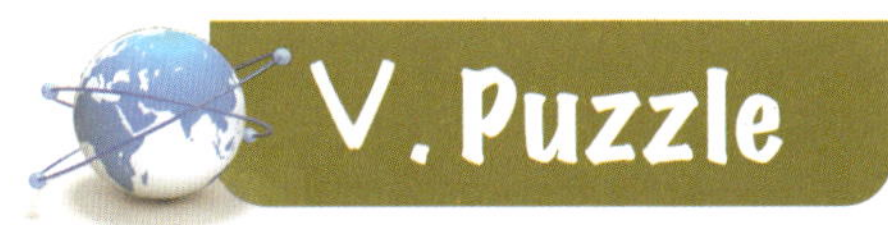

뜻풀이에 맞는 말을 〈보기〉에서 찾아 순서대로
한 자 한 자씩 칸에 써넣고 맨 아래 칸을 채워 새 단어를 완성하세요.

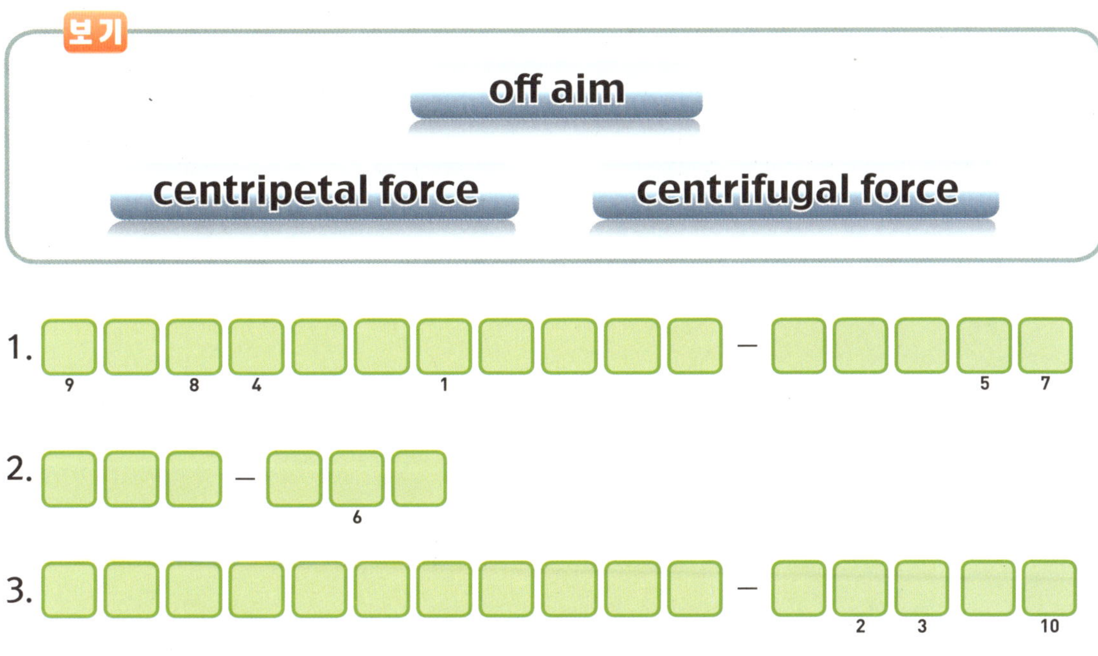

1. A force that is directed from an object in circular motion towards the center of the circle

2. An aim in a direction different from that of the target

3. A force that has the same intensity as the centripetal force but is applied in the opposite direction, from the center of the circle outwards

I. Vocabulary

밑줄 친 말의 뜻을 파악하고, 괄호 안의 표현을 이용하여 문장을 완성하세요.

1. <u>successive</u> (three / I / baskets! / successive / made)

2. <u>all of a sudden</u> (changed / The ball / all of a sudden! / its direction)

3. <u>keep ~ from ~ing</u>

(keep / The bumps / from / slipping away / easily / the ball)

4. <u>give it a try</u>

(I'll / this time, / so / give it a try / be a goalkeeper)

II. Reading Comprehension

A 다음 물음에 알맞은 답을 고르세요.

What is the story mainly about? (pp. 80–85)

A. How a soccer ball bends

B. The role of the pieces on the soccer ball

C. How to score a goal

D. All of the above

B 다음 물음에 알맞은 답을 고르세요.

1. **What does the following picture explain?** (p. 76)

The scope in which the center of the ball can move when a basket is scored.

A. The chance of making it in the basket decreases when the ball goes in from the side of the basket.

B. The chance of making it in the basket increases when the ball goes in from the side of the side.

C. The chance of making it in the basket increases when the ball falls from right above the basket.

D. The chance of making it in the basket decreases when the ball falls from right above the basket.

2. The following picture shows one kind of pass.
   What is it? (p. 87)

A. Space pass

B. Triangle pass

C. Instep pass

D. Obtuse angle pass

Fact

C 다음 물음에 알맞은 답을 고르세요.

Which of the following is NOT true? (pp. 74–89)

A. Jumping helps you make a basket because you can raise the shooting height.

B. Pentagons and hexagons on the soccer ball make the ball as spherical as possible.

C. The ball bends due to the change in the pressure on the rapidly spinning ball.

D. When the goalkeeper is far from you, your shooting angle is reduced.

III. Summary

다음 글의 빈칸에 들어갈 알맞은 단어를 〈보기〉에서 찾아 쓰세요.

banana	**train**	**ball**
feint	**principles**	**goalpost**

Spot opens the locked door of the sports science training center, where the kids are going to learn about __________ games. Gomji and Omji want to save the doctor, but they can't because Spot is programmed to __________ them first. Spot gives them tests. The first test is to make three consecutive baskets. Omji makes three successive baskets after learning the scientific __________ in basketball. Then the next course is soccer. Spot shows a __________ kick, and then tells the kids to kick the ball into the __________ with a goalkeeper. Gomji tries to score a goal but he fails. Spot tells the kids about some soccer techniques. Gomji tries to kick the ball with Spot as the goalkeeper, but he misses again. However, Gomji passes the test because the __________ that Gomij tricked Spot with counts as a technique. Finally, Spot explains about how soccer balls are made up of many pieces.

IV. Speaking

A 다음 물음에 답을 쓰고, 소리 내어 읽어 보세요.

1. When using the backboard, what technique do you need to score a basket? (p. 78)

2. How far is the penalty mark from the goal line in soccer? (p. 87)

3. The Teamgeist is a soccer ball made up of many pieces. What are the characteristics of the ball? (p. 89)

B 다음 대화의 빈칸에 들어갈 알맞은 말을 〈보기〉에서 찾아 쓰세요.

보기

tricked　　lightly　　method　　feints

A : First I kick the ball ＿＿＿＿＿. And now, shoot! (Swoosh)

B : No way!

A : He he, I ＿＿＿＿＿ you! (Tap)

B : Using ＿＿＿＿＿ counts as a technique. Since you learned the ＿＿＿＿＿ on your own, I'm going to pass you!

V. Puzzle

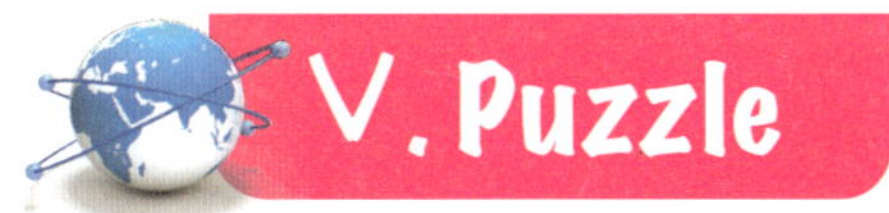

뜻풀이에 맞는 단어를 〈보기〉에서 찾아 퍼즐을 완성하세요.

보기

offense　opponent　horizontal
vertical　feint

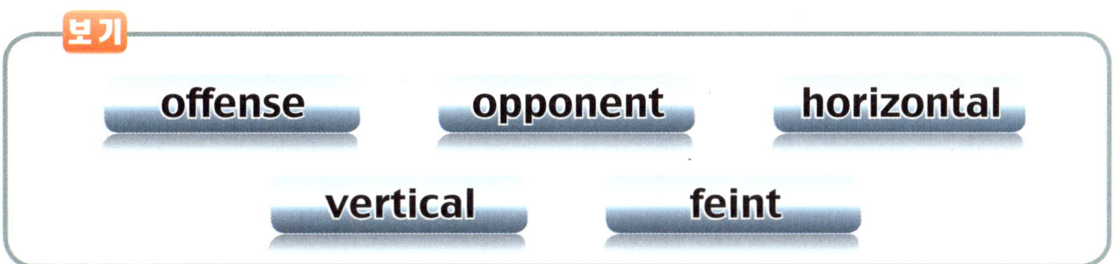

Across

2. the group of players on a team who try to score points or goals against an opponent
4. going straight up
5. a person, team, group, etc. that is competing against another in a contest

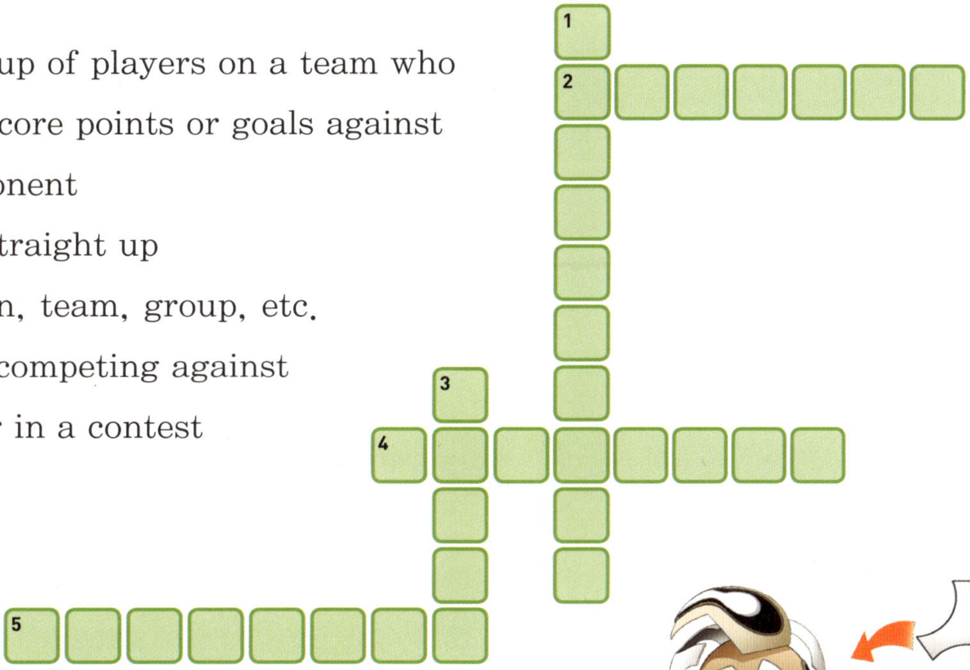

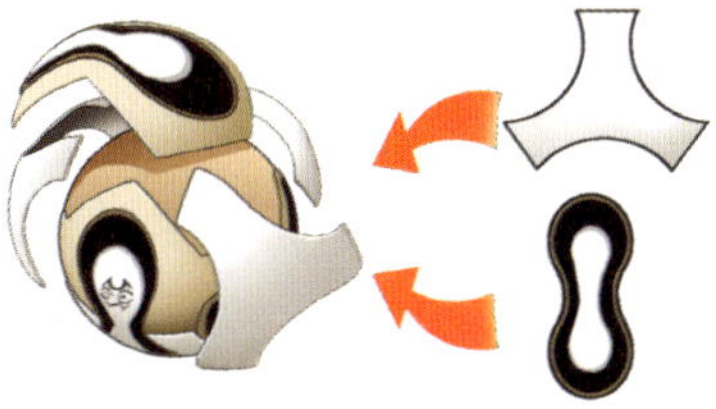

Down

1. parallel to the ground
3. a quick movement that you make to trick an opponent

Unit 7

- The Science in Volleyball
- The Science in Baseball

I. Vocabulary

밑줄 친 말의 뜻을 파악하고, 괄호 안의 표현을 이용하여 문장을 완성하세요.

1. <u>awesome</u> (awesome / You / my / pass! / wasted)

2. <u>coincidence</u> (just / That / a coincidence / was)

3. <u>be equipped with</u> (are equipped with / Helmets / ear protection / for amateurs / on both sides)

4. <u>so far</u> (and I saw / all your throws / I studied / a pattern / so far,)

II. Reading Comprehension

A 다음 물음에 알맞은 답을 고르세요.

What is the story mainly about? (pp. 93-95)

A. The movement of the volleyball

B. The different types of defenses in volleyball

C. How to receive balls in volleyball

D. How to make attacks in volleyball

B 다음 글의 빈칸에 차례대로 들어갈 알맞은 말을 고르세요.

1. In volleyball, you can make up to ________ contacts with the ball before sending the ball back to the opposite side of the court. One person can make no more than ________ successive contacts. (p. 90)

A. two, three   B. three, two

C. three, three   D. four, two

2. The stitches on a baseball help the ball fly ________ and ________. (p. 99)

A. faster, closer   B. slower, further

C. faster, further   D. slower, closer

C 다음 물음에 알맞은 답을 고르세요.

Which of the following is NOT true? (pp. 90–102)

A. In volleyball, if your arms are too tense, the ball can bounce off too far.

B. In volleyball, feints are used in the time lag attack.

C. Baseball pitches differ depending on how the pitcher grips the ball.

D. In baseball, exercising your arms is more important than legs.

D 각 그림을 보고 공 잡는 방법에 따른 야구공의 구질을 알맞게 연결하세요. (p. 100)

   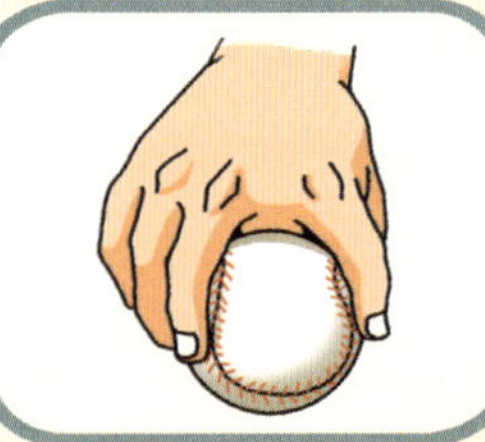

Slider	Fork Ball	Fast Ball	Curve Ball
It looks like a fast ball up to 60 cm away from the batter's box, then bends outwards of a right-handed batter.	It is slow, because the diverging fingers disperse the force, but it suddenly drops in front of the batter.	The ball is fast with less of a bend. A skilled pitcher can make the ball float or sink.	It looks like a fast ball but drops to the ground before the plate.

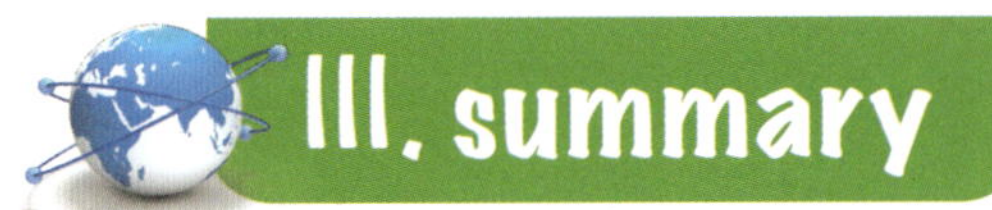

III. summary

다음 글의 빈칸에 들어갈 알맞은 단어를 〈보기〉에서 찾아 쓰세요.

At volleyball court, Spot teaches Gomji and Omji how to hit the balls that he throws over the ____________. Then he also teaches how to make ____________ in volleyball. Gomji passes the volleyball test since he made an ____________. After training for volleyball, they move to a batting cage, and Gomji puts on a baseball helmet with ear ____________ on one side. Spot tells Gomji how to hit a ball fast and accurately, and what a ____________ ball is. He shows the characteristics of a baseball, different pitches according to ____________, and how to throw a strong pass as well. Finally, Gomji can see a pattern after studying all Spot's throws so that he can ____________ what Spot's next throw will be like.

A 다음 물음에 답을 쓰고, 소리 내어 읽어 보세요.

1. In volleyball, when are feints usually used? (p. 95)

2. What is important for batters to hit the ball fast and accurately? (p. 98)

3. In baseball, what is the ball that bends as it comes in called? (p. 99)

B 다음 대화의 빈칸에 들어갈 알맞은 말을 〈보기〉에서 찾아 쓰세요.

보기

attitude   mistake   over   difficult

A : That might be a little ___________ for you, I imagine.

B : Let's do it ___________! I can do it! I never make the same ___________ twice!

A : All right, I like the ___________!

B : Oh, I missed again!

뜻풀이에 맞는 단어를 〈보기〉에서 찾아 퍼즐을 완성하세요.

보기

batter　　**setter**　　**toss**　　**breaking ball**

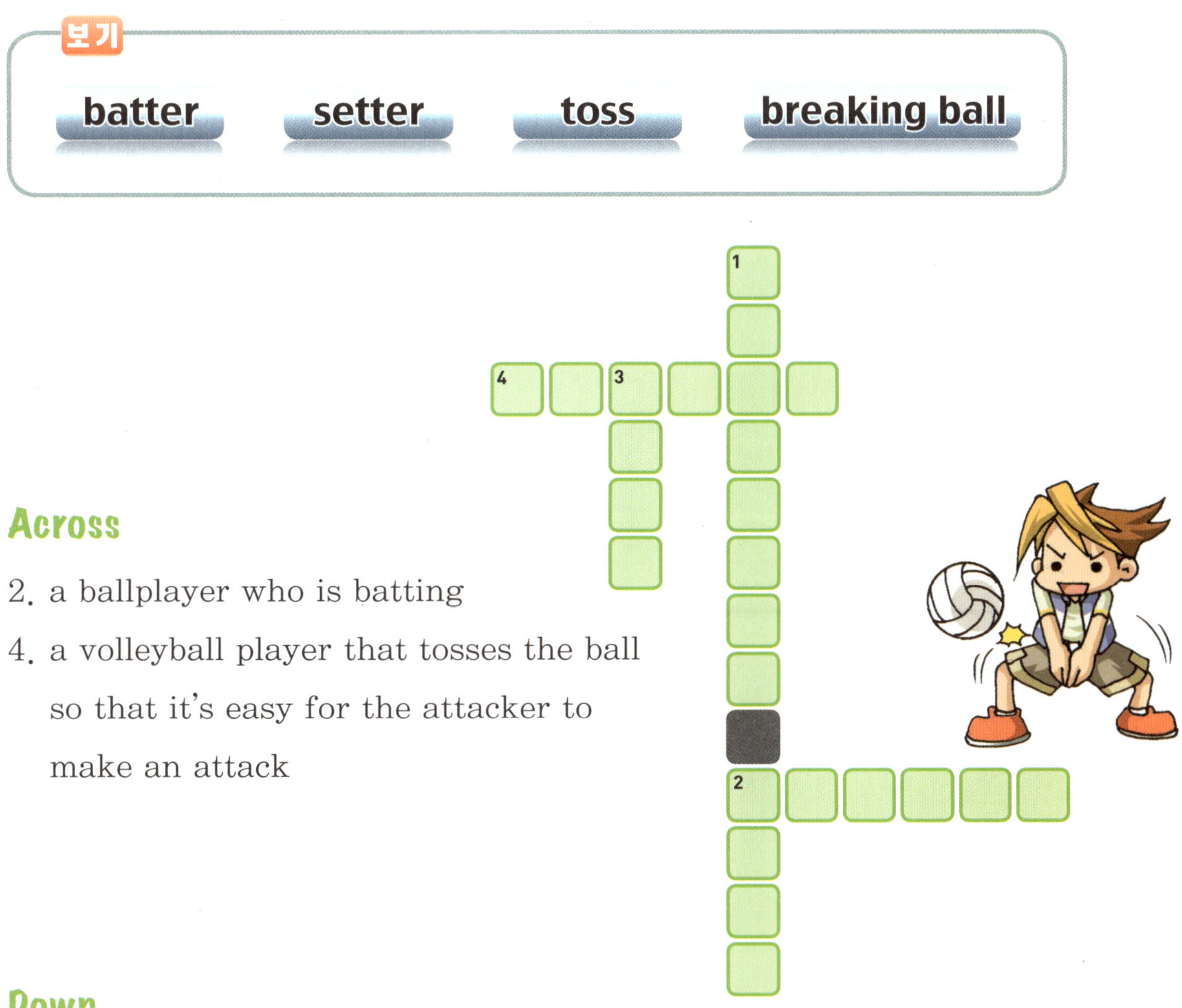

Across

2. a ballplayer who is batting

4. a volleyball player that tosses the ball so that it's easy for the attacker to make an attack

Down

1. a pitch of a baseball that is thrown with spin so that its path curves as it approaches the batter

3. an act of throwing the volleyball lightly up into the air so that it's easy for the attacker to make an attack

Unit 8

I. Vocabulary

밑줄 친 말의 뜻을 파악하고, 괄호 안의 표현을 이용하여 문장을 완성하세요.

1. require

(to see / thinking / that playing sports / They're starting / requires)

2. indicate (their weight / on bowling balls / The numbers / indicate)

3. attempt

(to knock / down / I'm going / in a single attempt! / them)

4. at once (them down / possible / Is / at once? / to knock / it)

II. Reading Comprehension

A 다음 물음에 알맞은 답을 고르세요.

What is the story mainly about? (pp. 103–104)

A. Why the dimples on golf ball are made on purpose

B. Why the golf ball is smaller than a baseball

C. Why golfers consider various factors when making a swing

D. Why playing sports requires thinking

B 다음 물음에 알맞은 답을 모두 고르세요.

Why are dimples put on a golf ball on purpose? (p. 104)

A. That's because the ball has been hit many times.

B. That's because a ball with dimples flies further than a ball without dimples.

C. That's because dimples make a greater difference in the pressure when the ball spins, making it easier to hit a curve ball.

D. That's because a ball with dimples is more beautiful than a ball without dimples.

C 다음 물음에 알맞은 답을 고르세요.

Which factor of the following should NOT be considered when making a swing in golf? (p. 105)

A. The direction from which the wind blows

B. The incline of the ground

C. The curve of the ground

D. The condition of clothes

E. The depth to which the ball is driven

D 꼼지가 볼링장에서 스트라이크를 치려 할 때 해야 할 행동으로 맞으면 True, 틀리면 False에 동그라미 표시를 하세요. (pp. 108-114)

A	He should choose a ball that's too heavy for him.	True	False
B	He should control his steps as he walks so that he'll be able to roll the ball on his third or fourth step.	True	False
C	He must bend his arm when making pendular movements.	True	False
D	He must keep his lower body stable so that his shoulder doesn't shake when he makes pendular movements.	True	False
E	He must roll the ball in between the #1 and #2 pins because he is right-handed.	True	False

III. Summary

다음 글의 빈칸에 들어갈 알맞은 단어를 〈보기〉에서 찾아 쓰세요.

보기

split	thinking	balance	pose
swing	bowling	wrist	dimples

Spot gives Gomji a golf club and asks him to hit a ball with grooves called ____________. He tells the kids where the ball is hit and goes, and he adds some factors that should be considered when making a ____________. The kids are starting to see that playing sports requires ____________. Omji tries to hit the ball into a hole and she makes it. Now, it's ____________, a game of knocking down ten pins by rolling a ball twice. Gomji wants to roll the ball once, but it rolls off to the side. So Spot shows the right ____________ and why the ball bends. On Omji's turn, the ball bends because of her ____________ movement. Since she has pins left over from her first go, which is called a ____________, Spot shows how to knock them down at once. At last, Gomji gives it a try again expecting a strike and he does it by keeping his ____________, rolling the ball in a stable pose.

A 다음 물음에 답을 쓰고, 소리 내어 읽어 보세요.

1. How can you hit a ball to make a double leap in golf? (p. 105)

2. How many times do you roll a bowling ball to knock down ten pins? (p. 108)

3. Why does the bowling ball curve all of a sudden? (p. 111)

B 다음 대화의 빈칸에 들어갈 알맞은 말을 〈보기〉에서 찾아 쓰세요.

보기

| pose | weird | pins | stable | embarrassing |

A : Oh, how __________! The ball rolled off to the side. That was __________. Let me try again!

B : Oh, look at your __________.

A : Oh, I came too close. Yikes!

B : Your steps are all wrong. You need to be in a __________ position to exert your energy towards the __________.

빈칸에 들어갈 알맞은 단어를 〈보기〉에서 찾아 퍼즐을 완성하세요.

보기

dimples double leap pendular split

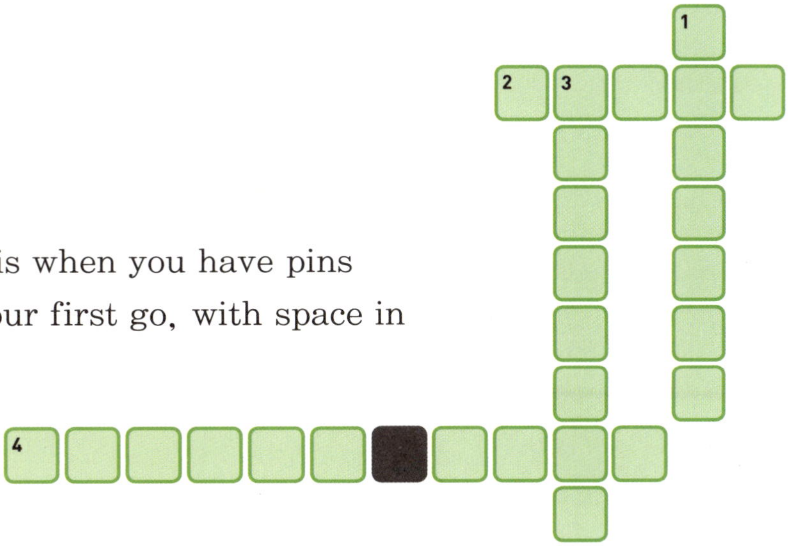

Across

2. A ____________ is when you have pins left over from your first go, with space in between.

4. Golf balls can make a ____________ because balls fly forward straight when the speed is high, and when balls slow down, the Magnus effect comes into play.

Down

1. The grooves on the golf ball are called ____________.

3. ____________ movement must be made in a straight line in the front and back, with the shoulder as the axis.

밑줄 친 말의 뜻을 파악하고, 괄호 안의 표현을 이용하여 문장을 완성하세요.

1. <u>similar to</u> (similar to / Tennis / volleyball / is)

2. <u>greedy</u> (I / was / guess / greedy / I)

3. <u>improve</u> (have / Your skills / improved / a lot)

4. <u>determine</u> (you / First, / need to / your spots / determine)

II. Reading Comprehension

A 다음 물음에 알맞은 답을 고르세요.

What is the story mainly about? (pp. 118–122)

A. How to try a sky serve

B. How to put a spin on the ball

C. How to repair a crashed-up ping-pong ball

D. How to play ping-pong and the science in table tennis

B 다음 표의 빈칸에 들어갈 알맞은 말을 순서대로 나열한 것을 고르세요.

[The Instantaneous Velocity of Balls in Sports Games] (p. 124)

1. 332 km/h	golf 310 km/h	2. 250 km/h
tennis (serve) 246 km/h	ice hokey 200 km/h	baseball (bat) 180 km/h
baseball (pitch) 164 km/h	soccer (kick) 150 km/h	3. 115 km/h

A. badminton – table tennis – volleyball (spike serve)

B. table tennis – badminton – volleyball (spike serve)

C. volleyball (spike serve) – table tennis – badminton

D. table tennis – volleyball (spike serve) – badminton

C 다음 물음에 알맞은 답을 고르세요.

Which of the following is NOT how you play ping-pong? (pp. 119–121)

A. When making a serve, you pass the ball right to the opponent's court.

B. To put a strong spin on the ball, the racket must touch the ball for a while.

C. When making a serve, you must first make the ball hit your side of the court.

D. To make the serve stronger, throw the ball high.

D 다음 결과의 원인에 해당하는 답을 고르세요. (pp. 116–117)

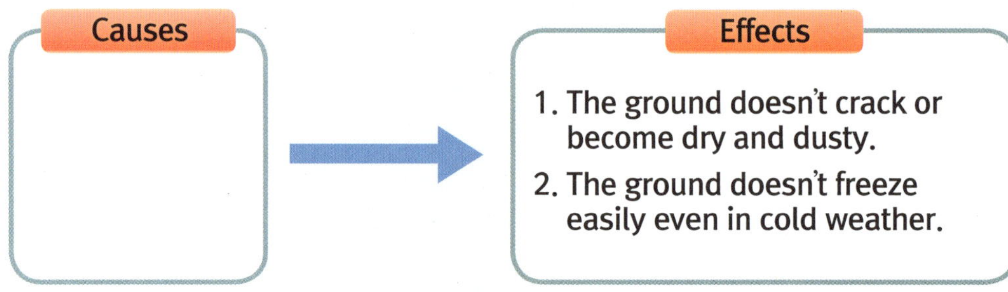

A. The dirt on the ground of tennis court is clay.

B. Salt is scattered over the ground of tennis court.

C. Water is sprinkled on the ground of tennis court.

D. The ground of tennis court is made of concrete.

다음 글의 빈칸에 들어갈 알맞은 단어를 〈보기〉에서 찾아 쓰세요.

보기

shuttlecock	velocity	improved
moist	expand	harder	hot

On the tennis court, Spot teaches Gomji and Omji how to play tennis and why the dirt on the court is ____________ and more ____________ than an ordinary one. In the next room, he teaches them how to play table tennis, and he explains the principle in which objects ____________ due to heat by placing the crushed-up ping-pong ball in ____________ water. When Gomji's ping-pong ball hits the corner of the table, Spot admits his skills have ____________. Now he asks the kids to try returning a badminton ____________. Gomji fails to return it because it's the highest instantaneous ____________ of all balls in sports. This time, Spot asks them to try returning his smash together. While Gomji misses the ball, Omji gets it. Since they learned to work together, Spot lets them pass the courses.

Ⅳ. Speaking

A 다음 물음에 답을 쓰고, 소리 내어 읽어 보세요.

1. Where is a crushed-up ping-pong ball placed to be straightened out? (p. 122)

2. Why is the shuttlecock fast only at the beginning and slow when it falls? (p. 125)

3. Why do you lower your position when you play badminton? (p. 126)

B 다음 대화의 빈칸에 들어갈 알맞은 말을 〈보기〉에서 찾아 쓰세요.

A : Wow,   is amazing!
B : Yeah, and it gives   to food.
A : When you make something with clay, you can mix in some salt   it doesn't   easily.
C : Oh, that's a good idea.

V. Puzzle

뜻풀이에 맞는 단어를 〈보기〉에서 찾아 퍼즐을 완성하세요.

iceberg   potential   smashing

serve   expand

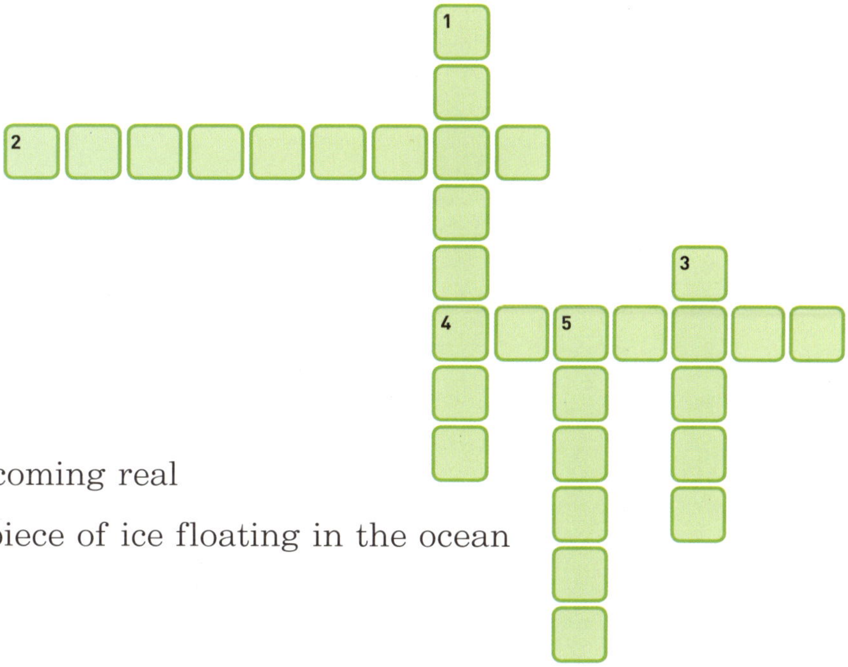

Across

2. capable of becoming real

4. a very large piece of ice floating in the ocean

Down

1. the strongest attack, sending the shuttlecock fast from up high over to the opponent's side of the court in badminton

3. to throw a ball into the air and hit it over a net to start play in tennis, volleyball, etc.

5. to become bigger

Unit 10

- The Science in Gliding
- The Science in Judo

I. Vocabulary

밑줄 친 말의 뜻을 파악하고, 괄호 안의 표현을 이용하여 문장을 완성하세요.

1. <u>beat</u> (Are / can beat / sure / you / him? / you)

2. <u>device</u> (I / a tracking device / on the assailants / put)

3. <u>no matter what</u>

(to train / The doctor / me / you first, / programmed / no matter what)

4. <u>rely on</u>

(that / relies on / is / a sport / the air current / Gliding)

II. Reading Comprehension

A 다음 물음에 알맞은 답을 고르세요.

What is the story mainly about? (pp. 130–137)

A. The kids learn techniques used in Judo on the
way to rescue the doctor.

B. The kids learn how to rescue the doctor.

C. The kids learn how to beat the assailants.

D. The kids learn the structure of the assailants' base.

B 다음의 각 글은 유도 기술을 설명합니다. 빈칸에 들어갈 알맞은 말을
〈보기〉에서 찾아 쓰세요. (pp. 132–136)

보기

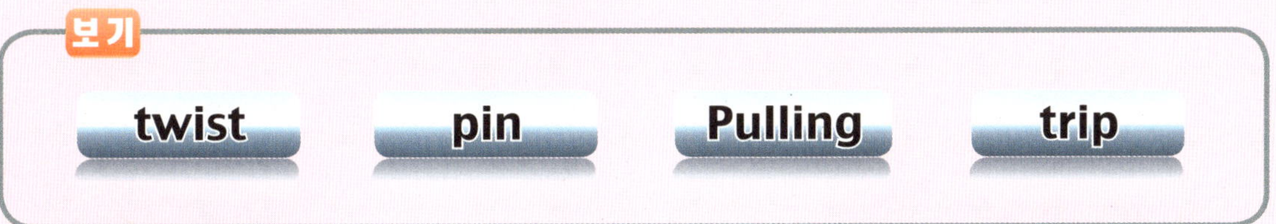

1. If you _______________ the opponent using the foot or waist,
the leverage effect occurs for even better results.

2. _______________ the opponent using the arms is a technique
used to throw off his center.

3. When you _______________ the opponent down, you should fix
his center on the floor so that he can't move.

4. A _______________ is a technique used to twist or wring the
opponent's joints, making him surrender due to pain.

C 다음 물음에 알맞은 답을 고르세요.

Which of the following is NOT true about gliding? (pp. 127–129)

A. A glider flies on the same principle on which an airplane takes off.

B. It's better for beginners to fly early in the morning when the wind is mild and the air current starts to move.

C. The weather is very important in gliding because it's a sport that relies on the air current.

D. You should fly at the back of mountains or valleys because the air current is regular when the wind blows.

Compare & Contrast

D 다음 표의 각 내용을 읽고 해당하는 칸에 표시하세요. (p. 128)

Attribute	Hang Glider	Paraglider
It has no propellers or engines.		
It flies using the lift force of the air.		
The strings are used to control the speed and direction.		
It flies fast at 40–120 km/h		
It moves slowly at 20–30 km/h		

다음 글의 빈칸에 들어갈 알맞은 단어를 〈보기〉에서 찾아 쓰세요.

보기

| dangerous | glider | twist |
| rescue | lift | judo | weather |

Spot and the kids fly a ___________ to the assailants' base to ___________ the doctor. While riding a glider, Spot says that a glider flies using ___________ force of the air and the ___________ is important in gliding because it's a sport that relies on the air current. Finally, they arrive at the base and encounter some assailants on the narrow path. Spot throws them using techniques in ___________. Inside the base, Spot pins an assailant down and tries to ___________ his joints so that the assailant can't help telling where the doctor is. Spot and the kids soon see the doctor trapped in a huge glass tube. The doctor tells them to run away from this ___________ place, but they can't do that.

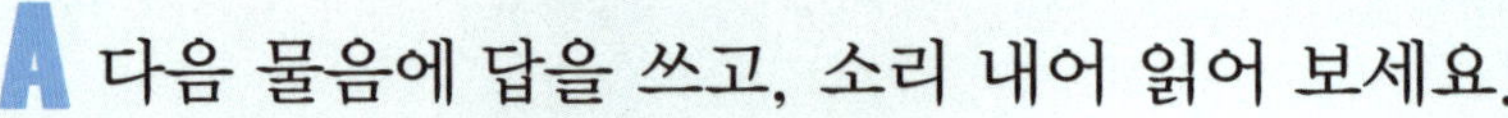

A 다음 물음에 답을 쓰고, 소리 내어 읽어 보세요.

1. How did Spot know where the doctor was? (p. 127)

2. Why is it difficult to throw someone standing still? (p. 132)

3. Why is it difficult to stand when someone pushes down on your forehead with a finger? (p. 135)

B 다음 대화의 빈칸에 들어갈 알맞은 말을 〈보기〉에서 찾아 쓰세요.

보기

narrow   **figured out**   **ocean**   **leads**

A : There it is! That's their base.

B : It's in the middle of the ___________.

A : Come this way!

C : The path is so ___________ and scary!

A : This path ___________ to the back door.

B : How did you know?

A : When we were up high, I ___________ the structure of the base.

빈칸에 들어갈 알맞은 단어를 〈보기〉에서 찾아 퍼즐을 완성하세요.

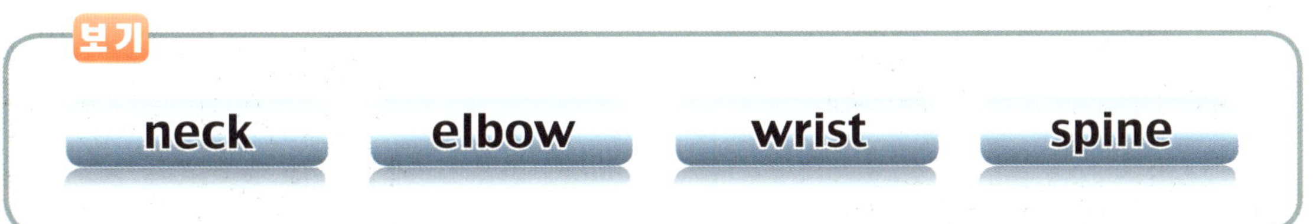

Across

3. The ___________ bone can move in diverse directions, like a pen holder.

4. The ___________ bone is joined together like a millstone and can be turned around.

Down

1. The ___________ bone can move only in one direction like a hinge.

2. The bones that make up the ___________ are connected through cartilage, like the support of a desk lamp, and can move forward and backward.

Unit 11

- The Science in a Taekwondo Smash
- The Science in Boxing

I. Vocabulary

밑줄 친 말의 뜻을 파악하고, 괄호 안의 표현을 이용하여 문장을 완성하세요.

1. <u>fulfill</u> (yet / I / fulfilled / haven't / my mission)

2. <u>last</u> (long / It's / going to / not / last)

3. <u>all at once</u> (hit / We're / all at once! / going to)

4. <u>laugh at</u> (you / How / laugh at / dare / me!)

II. Reading Comprehension

A 다음 물음에 알맞은 답을 고르세요.

What is the story mainly about? (pp. 138–141)

A. How to do Taekwondo

B. The mission of rescuing the doctor

C. The principle of Taekwondo smashing

D. How to save energy for Spot

B 다음 물음에 알맞은 답을 고르세요.

1. **What principle of Taekwondo smashing is explained?** (p. 139)

> When smashing bricks, use the blade of your hand to reduce the beating point.

A. The pressure increases as the beating point decreases when the same force is applied.

B. The direction and point of application of the force

C. Momentum increases with speed.

D. Reduce the buffer effect

2. **What principle of Taekwondo smashing is explained?** (p. 140)

> Legs have a greater destructive power than fists because they have a greater mass.

A. The pressure increases as the beating point decreases.

B. The direction and point of application of the force

C. Reduce the buffer effect

D. Increase the mass

C 다음 물음에 알맞은 답을 고르세요.

Which of the following is NOT true about boxing? (pp. 142–147)

A. The mouthpiece protects the teeth from external shock.

B. Weaving is a technique in which you can throw off your opponent by moving and can dodge your opponent's fists.

C. Boxing is very dangerous exercise because you might get a concussion.

D. A boxer can lose his balance due to the shock transferred from the chin to the brain.

D 다음 물음에 알맞은 답을 고르세요.

What technique in boxing does Gomji imply? (p. 145)

A. Weaving

B. Turning

C. Blocking

D. Covering-up

다음 글의 빈칸에 들어갈 알맞은 단어를 〈보기〉에서 찾아 쓰세요.

보기

smashing   weaving   without

rescue   boxer

Dr. Teunteun orders Spot to take the kids and run. Since Spot hasn't fulfilled his mission, he tries to ________ the doctor even though he has enough energy left for only one hit. Spot asks the kids to help him by teaching them the principles of ________ used in Taekwondo: the direction and point of application of the force, pressure, speed, reduce the buffer effect, and increase the mass. After that, Spot and the kids hit the glass all at once and free the doctor. However, the assailants' boss brings a big ________ to get them. At first, Spot stops the boxer using his emergency energy and then he dodges the boxer's fist using the ________ technique in boxing. Finally Spot knocks the boxer down with only one punch, but he can't move because he used up all his energy. So the doctor and the kids have no choice but to run ________ Spot.

IV. Speaking

A 다음 물음에 답을 쓰고, 소리 내어 읽어 보세요.

1. When does an object break easily? (p. 138)

2. Why do you place the object for smashing on hard ground? (p. 140)

3. When an object is supported on both sides, where should it be hit for smashing? (p. 139)

B 다음 대화의 빈칸에 들어갈 알맞은 말을 〈보기〉에서 찾아 쓰세요.

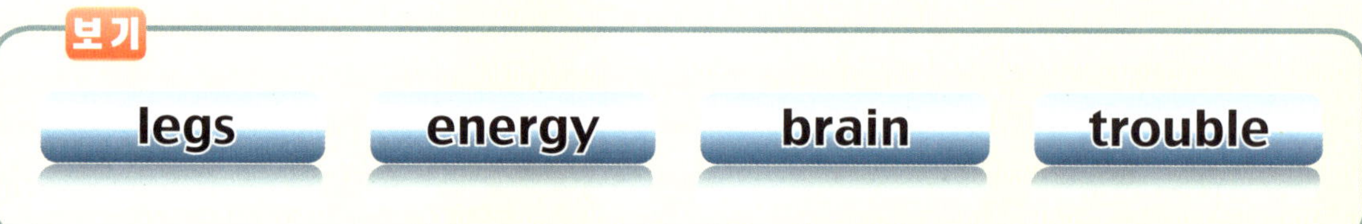

A : Spot is not moving!

B : He used up all his   .

C : Boxer, get up and get them!

A : Oh, we're in   !

Boxer : Oh, no, my legs…

A : Why can't he move his   , when he was hit on the chin?

B : That's because the shock is transferred to the   .

V. Puzzle

뜻풀이에 맞는 단어를 〈보기〉에서 찾아 퍼즐을 완성하세요.

Across

2. to cause force, pressure, etc. to have an effect or to be felt

4. to change something so that it no longer has its normal or original shape

Down

1. to move someone or something from one place to another

3. to move quickly to one side in order to avoid being hit by someone or something

5. the strength or force that something has when it is moving

I. Vocabulary

밑줄 친 말의 뜻을 파악하고, 괄호 안의 표현을 이용하여 문장을 완성하세요.

1. <u>develop</u> (is a way / Exercise / using energy / the body / to develop)

2. <u>prevent</u>

(If you / you can / a little care, / prevent / most accidents / take)

3. <u>confident</u>

(working out / I've felt / since / more confident / I started)

4. <u>put away</u>

(you're done / put away / after / You should / the equipment)

II. Reading Comprehension

A 다음 물음에 알맞은 답을 고르세요.

What is the story mainly about? (pp. 152–155)

A. Good eating habits help you to enjoy sports.

B. Sports and eating are important for health, both in mind and body.

C. Exercising and eating food relieve the stress.

D. Sports is important for health, both in mind and body.

B 다음 물음에 알맞은 답을 고르세요.

1. **What is the following first aid measure for?** (p. 150)

> Bend the head forward, and pinch the part below the nasal bone with the thumb and the index finger. Wipe the blood with a clean towel.

A. Food poisoning   B. Heatstroke

C. Concussion   D. Nosebleed

2. **Which is the function of carbohydrates?** (p. 153)

A. Main source of energy; develops good reflexes

B. Main component of bodily tissues (muscles, hormones)

C. Main source of energy during long hours of exercise

D. Regulates osmotic pressure and body fluids

C 다음 물음에 알맞은 답을 고르세요.

Which of the following is NOT true about the food bicycle? (p. 153)

A. The food bicycle shows a distribution of the seven food groups including water.

B. The back wheel shows the importance of having balanced meals.

C. The front wheel shows the importance of water intake.

D. The bicycle shows the prevention of obesity through proper exercise.

D 인공 호흡하는 순서를 빈칸에 올바르게 써넣으세요.

Breathe forcibly into the mouth, breathing air into the lungs.

Tilt the head back and raise the chin to secure the airway, and pinch the nose with one hand.

Check the chest to see if breathing has returned, and listen for the sound of breathing.

다음 글의 빈칸에 들어갈 알맞은 단어를 〈보기〉에서 찾아 쓰세요.

보기

switched	prevent	exercising
eating	good	first aid

Gomji enjoys exercising after he learned about the scientific principles in sports. Dr. Teunteun tells him how to __________ accidents caused in exercising. He also shows the kids various __________ measures, especially artificial respiration using a dummy. In addition, he says that sports and __________ are very important to become healthier, both in mind and body. According to him, we should eat a wide variety of foods to get the main nutrients. We can also relieve stress and have more confidence and better relationships with people through __________. When Gomji misses Spot, Spot comes back looking different because the doctor __________ programs. In the meantime, the original Spot with a new program that makes the assailants __________ helps them out a lot at the villains' headquarters.

IV. Speaking

A 다음 물음에 답을 쓰고, 소리 내어 읽어 보세요.

1. If someone has broken a bone, what should you do? (p. 150)

2. What are the main nutrients from foods? (p. 152)

3. How did the doctor bring Spot back? (p. 156)

B 다음 대화의 빈칸에 들어갈 알맞은 말을 〈보기〉에서 찾아 쓰세요.

보기

make up   as usual   regularly

overboard   scientific

A : Hey Gomji, what's up? You're exercising   , huh?

B : After I learned about the   principles in sports, I began to enjoy exercising.

A : You shouldn't go   , though.

B : I'm going to   for lost time!

C : No, you shouldn't do too much at once because you didn't exercise   before.

뜻풀이에 맞는 단어를 〈보기〉에서 찾아 퍼즐을 완성하세요.

보기

injury　　　concussion　　　respiration

dummy　　　nutrient　　　orphanage

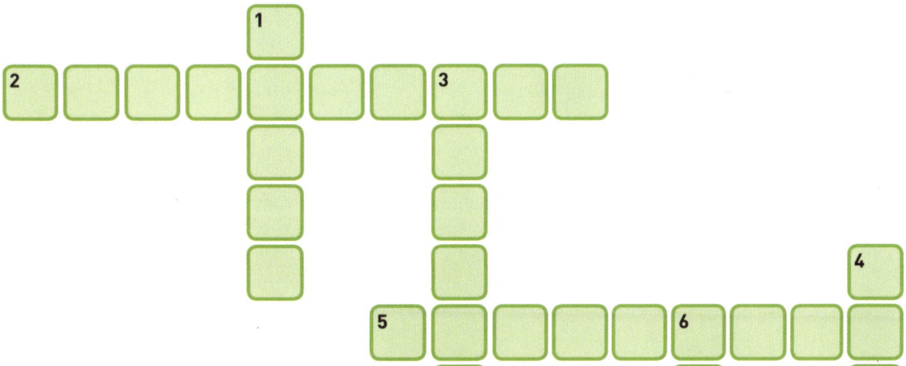

Across

2. an injury to the brain that is

   caused by something hitting the head very hard

5. a place where children whose parents have

   died can live and be cared for

Down

1. a doll that is shaped like and is as large as a person

3. any physical damage to the body caused by

   violence or an accident, etc.

4. the act or process of breathing

6. a substance that plants, animals, and people need to live and grow

정답 및 해설

Unit 1 pp. 8-13

I. Vocabulary

1. You should get rid of your potbelly first!
   (먼저, 네 똥배부터 빼야겠어!)

2. Look how stiff you are! (네가 얼마나 뻣뻣한지 좀 봐!)

3. I'm healthy even if I don't exercise.
   (난 운동하지 않아도 건강해.)

4. You need to exercise on a regular basis.
   (운동은 규칙적으로 해야 해.)

II. Reading Comprehension

A 1. C 과학적인 운동의 다섯 가지 원리
   2. B 인체의 구조와 기능

B A 유산소의

C A 성장기 때 운동하면 키가 크지 않는다.

D D 과부하의 원칙

III. Summary

fat – scientific – oxygen – loss – muscular
(엄지는 꼼지를 스포츠 과학 연구소에 계신 그의 할아버지께 데려간
다. 그의 할아버지 튼튼 박사님은 그들의 체지방을 측정하고 스포츠
는 과학적이므로 과학적으로 운동하면 몸에 다양한 효과를 얻을 수
있다고 말한다. 또한 과학적인 운동은 5가지 원칙(과부하의 원칙,
점진성의 원칙, 반복성의 원칙, 개별성의 원칙, 특이성의 원칙)으로
요약할 수 있다고 가르쳐 준다. 엄지와 꼼지는 유산소 운동과 무산
소 운동에 관해서도 배운다. 유산소 운동은 산소가 필요하지만, 무
산소 운동은 그렇지 않다. 걷기, 자전거 타기, 수영은 몸무게를 줄이
는 데 효과적인 유산소 운동이다. 반면, 웨이트 트레이닝 같은 근육
운동은 가장 대표적인 무산소 운동이다.)

IV. Speaking

A 1. That's because all he does is sit in front of the computer
   all day. (그것은 하루 종일 그가 하는 일이 컴퓨터 앞에 앉아
   있는 것이기 때문이다.)

2. Body fat percentage refers to the amount of fat in a
   person's total weight. (체지방 비율은 한 사람의 전체 체중
   에서 지방이 차지하는 양이다.)

---

3. An increase in height indicates the growth of bones in
   the body. Height increases when the growth plate at
   the end of a bone expands.
   (키가 큰다는 것은 몸의 뼈가 성장하는 것이다. 키는 뼈의 끝 부분
   에 있는 성장판이 확장하면서 큰다.)

B why – muscles – healthy – good
   A : 사람들이 왜 운동하는지 아니?
   B : 근육을 만들기 위해서겠죠.
   C : 운동이 재미있고 우리 몸을 건강하게 하니까요.
   A : 그래, 사람마다 운동하는 이유가 다르지만, 운동이 좋다는 건
       다 알고 있어. 그렇지?

V. Puzzle

1. obesity (비만: 평균 이상의 뚱뚱함)

2. respiration (호흡: 숨 쉬는 행위나 과정)

3. bowels (창자, 장: 음식의 소화를 돕고 고형 폐기물을 몸 밖으
   로 내보내는 것을 돕는 몸속의 긴 관)

4. stamina (체력, 정력, 지구력: 신체가 산소를 받아들여 운동을
   지속할 수 있는 능력)

5. circulation ([혈액] 순환: 심장 박동에 의해 일어나는, 몸속을
   흐르는 혈액의 이동)

Unit 2 pp.14-19

I. Vocabulary

1. Don't fall for me when I'm all trim and fit.
   (내가 날씬하고 탄탄해지면 나에게 반하지 마.)

2. I wonder how long your resolve will last.
   (네 결심이 얼마나 오래갈까 궁금하네.)

3. Gomji needs a strict instructor who scolds him every
   day. (꼼지에게는 그를 날마다 혼내는 엄한 지도자가 필요해요.)

4. Ji-Sung Park is famous for never growing tired!
   (박지성은 지치지 않기로 유명하잖아!)

II. Reading Comprehension

A 1. C 근육 피로의 원인인 젖산을 없애는 방법
   2. B 산소

B C 따뜻한 물에 샤워한다.

C B 허리를 심하게 돌린다.

D A 운동으로 젖산이 쌓이면 근육이 피로해진다.

III. Summary

fatigue – warming – oxygen – heart – straight – abducted
(튼튼 박사님은 근육 피로의 원인인 젖산을 없애는 방법을 설명한

다. 가벼운 유산소 운동과 운동 후 몸을 따뜻하게 하는 것은 젖산을
빨리 분해한다. 또한 규칙적인 유산소 운동으로 산소 소비량을 늘리
면 피로에서 빨리 회복할 수 있다. 만약 심장이 튼튼하면 많은 산소
를 짧은 시간에 온몸으로 공급할 수 있다. 그러면 많은 에너지가 만
들어져 피로가 빨리 사라질 것이다. 박사님은 파워 워킹이 곧은 체
형을 유지하게 도와줄 것이며 근력과 심폐 기능이 좋아질 거라고 덧
붙인다. 그러나 그가 꼼지를 위해 지도자를 찾았다고 말한 후 그는
갑자기 납치된다. 엄지와 꼼지는 튼튼 박사님의 연구실 열쇠를 발견
한다. 그들은 곧 꼼지를 훈련하도록 프로그램화된 스폿을 만난다.)

IV. Speaking

A 1. An athletic heart beats slower than an ordinary heart.
The heart of an ordinary person beats about 70–80
times per minute, and the heart of an athlete beats
about 40–50 times per minute. (스포츠 심장은 보통 심장
보다 더 느리게 뛴다. 일반인의 심장은 1분에 70~80회 정도
뛰고, 운동선수의 심장은 1분에 40~50회 정도 뛴다.)

2. When we breathe air in, it passes the trachea and
enters the lungs.
(공기를 들이마시면 기관을 지나 폐로 들어간다.)

3. The red blood cells in the blood carry oxygen through
blood vessels.
(피 속의 적혈구가 혈관을 통해 산소를 운반한다.)

B improvement – Power – fat – longer
A : 네 한 가지 습관만 바꾸어도 놀랍도록 좋아질 거야.
B : 정말요? 어떤 습관이요?
A : 걷는 방법이지! 체지방을 줄이는 데는 달리기보다 파워 워킹이
더 좋아. 왜냐하면 더 쉽고 오래 할 수 있거든.

V. Puzzle

1. consumption (소비, 소모: 무언가를 먹거나 마시는 행위)
2. laboratory (실험실, 연구실: 과학적인 실험이나 테스트를 하
기 위해 특수한 장비를 갖춘 방이나 건물)
3. 가로 – fatigue (피로: 아주 피곤한 상태)
세로 – function (기능: 어떤 것이 존재하거나 쓰이기 위한 특
별한 목적이나 활동)

Unit 3 pp.20-25

I. Vocabulary

1. I have cramps in my leg. (내 다리에 쥐가 났어.)
2. You tried to fool us with a wrestling dummy!
(레슬링 연습용 인형으로 감히 우릴 속이려 들다니!)
3. Your arms are elastic like rubber bands!
(네 팔은 마치 고무줄처럼 탄력이 있구나!)
4. It is supposed to knock you out.
(그것이 널 때려 눕혔을 텐데.)

II. Reading Comprehension

A D 육상 경기 속 과학
B B 단거리달리기 – 오래달리기 – 멀리뛰기 – 포환던지기, 원반던
지기, 해머던지기 – 장대높이뛰기
C A 머리를 오랫동안 숙인 채로 있다.
D D 제출하다, 제기하다

III. Summary

short – long – long jump – throwing – pole vault
(스폿은 훈련을 시작하기 전에 꼼지에게 준비 운동과 스트레칭을
하게 한다. 갑자기 튼튼 박사님을 납치한 괴한들이 나타나 아이들
을 잡으려 한다. 하지만 스폿은 단거리달리기 출발 자세로 뛰게 하
면서 아이들을 훈련하기 시작한다. 곧 스폿은 장거리를 달리면서
아이들에게 뒤꿈치를 먼저 땅에 닿게 하고 코와 입으로 동시에 숨
을 쉬라고 말해 준다. 도랑에 이르렀을 때 그들은 괴한들에게 갇히
고 만다. 스폿은 도랑을 건너려고 멀리뛰기를 훈련한다. 그러고 나
서 스폿은 괴한들에게 돌을 던질 때, 던지기에서 선수들이 도움닫
기와 회전을 하는 이유를 아이들에게 말해 준다. 아이들은 다시 막
다른 골목에 갇힌다. 다행히 이곳으로 온 것은 장대높이뛰기 속 과
학을 가르치기 위한 스폿의 계획이다.)

IV. Speaking

A 1. By warming up, they can prepare their body for
exercise, and use their capacity to its fullest.
(준비 운동을 함으로써 그들은 자신의 몸을 운동에 맞게 준비할
수 있고, 자신의 능력을 최대한 쓸 수 있다.)

2. When an object with mass pushes at something, it is
pushed back by the same amount of force. The two
forces are the same in size but opposite in direction.
(질량이 있는 물체가 어떤 것을 밀면, 그것은 같은 양의 힘에 의
해 다시 밀린다. 두 힘은 방향이 반대지만, 크기는 같다.)

3. They can throw further because they gain acceleration.
(그들은 가속도를 얻기 때문에 더 멀리 던질 수 있다.)

B dead – trapped – on purpose – Calm – tight
A : 앗, 막다른 골목이야.
D : 하하, 이번에야 너희는 확실히 잡혔다!
C : 걱정하지 마. 일부러 이쪽으로 온 거니까.
A : 뭐? 일부러 우릴 잡히게 했다고!
B : 진정해, 스폿에게 이유가 있는 게 확실해!
C : 물론 있지. 이 장대 좀 봐! 우리는 이 장대를 이용해서 뛰어넘
을 거야. 꽉 잡아!

Ⅴ. Puzzle

1. (the) javelin (창던지기)
2. (the) pole vault (장대높이뛰기)
3. (the) long jump (멀리뛰기)
4. (the) discus throw (원반던지기)
5. running (달리기)

Unit 4 pp.26-31

Ⅰ. Vocabulary

1. We have to rescue my grandfather!
   (우리 할아버지를 구해야 해!)
2. People with more fat float better.
   (지방이 더 많은 사람이 물에 더 잘 뜬다.)
3. Water is different from the ground!
   (물은 땅과 다르잖아!)
4. Is there anything you are good at?
   (네가 잘하는 것이 있니?)

Ⅱ. Reading Comprehension

A B 물속에서 앞으로 나아가는 방법
B C 마찰
C A 물에서 몸을 수평으로 누이면 더 잘 뜰 수 없다.
D 1. Air Gun (공기 소총)
    2. Rifle (라이플총, 소총)

Ⅲ. Summary

running – fast – hypothermia – shoots – covers
(스폿, 꼼지, 엄지는 물 쪽으로 계속 달린다. 스폿은 아이들에게 물
에 뛰어들게 하고 수영하는 방법을 가르친다. 그는 또한 다양한 수
영법과 전신 수영복을 입은 선수들이 왜 빨리 수영할 수 있는지를
알려 준다. 얼마 후, 그들은 추위를 느끼며 물 밖으로 나온다. 스폿
은 아이들이 저체온증에 걸리지 않도록 말려 준다. 한편, 괴한들은
여전히 배를 타고 그들을 쫓고 있다. 스폿은 아이들을 스포츠 아일
랜드로 데리고 간다. 거기서 꼼지는 서바이벌 게임용 총으로 괴한
들을 쏜다. 그러나 꼼지가 목표를 맞히지 못하자 스폿은 사격 속 과
학을 가르쳐 준다. 그리고 나서 그는 아이들이 구멍이 있는 뒤쪽으
로 도망칠 수 있도록 엄호한다.)

Ⅳ. Speaking

A 1. The difference in the density of the water and that of
     the object makes an object float or sink. (물과 물체의 밀
     도 차이가 물체를 물에 뜨게 하거나 가라앉게 한다.)

2. That is because outer space is almost a vacuum.
   (그것은 우주가 거의 진공 상태이기 때문이다.)
3. Symptoms of hypothermia include chill, reduced
   muscle activity, and disturbance of consciousness.
   (저체온증의 증상에는 오한, 근육 운동 저하, 의식 장애 등이 있다.)

B long – heat – hypothermia – breeze
   A : 우리가 물에 너무 오래 있었나? 어서 와!
   B : 으~, 추워!
   A : 찬물 속에 오래 있으면 열을 빼앗겨 저체온증이 일어날 수 있어.
   B : 덜~덜!
   A : 내가 따뜻한 바람으로 말려 줄게! (후아아아~)
   B : 와, 따뜻해!

Ⅴ. Puzzle

1. backstroke (배영: 배영은 얼굴을 물 위에 내놓고 반듯이 누운
   자세로 헤엄치는 영법이다.)
2. freestyle (자유형: 자유형에서, 얼굴이 물속에 들어갔다 물 밖으
   로 나오기 때문에 크롤 영법에서는 호흡 조절이 매우 중요하다.)
3. 가로 – breaststroke (평영: 평영은 개구리처럼 팔다리를 오므
              렸다 펴면서 앞으로 나아가는 영법이다.)
   세로 – butterfly (접영: 접영은 팔다리를 동시에 움직여 물결
              모양처럼 몸을 앞으로 나아가는 영법이다.)

Unit 5 pp.32-37

Ⅰ. Vocabulary

1. I've set up some scarecrows to have time.
   (시간을 벌려고 허수아비를 세워 놓았어.)
2. You can't play with the equipment!
   (그 장비를 가지고 놀면 안 돼!)
3. We'll have the advantage if we pour sand on the ice.
   (얼음판에 모래를 뿌리면 우리가 더 유리할 거야.)
4. A bullet crashes due to the resistance of bulletproof
   clothing. (방탄복의 저항 때문에 총알이 뭉개진다.)

Ⅱ. Reading Comprehension

A D 위에 언급된 모든 것
B A. True 양궁은 활의 탄성을 이용한 운동이다.
   B. False 달리기 시작할 때나 오르막길을 오를 때 힘이 덜 들게 자
         전거를 타려면 페달 기어를 높여 줘야 한다.
   C. True 사이클 선수는 운동 방향과 반대로 작용하는 항력을 줄이
         려고 몸을 앞쪽으로 숙인다.
   D. False 얼음이 녹아 물이 되면 훨씬 덜 미끄럽다.
   E. False 일정 영역의 압력은 그 면적이 축소될 때 줄어든다.

C B 벨로드롬용 자전거는 바람과 많은 마찰이 발생되도록 만들어
졌다.

D

특성	Figure Skating	Speed Skating
스케이트 선수들은 마찰을 최소화하고 관성과 균형을 유지하면서 힘을 오래 유지할 수 있다.	○	○
날이 짧고 두껍다.	○	
날이 길고 가늘다.		○
다양한 동작이 필요하다.	○	
날이 스케이트 선수가 진로에서 벗어나지 않게 막아 준다.		○

III. Summary

elasticity – arrows – bicycles – skating – artificial – control
(스폿은 꼼지와 엄지를 양궁장으로 데려가 활의 탄성을 이용한 양
궁에 관해 가르쳐 준다. 또한 화살이 심지어 방탄조끼도 뚫을 수
있음을 말해 준다. 곧 그들은 괴한들이 자신들 바로 뒤에 숨어 있
는 것을 알고 자전거를 타고 도망간다. 스폿은 경주용 자전거를 탈
때 속력을 내는 방법, 안전을 위해 쓰는 스포츠 헬멧에 관하여 말
해 준다. 괴한들이 오토바이를 타고 쫓아오지만, 아이들은 스폿을
따라 실내 스케이트장으로 들어간다. 스폿은 스케이트 타는 방법,
피겨 스케이팅과 스피드 스케이팅의 차이점을 아이들에게 알려
준다. 그러고 나서 아이들을 다음 문으로 데려가는데, 그곳은 인공
눈으로 가득 차 있다. 거기서 아이들은 속도를 조절하는 방법을 배
우면서 스키를 타고 내려가 어느 잠긴 문에 도달한다.)

IV. Speaking

A 1. We must tilt the bow and take an off aim in the direction from
which the wind comes.
(활을 기울여 바람이 불어오는 방향으로 오조준해야 한다.)

2. You can't speed bike up, no matter how fast you pedal.
(페달을 아무리 빨리 밟아도 자전거 속도를 올릴 수 없다.)

3. The lower I bend, the easier it becomes to find my balance
because the center of gravity becomes lower.
(몸을 낮게 구부릴수록 무게 중심이 낮아지므로 균형을 찾기가 더
쉬워진다.)

B supposed – advantage – Hold
A : 하하, 얼음 위에서는 스케이트를 타야지.
B & C : 어이쿠! 얼음판에 모래를 뿌리면 되겠다. 그럼 우리가 더
유리해질 거야! 저 녀석들이 다시 도망간다! 잡아라!
A : 모두 날 꽉 붙잡아!

V. Puzzle

1. centripetal force (구심력: 원 운동하는 물체에서 원 중심 방
향으로 작용하는 힘)

2. off aim (오조준: 표적 방향과 다르게 조준하는 것)

3. centrifugal force (원심력: 구심력과 크기가 같고 방향은 반대
로, 원의 중심에서 밖으로 작용하는 힘)
SPORTS SCIENCE

Unit 6 pp.38-43

I. Vocabulary

1. I made three successive baskets!
(내가 세 골을 연속 넣었어!)

2. The ball changed its direction all of a sudden! (공이 갑자
기 방향을 바꾸었어!)

3. The bumps keep the ball from slipping away easily.
(그 돌기들은 공이 쉽게 미끄러지지 않게 막아 준다.)

4. I'll be a goalkeeper this time, so give it a try.
(이번에 내가 골키퍼를 할 테니, 한번 시도해 봐.)

II. Reading Comprehension

A A 축구공은 어떻게 휘는가
B 1. C 공이 골대 위에서 바로 떨어질 때 득점 기회가 높아진다.
2. B 삼각 패스
C D 골키퍼가 멀리 있을 때 슈팅 각도는 줄어든다.

III. Summary

ball – train – principles – banana – goalpost – feint
(스폿은 아이들이 공으로 하는 스포츠를 배우게 될 스포츠 과학 훈련
장의 잠긴 문을 연다. 꼼지와 엄지는 박사님을 구하길 원하지만, 스폿
이 먼저 그들을 훈련하도록 프로그램화된 탓에 그렇게 할 수가 없다.
스폿은 아이들에게 시험을 제시한다. 첫 번째 시험은 세 번 연속 득점
하는 것이다. 엄지는 농구의 과학적인 원리를 배운 후 연속 세 골을
성공한다. 다음 과정은 축구다. 스폿은 바나나킥을 보여 주고 나서 아
이들에게 골키퍼가 있는 골대에 공을 차 넣으라고 말한다. 꼼지가 골
을 넣으려고 시도하지만 실패한다. 스폿은 아이들에게 몇몇 축구 기
술을 말해 준다. 꼼지는 스폿을 골키퍼로 세우고 공을 차 보지만, 다
시 빗맞힌다. 하지만 꼼지가 스폿을 속인 속임동작이 하나의 기술로
인정되어 꼼지는 시험을 통과한다. 마지막으로 스폿은 축구공이 어
떻게 여러 조각으로 이루어졌는지에 관해 설명한다.)

IV. Speaking

A 1. We have to put a backspin on the ball using our wrist
and fingers.
(손목과 손가락을 이용해 공을 거꾸로 회전해 줘야 한다.)

2. It is made 11 m away from the goal line.
(그것은 골라인에서 11m 떨어진 지점에 정해진다.)

3. The Teamgeist is even more spherical with 14 separate

pieces and more stable with less joints. It has great elasticity and turning effect. (팀가이스트는 14개 조각으로 돼 있어 더욱 구에 가깝고, 이음새가 줄어들어 더욱 안정적이다. 그것은 탄력과 회전 효과가 좋다.)

B lightly – tricked – feints – method

A : 먼저 공을 가볍게 찬다. 그리고 이제, 슛! (휙)

B : 안 돼!

A : 헤헤, 속임수지요! (툭)

B : 속임 동작을 쓰는 것도 기술로 인정한다. 스스로 방법을 깨우쳤으니 합격시켜 주겠다!

V. Puzzle

1. horizontal (수평의: 지면과 평행한)
2. offense (공격진: 상대팀에 대항해서 자신의 팀이 점수나 골을 얻게 하려고 노력하는 선수 그룹)
3. feint (속임 동작: 상대를 속이려고 하는 빠른 동작)
4. vertical (수직의: 위로 곧게 뻗은)
5. opponent (상대, 적수: 시합에서 다른 쪽과 경쟁하는 사람이나 팀, 그룹 등)

Unit 7 pp.44-49

I. Vocabulary

1. You wasted my awesome pass! (네가 내 멋진 패스를 망쳤어!)
2. That was just a coincidence. (그건 단지 우연일 뿐이야.)
3. Helmets for amateurs are equipped with ear protection on both sides.
   (아마추어용 헬멧은 양쪽에 귀 보호대를 갖추고 있어.)
4. I studied all your throws so far, and I saw a pattern.
   (지금까지 네가 던진 것을 연구했더니 규칙이 보였어.)

II. Reading Comprehension

A D 배구에서 공격 방법

B 1. B 세 번, 두 번

2. C 더 빠르고, 더 멀리

C D 야구에서는 다리보다 팔 운동이 더 중요하다.

D

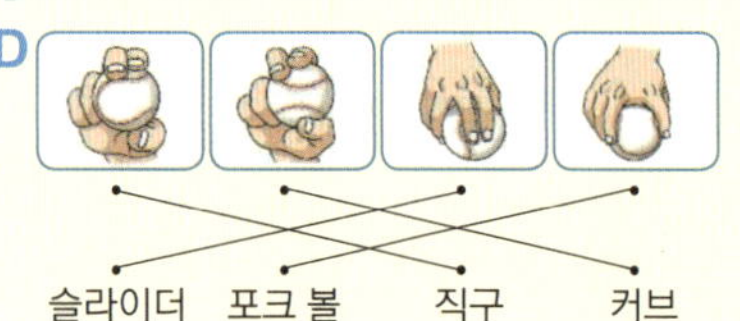

III. Summary

net – attacks – effort – protection – breaking – grip – predict

(배구장에서 스폿은 꼼지와 엄지에게 그가 네트 위로 넘겨 준 공을 받아치는 방법을 가르쳐 준다. 그러고 나서 배구에서 공격하는 방법도 가르쳐 준다. 꼼지는 노력한 덕분에 배구 시험에서 합격한다. 배구 훈련을 한 뒤, 그들은 야구 타격장으로 가고, 꼼지는 한쪽에 귀 보호대가 있는 야구 헬멧을 쓴다. 스폿은 꼼지에게 빠르고 정확하게 공을 치는 법과 변화구가 무엇인지 알려 준다. 그는 또한 야구공의 특징, 공을 잡는 방법에 따라 다른 투구, 강한 공 던지기 요령 등을 알려 준다. 결국 꼼지는 스폿이 던진 모든 공을 연구한 뒤 어떤 규칙을 찾아내어 스폿의 다음 공이 어떨지 예상할 수 있게 된다.)

IV. Speaking

A 1. Feints are usually used in the 'time lag attack', in which 2-3 attackers feint and the last attacker makes an attack in safety. (속임 동작은 2~3명의 공격수가 속이고 마지막 공격수가 안전하게 공격하는 '시간차 공격'에서 주로 쓰인다.)

2. It's important that the timing of the swing and the spot on the bat that hits the ball. (방망이를 휘두르는 타이밍과 공을 때리는 방망이 부분이 중요하다.)

3. It is called a breaking ball. (그것은 변화구라고 부른다.)

B difficult – over – mistake – attitude

A : 내 생각에 그것이 너희에겐 좀 어렵겠다.

B : 다시 하자! 난 할 수 있어! 나는 같은 실수를 두 번은 안 해!

A : 좋아, 그 태도가 좋아!

B : 으아, 또 공이 빗나갔어!

V. Puzzle

1. breaking ball (변화구: 스핀 있게 던져져 타자에게 다가감에 따라 그 진로가 휘는 야구의 투구)
2. batter (타자: 공을 치는 야구 선수)
3. toss (토스: 공격수가 공격하기 쉽도록 배구공을 가볍게 공중으로 띄우는 행동)
4. setter (세터: 공격수가 공격하기 쉽도록 공을 가볍게 공중으로 던져 올리는 배구 선수)

Unit 8 pp.50-55

I. Vocabulary

1. They're starting to see that playing sports requires thinking. (스포츠를 하려면 생각이 필요하다는 것을 그들이 알기 시작하는구나.)

2. The numbers on bowling balls indicate their weight.
(볼링 공 위의 숫자들은 공의 무게를 나타낸다.)

3. I'm going to knock them down in a single attempt!
(내가 단 한 번의 시도로 다 넘겨 버릴 테야!)

4. Is it possible to knock them down at once?
(저것들을 한꺼번에 넘길 수 있을까?)

II. Reading Comprehension

A A 골프 공 위의 딤플이 일부러 만들어진 이유

B B 딤플이 있는 공은 딤플이 없는 공보다 더 멀리 날아가기 때문이다.
   C 딤플은 공이 회전할 때 압력 차이를 더 크게 하여 커브 볼을 더
   쉽게 치게 해 주기 때문이다.

C D 옷의 상태

D A. False 그는 그에게 아주 무거운 공을 선택해야 한다.
   B. True 그는 세 번째나 네 번째 걸음에 공을 굴릴 수 있도록 걸을
   때 보폭을 조정해야 한다.
   C. False 진자 운동을 할 때 그는 팔을 굽혀야 한다.
   D. True 그는 진자 운동을 할 때 어깨가 흔들리지 않도록 하체를
   안정감 있게 유지해야 한다.
   E. False 그는 오른손잡이이기 때문에 1번과 2번 핀 사이로 공을
   굴려야 한다.

III. Summary

dimples – swing – thinking – bowling – pose – wrist
– split – balance
(스폿은 꼼지에게 골프채를 주고 딤플이라 부르는 홈이 있는 공을
쳐 보라고 한다. 그는 아이들에게 공이 맞는 위치와 어디로 나아가
는지를 이야기해 주고 스윙할 때 고려해야 할 몇몇 사항을 덧붙인
다. 아이들은 스포츠를 하는 데 생각이 필요하다는 것을 알기 시작
한다. 엄지는 구멍 속으로 공을 쳐 넣으려 애쓰고, 그것을 이뤄 낸
다. 이제, 공을 두 번 굴려 열 개의 핀을 쓰러뜨리는 게임인 볼링이
다. 꼼지는 공을 한 번만 굴리고 싶지만, 공이 옆으로 빠져 버린다.
그래서 스폿은 올바른 자세와 공이 휘는 이유를 알려 준다. 엄지
차례에서는 엄지의 손목 동작 때문에 공이 휜다. 엄지의 첫 번째
시도에서 남은 핀, 즉 스플릿이라 부르는 핀이 있어 스폿은 그것을
한꺼번에 넘어뜨리는 방법을 알려 준다. 마침내, 꼼지가 스트라이
크를 기대하며 다시 시도하는데, 그는 균형을 유지하고 안정된 자
세로 공을 굴려 성공해 낸다.)

IV. Speaking

A 1. The ball must be fast, so I'll use centrifugal force,
   making a big, fast swing. (공이 빨라야 한다. 그래서 나는
   크고 빠른 스윙을 하게 하는 원심력을 이용할 것이다.)

   2. I can roll the ball twice or once

(나는 공을 두 번이나 한 번 굴릴 수 있다.)

3. That's because of wrist movement. The ball spins in
the direction of the wrist and it turns due to the friction
with the floor. (그것은 손목 동작 때문이다. 공은 손목의 방향
으로 돌고, 바닥의 마찰 때문에 휘게 된다.)

B embarrassing – weird – pose – stable – pins
   A : 으악, 창피해! 공이 옆으로 빠져서 굴러갔잖아. 이상하다. 다시
   한 번 해 봐야지!
   B : 어이구, 자세 좀 봐라.
   A : 으아, 너무 가까이 왔네. 아이코!
   B : 네 스텝은 모두 엉망이야. 핀을 향해 힘을 가하려면 안정된 자
   세를 취하는 게 필요해.

V. Puzzle

1. dimples (딤플: 골프 공 위의 홈들을 딤플이라고 부른다.)

2. split (스플릿: 첫 번째 시도에서 핀들이 사이에 간격을 두고 남
은 것을 스플릿이라고 한다.)

3. pendular (진자의, 진자처럼 운동하는: 진자 운동은 어깨를 축
으로 앞뒤에서 일직선으로 이루어져야 한다.)

4. double leap (2단 도약: 골프 공은 2단 도약을 하는데, 공의
속도가 빠를 땐 공이 앞으로 곧게 날아가고, 속도가 줄면 마그
누스 효과가 나타나기 때문이다.)

Unit 9 pp.56-61

I. Vocabulary

1. Tennis is similar to volleyball. (테니스는 배구하고 비슷하다.)

2. I guess I was greedy. (내가 욕심을 부린 것 같아.)

3. Your skills have improved a lot. (네 실력이 많이 늘었다.)

4. First, you need to determine your spots.
(먼저 너희 구역을 정해야 해.)

II. Reading Comprehension

A D 탁구 치는 방법과 탁구 속 과학

B A 배드민턴 – 탁구 – 배구(스파이크 서브)

C A 서브할 때 공을 상대 코트로 바로 넘긴다.

D B 테니스 코트의 땅 위에 소금을 뿌렸다.

III. Summary

harder – moist – expand – hot – improved – shuttlecock
– velocity
(테니스 코트에서 스폿은 꼼지와 엄지에게 테니스 치는 법과 코트
의 흙이 보통 흙보다 더 단단하고 습기 많은 이유를 가르쳐 준다.
다음 방에서 그는 아이들에게 탁구 치는 법을 가르쳐 주고 찌그러

진 탁구공을 뜨거운 물에 넣어서 물체가 열 때문에 팽창하는 원리를 설명한다. 꼼지의 탁구공이 탁구대 모서리를 치자 스폿은 꼼지의 실력이 향상했다고 인정한다. 이제 스폿은 아이들에게 배드민턴 셔틀콕을 받아치라고 한다. 셔틀콕이 스포츠의 모든 공 중에서 순간 속도가 가장 높은 탓에 꼼지는 그것을 받아치는 데 실패한다. 이제 스폿은 그들에게 함께 그의 스매시를 받아치라고 한다. 꼼지는 공을 놓치지만 엄지가 받아 낸다. 스폿은 함께 협력하는 방법을 터득했다고 그들을 합격시켜 준다.)

IV. Speaking

A 1. It is placed in hot water. (그것은 뜨거운 물속에 넣어진다.)

2. The shuttlecock flies fast when hit hard, due to the elasticity of the racket strings, but the feathers, which cause friction with the air, reduce its speed.
(셔틀콕은 강하게 치면 라켓 줄의 탄성 덕분에 빠르게 날아가지만, 깃털은 공기와 마찰을 일으켜 공의 속도를 줄여 준다.)

3. That's because we can react quickly to the ball that comes flying fast. (그것은 빠르게 날아오는 공에 빠르게 반응할 수 있기 때문이다.)

B salt – flavor – so that – break
A : 우아, 소금이 대단한데!
B : 그래, 그리고 음식에 맛을 더해 주잖아.
A : 찰흙으로 뭔가를 만들 때 소금이랑 섞으면 쉽게 부서지지 않겠다.
C : 오, 그것 좋은 생각인데.

V. Puzzle

1. smashing (스매시, 스매싱: 배드민턴에서, 높은 위치에서 상대방 코트로 셔틀콕을 빠르게 보내는 가장 강력한 공격)

2. potential (일어날 수 있는: 실현될 가능성이 있는)

3. serve (서브하다: 테니스, 배구 등에서 경기를 진행하려고 공을 공중으로 던져 네트 위로 치다)

4. iceberg (빙산: 바다에 떠다니는 아주 큰 얼음 덩어리)

5. expand (팽창하다, 확장하다: 더 커지다)

Unit 10 pp.62-67

I. Vocabulary

1. Are you sure you can beat him?
(그를 확실히 이길 수 있겠어?)

2. I put a tracking device on the assailants.
(내가 괴한들에게 추적 장치를 붙여 뒀다.)

3. The doctor programmed me to train you first, no matter what. (박사님은 어떤 일이 있어도, 먼저 너를 훈련하도록 날 프로그램하셨어.)

4. Gliding is a sport that relies on the air current.
(글라이딩은 기류에 의존하는 스포츠다.)

II. Reading Comprehension

A A 박사님을 구하러 가는 길에 아이들은 유도에서 쓰는 기술을 배운다.

B 1. trip 발이나 허리를 이용하여 상대를 걸어 넘어뜨리면 지렛대 효과로 훨씬 더 나은 결과가 나온다.

2. Pulling 팔을 이용해 상대를 잡아당기는 것은 상대의 중심을 불안정하게 하려고 쓰는 기술이다.

3. pin 상대를 누르기 할 때, 상대의 몸 중심을 반드시 바닥에 고정하여 움직이지 못하게 한다.

4. twist 꺾기는 상대의 관절을 꺾거나 비틀어서 상대가 고통으로 항복하게 하려고 쓰는 기술이다.

C D 바람이 불 때는 기류가 규칙적이므로 산 뒤쪽이나 계곡에서 날아야 한다.

D

특성	Hang Glider	Paraglider
프로펠러도 엔진도 없다.	○	○
공기의 양력을 이용해 비행한다.	○	○
속도와 방향을 조절하는 데 줄을 쓴다.		○
시속 40 ~120km로 빨리 난다.	○	
시속 20 ~30km로 천천히 움직인다.		○

III. Summary

glider – rescue – lift – weather – judo – twist – dangerous
(스폿과 아이들은 박사님을 구하려고 괴한들의 기지로 글라이더를 타고 간다. 글라이더를 타면서 스폿은 글라이더가 공기 양력으로 하늘을 날며, 글라이딩은 기류에 의존하는 스포츠라 날씨가 중요하다고 말해 준다. 마침내, 그들은 기지에 도착하여 좁은 길 위에서 괴한들과 마주친다. 스폿은 유도 기술을 이용하여 그들을 던져 버린다. 기지 안에서 스폿이 한 괴한을 누르기로 공격하고 관절 꺾기를 시도하자, 괴한은 박사님이 있는 곳을 말하지 않고는 못 배긴다. 스폿과 아이들은 곧 거대한 유리관에 갇힌 박사님을 만난다. 박사님은 위험한 이곳을 떠나라고 말하지만, 그들은 그럴 수 없다.)

IV. Speaking

A 1. He knew that because he put a tracking device on the assailants when they first started chasing after him.
(괴한들이 맨 처음 그를 뒤쫓기 시작했을 때 그가 추적 장치를 붙여 놓았기 때문에 알았다.)

2. That's because you can't use the opponent's strength.
(그것은 상대의 힘을 이용할 수 없기 때문이다.)

3. That's because we must rise our head first to stand.
(그것은 일어서려면 먼저 머리부터 올라가게 해야 하기 때문이다.)

B ocean – narrow – leads – figured out

A : 저기 있다! 저것이 그들의 기지야.

B : 바다 한가운데에 있구나.

A : 이쪽으로 와!

C : 길이 너무 좁고 무섭다!

A : 이 길이 뒷문으로 연결돼 있어.

B : 그걸 어떻게 알아?

A : 우리가 높은 곳에 있을 때 기지의 구조를 파악해 뒀지.

V. Puzzle

1. elbow (팔꿈치: 팔꿈치 뼈는 경첩처럼 한 방향으로만 움직일 수 있다.)

2. spine (등뼈: 등뼈를 형성하는 뼈들은 책상 스탠드의 기둥처럼 연골로 이어져 있어 앞뒤로 움직일 수 있다.)

3. wrist (손목: 손목뼈는 펜 꽂이처럼 여러 방향으로 움직일 수 있다.)

4. neck (목: 목뼈는 맷돌처럼 연결되어 있어 돌릴 수 있다.)

Unit 11 pp.68-73

I. Vocabulary

1. I haven't fulfilled my mission yet.
   (나는 아직 내 임무를 다 수행하지 못했어.)

2. It's not going to last long. (그렇게 오래가지는 않을 거야.)

3. We're going to hit all at once! (우리가 동시에 칠 거야!)

4. How dare you laugh at me! (감히 나를 비웃다니!)

II. Reading Comprehension

A C 태권도 격파의 원리

B 1. A 같은 힘이 가해질 때 타점이 줄어듦에 따라 압력은 강해진다.
2. D 질량 늘리기

C C 권투는 뇌진탕이 올 수 있으므로 아주 위험한 운동이다.

D A 위빙

III. Summary

rescue – smashing – boxer – weaving – without
(튼튼 박사님은 스폿에게 아이들을 데리고 도망가라고 명령한다. 스폿은 그의 임무를 다하지 못했으므로 비록 겨우 한 방 때릴 에너지만 남았지만 박사님을 구하려고 한다. 스폿은 아이들에게 태권도에서 쓰는 격파 원리(힘의 방향과 작용점, 압력, 속도, 완충 효과 줄이기, 질량 늘리기)를 가르쳐 주며 도움을 청한다. 그러고 나서 모두 함께 동시에 유리를 쳐서 박사님을 구한다. 하지만 괴한 두목이 덩치 큰 복서를 데려와 그들을 붙잡으려고 한다. 처음에 스폿은 그의 비상 에너지를 이용하여 복서를 막고 그런 다음에는 복싱의

위빙 기술을 이용하여 복서의 주먹을 잽싸게 피한다. 마지막으로 스폿은 펀치 한 방으로 복서를 넘어뜨리지만, 그는 에너지를 다 써 버려 움직이지 못한다. 그래서 박사님과 아이들은 어쩔 수 없이 스폿 없이 도망간다.)

IV. Speaking

A 1. An object breaks easily when the force applied exceeds its deformation limit. (물체는 가해지는 힘이 그것의 변형 한계를 넘어설 때 쉽게 깨어진다.)

2. That's because the object on hard ground breaks more easily to reduce the buffer effect. (그것은 딱딱한 바닥 위의 물체가 완충 효과를 줄여서 더 잘 깨어지기 때문이다.)

3. It should be hit in the center. (그것의 중심을 쳐야 한다.)

B energy – trouble – legs – brain

A : 스폿이 움직이질 않아요!

B : 그의 에너지를 다 써 버린 거다.

C : 복서, 일어나서 놈들을 잡아!

A : 으아, 우리 이제 큰일이다!

Boxer : 오, 안 돼, 내 다리가……

A : 턱을 맞았을 때 그는 왜 다리를 움직이지 못한 거죠?

B : 그건 충격이 뇌까지 전달되기 때문이야.

V. Puzzle

1. transfer (~를 옮기다: 한 곳에서 다른 곳으로 사물이나 사람을 이동하게 하다)

2. apply ([힘·압력·열 등을] 가하다: 힘이나 압력 등이 효과를 발휘하게 하거나 느껴지게 하다)

3. dodge (잽싸게 몸을 비키다: 사물이나 사람에게 맞는 것을 피하려고 재빨리 한쪽으로 움직이다)

4. deform (~을 변형하다: 어떤 것을 정상적인 모양이나 본디 모양이 더 나타나지 않게 바꾸다)

5. momentum (운동량: 어떤 물체가 움직일 때 지니는 힘이나 기세)

Unit 12 pp.74-79

I. Vocabulary

1. Exercise is a way to develop the body using energy.
   (운동은 에너지를 이용하여 신체를 발달시키는 방법이다.)

2. If you take a little care, you can prevent most accidents.
   (조금만 주의하면 대부분의 사고를 막을 수 있어.)

3. I've felt more confident since I started working out.
   (운동을 시작한 이후로 나는 더 많은 자신감을 느꼈다.)

4. You should put away the equipment after you're done.
   (네가 끝마친 뒤에는 기구를 잘 치워 둬야 해.)

II. Reading Comprehension

A B 스포츠와 먹는 것은 신체와 정신 건강 둘 다를 위해 중요하다.

B 1. D 코피가 날 때
   2. A 주 에너지원; 좋은 반사 신경을 발현하게 한다.

C A 식품 자전거는 물을 포함한 일곱 가지 식품군의 분포를 나타낸다.

D (2) 폐 속으로 공기를 불어넣기 위해 입속으로 힘차게 숨을 불어 넣는다.
   (1) 머리를 뒤로 젖히고 턱을 들어 기도를 확보하고, 한 손으로 코를 쥔다.
   (3) 호흡이 돌아오는지 보기 위해 가슴을 확인하고 숨소리를 듣는다.

2. concussion (뇌진탕: 뭔가가 머리를 세게 쳐서 뇌에 생긴 부상)
3. injury (부상, 상처: 폭력, 사고 등에 의해 몸에 입은 신체적 손상)
4. respiration (호흡: 숨 쉬는 동작이나 과정)
5. orphanage (고아원: 부모가 죽고 없는 아이들이 살거나 돌봄을 받는 곳)
6. nutrient (영양소, 영양분: 식물, 동물, 사람이 생존하고 성장하는 데 필요한 물질)

III. Summary

prevent – first aid – eating – exercising – switched – good
(꼼지는 스포츠 속 과학 원리를 배운 후 운동하는 것을 즐긴다. 튼튼 박사님은 꼼지에게 운동하면서 생기는 사고 예방법을 말해 준다. 그는 또한 아이들에게 여러 가지 응급 처치법, 특히 인형을 이용한 인공호흡법을 보여 준다. 게다가 스포츠와 먹는 것은 몸과 마음을 더 건강하게 하는 데 아주 중요하다고 말한다. 그에 따르면 우리는 주요한 영양을 섭취하기 위해 다양한 음식을 먹어야 한다. 또한 우리는 운동을 통해 스트레스를 덜고 자신감을 더 키우며 사람들과의 관계를 더 좋게 할 수 있다고 한다. 꼼지가 스폿을 보고 싶어할 때 스폿이 다른 모습으로 돌아오는데, 박사님이 프로그램을 바꾸어 놓았기 때문이다. 한편, 괴한들의 본부에서는 괴한들을 착하게 하는 새로운 프로그램이 설치된 원래 스폿이 괴한들을 크게 돕는다.)

IV. Speaking

A 1. We should call the hospital right away and take first aid measures. (바로 병원에 연락하고 응급 처치를 해야 한다.)
   2. They are carbohydrates, vitamins and minerals, water, fat, and protein. (그것들은 탄수화물, 비타민과 무기질, 물, 지방, 그리고 단백질이다.)
   3. He brought Spot by switching programs during the commotion. (그는 북새통에 프로그램을 바꿔 넣어서 스폿을 데려왔다.)

B as usual – scientific – overboard – make up – regularly
   A : 꼼지야, 무슨 일이야? 오호, 평소처럼 운동하니?
   B : 스포츠 속 과학 원리를 알고 나니 운동을 즐기기 시작했어.
   A : 그래도 너무 무리하면 안 돼.
   B : 잃어버린 시간을 만회해야지!
   C : 아니다, 넌 전에 꾸준히 운동한 것이 아니라서 한꺼번에 너무 많이 하면 안 돼.

V. Puzzle

1. dummy (인체 모형: 사람처럼 생기고 사람만큼 큰 인형)

Why?
Sports Science

Vocabulary List

McGraw Hill · YeaRimDang

evaluation	**n.** 평가, 측정, 값 구하기
beat	**v.** 이기다, 통제하다 **n.** 울림, 리듬
wonder	**v.** 궁금하다, ~일지 모르겠다
share	**v.** 공유하다, 함께 쓰다 **n.** 몫, 지분
in front of	~의 앞에
stiff	**adj.** 뻣뻣한, 뻑뻑한
exercise	**n.** 운동, 연습, 일 **v.** 운동하다, 연습하다
ideal weight	이상 체중, 적정 체중
exceed	**v.** 초과하다, 넘어서다
overweight	**adj.** 과체중인, 중량 초과의
obese (obesity)	**adj.** 비만인, 뚱뚱한 (**n.** 비만, 비대)

morbidly	**adv.** 병적으로, 끔찍하게

make sure	반드시 ～하도록 하다

In any case, Dr. Teunteun told me to **make sure** you come with me, because you need an **evaluation**.

어쨌든 오늘 너 체력 측정해야 한다고 튼튼 박사님이 꼭 너랑 함께 오라고 하셨어.

sweat	**n.** 땀, 식은땀 **v.** 땀을 흘리다
institute	**n.** 기관, 협회, 학회, 연구소
scientific(ally)	**adj.** 과학의, 과학적인 (**adv.** 과학적으로)
grandson	**n.** 손자, 외손자
have to do with	～와 관계가 있다, 관련되다
structure	**n.** 구조, 구조물
function	**n.** (사람·사물의) 기능 **v.** 기능하다, 작용하다
psychology	**n.** 심리학
physiology	**n.** 생리학
muscle	**n.** 근육, 근력
disease	**n.** 질병, 질환

So if you don't get enough **exercise**, you can come down with various **diseases**, such as **obesity** and diabetes.

그래서 충분히 운동하지 않으면 비만, 당뇨 같은 여러 질병에 걸릴 수 있는 거야.

body fat	체지방
refer to	～을 나타내다, ～와 관련 있다
agility	**n.** 민첩성, 명민함
endurance	**n.** 참을성, 지구력
prescribe	**v.** 처방을 내리다, 규정하다
properly	**adv.** 제대로, 적절히

If you're weak, it means your body isn't **functioning properly**.
체력이 약하다는 건 신체가 제대로 기능하지 않는다는 뜻이지.

indicate	**v.** (사실임을) 나타내다, 가리키다
nonsense	**n.** 터무니없는 생각(말), 난센스
vital	**adj.** 필수적인, 생명의, 중요한
growth plate	성장판
bone marrow	골수
articular	**adj.** 관절의
stimulate	**v.** 자극하다, 활발하게 하다
contribute	**v.** 기부하다, 기여하다, 도움이 되다
interfere with	～을 방해하다, 협박하다

hinder	v. ~을 못하게 하다, 방해하다
undertake	v. 착수하다, 약속하다
thoughtlessly	adv. 생각 없이, 경솔하게
determine	v. 알아내다, 결정하다, 결심하다
capacity	n. 능력, 수용력, 용량
summarize	v. 요약하다, 간략하게 말하다
principle	n. 원칙, 원리
overload	v. 너무 많이 주다, 과적하다 n. 과부화
strengthen	v. 강화하다, 더 튼튼하게 하다
gradualness	n. 점진적임, 점진성
exhausted	adj. 기진맥진한, 다 써 버린
repetition	n. 반복, 되풀이, 중복
consistently	adv. 일관하여, 지속적으로
cram	v. 밀어(쑤셔) 넣다, 벼락치기 공부를 하다
soon after	바로, 머지않아
individuality	n. 개성, 특성
singularity	n. 특이(성), 드문 일

stamina	**n.** 체력, 원기, 지구력
oxygen	**n.** 산소
effect	**v.** (어떤 결과를) 가져오다 **n.** 영향, 효과, 결과
brain	**n.** 뇌, 두뇌, 머리
heart	**n.** 심장, 마음, 가슴
prevent	**v.** 예방하다, 막다, 방지하다

It can **prevent** the hardening of the arteries and **heart** diseases.
그것은 동맥 경화나 심장병을 예방할 수 있다.

lung	**n.** 폐, 허파
respiration	**n.** 호흡, 호흡 작용
consumption	**n.** 소비(량), 소모(량)
decrease	**v.** 줄다, 감소하다
abdominal	**adj.** (명사 앞에만 씀) 복부의
immune system	면역 체계, 면역 기능
organ	**n.** 기관, 장기
colorectal	**adj.** 직장의, 결장의
bowel(s)	**n.** (주로 복수로) 창자, 장

aerobic ↔ anaerobic	**adj.** 유산소의 ↔ 무산소의
simply put	간단히 말해서
prolonged	**adj.** 오래 계속되는, 장기적인
convert	**v.** 전환시키다, 바꾸다
carbohydrate	**n.** 탄수화물, (복수) 탄수화물 식품
lactic acid	젖산
exertion	**n.** 힘 내기, 노력, 진력, 격렬한 활동
break down	(물질을) 분해하다, 부수다, 고장 나다
fuse	**n.** 퓨즈, 도화선 **v.** 융합(결합)하다
midget	**n.** (모욕적 용어) 난쟁이
get rid of	~을 없애다

focus on
~에 주력하다, 집중하다

It's better to do both **aerobic** and **anaerobic** exercises together than to **focus on** just one.

오직 하나에만 집중하기보다는 유산소, 무산소 운동을 둘 다 같이 하는 게 더 좋지.

potbelly
n. 올챙이배, 똥배

muscular exercise
근육 운동

protein
n. 단백질

lack of
~이 부족한

fit (비교급: fitter)
v. (모양·크기가 사람·사물에) 맞다

adj. 건강한, 튼튼한, 적당한, 적합한

ache
v. (계속) 아프다 **n.** 아픔

accumulation
n. 축적, 누적

fatigue
n. 피로, 피곤

That's because you don't exercise regularly and have an **accumulation** of **fatigue** in your body.

그건 네가 운동을 꾸준히 하지 않아서 몸에 피로가 쌓였기 때문이야.

build up
쌓아 올리다, 강화하다

melting point
녹는점, 용해점

The **melting point** for **lactic acids** is 25-26°C, so it **breaks down** quickly if you warm yourself up after exercise.

젖산은 녹는점이 25~26℃이므로, 운동 후 몸을 따뜻하게 하면 젖산이 빨리 분해된다.

remove	**v.** 제거하다, 치우다
athlete	**n.** 운동선수, 스포츠맨
trachea	**n.** 기도, 기관
spread	**v.** 펼치다, 퍼지다 **n.** 확산, 전파
throughout	**prep.** 도처에, ~하는 동안 쭉

How does the oxygen, then, **spread throughout** the body?
그러면 산소는 어떻게 온몸으로 퍼질까?

carry out	~을 수행하다, 실시하다
aorta	**n.** 대동맥
atrium	**n.** 심방, 아트리움
ventricle	**n.** 심실
pump	**n.** 펌프, 심장 **v.** 펌프로 퍼 올리다
heartbeat	**n.** 심장 박동, 심박(수)
enlarge	**v.** 커지다, 확장되다, ~을 크게 하다
enhance	**v.** ~을 높이다, 강화하다, 늘리다
entire	**adj.** 전체의
contraction	**n.** 수축, 축소

habit	**n.** 버릇, 습관
gain	**v.** 얻다, 증가하다 **n.** 증가, 이득
maintain	**v.** 유지하다, 지속하다
lie down	(자거나 쉬려고) 눕다
tend to	~하는 경향이 있다

> People who are not very active and like to sit or **lie down tend to gain** weight.
>
> 활동적이지 않고 앉거나 눕기 좋아하는 사람은 몸무게가 느는 경향이 있다.

dramatic	**adj.** 극적인
improvement	**n.** 향상, 개선
vigorously	**adv.** 발랄하게, 힘차게
upright	**adj.** (자세가) 똑바른, 꼿꼿한

figure	n. 모습, 모양, 인물, 수치
stability	n. 안정, 안정감
stooped posture	구부정한 자세
abnormal	adj. 비정상적인
spine	n. 척추, 등뼈
waist	n. 허리, (옷의) 허리 부분
briskly	adv. 활발하게, 기분 좋게
breathing	n. 호흡, 한숨
inhale ↔ exhale	v. 숨을 들이마시다 ↔ 숨을 내쉬다
bend	v. (몸이나 머리를) 굽히다, 휘다, 굴복시키다

Bend your body forward at a 5° angle.
몸을 5° 앞으로 기울인다.

parallel	adj. 평행한, 비슷한 n. 평행, 유사
attack(er)	n. 공격, 습격 v. 공격하다 (n. 공격자)
unidentified	adj. 정체불명의, 불확실한
assailant	n. 공격자, 가해자
trim	adj. 늘씬한, 깔끔한 v. 다듬다, 손질하다

resolve	**n.** 결심, 결의 **v.** 해결하다, 결심하다
last	**v.** 계속하다, 지속하다 **adj.** 마지막의
perseverance	**n.** 인내(력), 참을성
strict	**adj.** 엄격한, 엄한
instructor	**n.** 강사, 지도자, 교관
scold	**v.** 야단치다, 꾸짖다
run away	도망치다
scary	**adj.** 무서운, 겁나는, 잘 놀라는
gym	**n.** 체육관, 체조, 체육
abduct	**v.** 납치하다, 유괴하다
universal	**adj.** 일반적인, 전 세계의, 우주의, 만능인
security guard	경비원, 경호원
encounter	**v.** 맞닥뜨리다, 부딪히다 **n.** 마주침
laboratory	**n.** 실험실, 연구실
target	**n.** 목표, 표적, 목표물
detect	**v.** 발견하다, 탐지하다, 간파하다
programmed	**adj.** 미리 프로그램으로 짜여진

Chapter 4

II. The Hidden Sports in Science
•Stretching and Physical Balance

stretch	**v.** 늘이다, 뻗다
stretching	**n.** 스트레칭
physical	**adj.** 신체의, 물리(학)의, 물질의
balance	**n.** 균형, 평형, 천칭, 저울
police station	경찰서
run after	～를 뒤쫓다
warm up	준비 운동을 하다
dramatically	**adv.** 극적으로
loosen up	느슨하게 하다(되다), 몸을 풀어 주다
tension	**n.** (사람들 사이의) 긴장 상태, 불안
facilitate	**v.** 가능하게(용이하게) 하다

| spasm | **n.** 경련, 쥐 |

| injury | **n.** 부상, 손상, 상처, 피해 |

| ligament | **n.** (관절의) 인대 |

Warming up before exercise can prevent **spasms** or **injury**, such as a **stretched ligament**.

운동 전에 준비 운동을 하면 인대가 늘어나는 등의 경련이나 부상을 예방할 수 있다.

| cramp | **n.** (근육에 생기는) 경련, 쥐 |

Oh, I have **cramps** in my leg…

오, 내 다리에 쥐가 나는데….

| prepare | **v.** 준비하다, 대비하다, 마련하다 |

| in addition | 게다가, 더욱이, 더구나 |

| normal | **adj.** 보통의, 평범한 **n.** 보통, 평균, 정상 |

| shape | **n.** 모양, 형태 |

| neck | **n.** 목, 목뼈, 목 부분 |

| shoulder | **n.** 어깨 **v.** (책임을) 짊어지다 |

| behind | **prep.** 뒤에 |

| support | **v.** 지지하다, 지탱하다, 지원하다 |

| curved | **adj.** 곡선의, 약간 굽은 |

straighten	v. ~을 곧게 하다, 바르게 되다
curvature	n. 굽음
pressure	n. 압박, 압력
hard to	~하기 어려운
cause	v. 일으키다, 원인이 되다 n. 원인
spinal disc	척추 디스크
herniation	n. 탈장됨, 탈장의 형성
lean	v. 기대다, 기울이다, 숙이다
backwards	adv. 뒤로, 거꾸로, 반대 방향으로
philosophy	n. 철학

If you're bent, **straighten** yourself out, and if you're stooped, **lean backwards**! This is the **philosophy** of **stretching**!

굽힌 만큼 펴 주고, 숙인 만큼 뒤로 젖혀라! 이것이 바로 스트레칭의 철학이야!

overcome	v. 극복하다, 이기다
tense	adj. 긴장한, 신경이 날카로운 v. 긴장하다
accelerate	v. 가속화되다, 가속화하다
buttock(s)	n. (주로 복수로) 궁둥이, 둔부
abdomen	n. 배, 복부, 복강

sprinting	**n.** 단거리달리기
training	**n.** 훈련, 훈육, 양성
file	**n.** 파일, 서류철 **v.** 보관하다, 제출하다, 발송하다
report	**n.** 보도, 보고서, 기록 **v.** 보고하다, 알리다
try to	～하려고 노력하다
fool	**n.** 바보 **v.** 속이다, 기만하다
dummy	**n.** 인체 모형, 모조품 **adj.** 모조의

You **tried to fool** us with a wrestling **dummy**!
레슬링 훈련용 인형으로 감히 우릴 속이려고 했다니!

quick	**adj.** 빠른, 신속한 **adv.** 재빨리
grab	**v.** (와락·단단히) 붙잡다, 움켜잡다

gasp	**v.** 숨이 턱 막히다, 헉헉거리다
give in	항복하다, (마지못해) 동의하다
wrong	**adj.** 틀린, 잘못된
starting posture	출발 자세
short distance running	단거리달리기
crucial	**adj.** 중대한, 결정적인
record	**n.** 기록, 음반 **v.** 기록하다, 녹음하다
gravity	**n.** (물리) 중력, 무게, 중대함
inertia	**n.** (물리) 관성, 타성, 활발치 못함
stable	**adj.** 안정된, 견실한

You bend your body forward when you start out because when your waist is bent, the center of **gravity** becomes lower, decreasing **inertia** and allowing you to run faster in a **stable** posture.

출발할 때는 몸을 앞으로 기울이는데, 허리를 굽혀 주면 무게 중심이 낮아지고 관성이 작아져서 안정된 자세로 빨리 뛸 수 있기 때문이다.

advantage	**n.** 이점, 장점, 유리, 이익, 우위
the law of action and reaction	작용 · 반작용 법칙
force	**n.** 힘, 물리력 **v.** ～하게 하다
propel	**v.** ～을 나아가게 하다, 추진하다, 몰아대다

uncomfortable

adj. 불편한, 불안정한

The posture looks very **uncomfortable**, though.

그래도 자세가 매우 불편해 보인다.

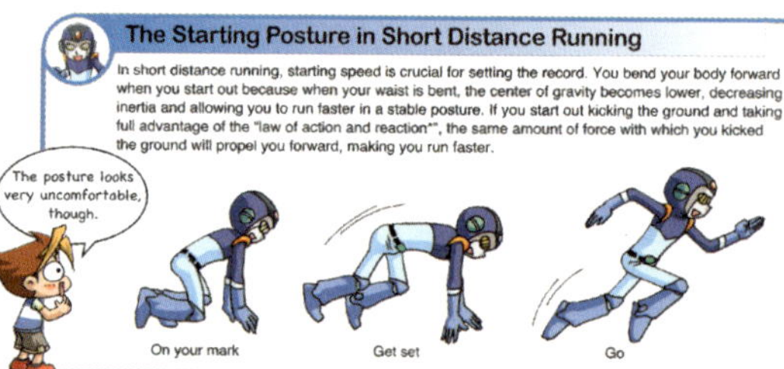

object

n. 물건, 물체

push

v. 밀다, 떠밀다, 추진하다

opposite

n. 정반대의 것 **adj.** 정반대의, 맞은편의

direction

n. (이동의) 방향, 지시

increase

v. 늘리다, 증가하다

control

n. 통제, 지배 **v.** 지배하다, 제어하다

swing

v. (전후좌우로) 흔들다, 휘두르다

movement

n. 움직임, 동작, 운동, 이동

Effective arm **movement** can help maintain the balance of the body.

효과적인 팔 동작은 신체의 균형을 유지하도록 도와줄 수 있다.

long distance running

오래달리기

key	**n.** 열쇠, 비결
strength	**n.** 힘, 기운, 기세
choice	**n.** 선택, 선택권 **adj.** 질 좋은, 고급의
tranquilize	**v.** (마음을) 안정시키다, 조용하게 하다
What's going on!	무슨 일이야!
be supposed to	～하기로 되어 있다
knock out	나가 떨어지다, 의식을 잃다
must be	～임이 틀림없다

He **must be** the universal sports robot!
그는 만능 스포츠 로봇임이 틀림없다!

through	**prep.** ～를 통하여
avoid	**v.** 방지하다, 막다, 피하다, 회피하다
strain	**n.** 부담, 중압 **v.** 무리하다, 무리를 주다
throat	**n.** 목, 목구멍
require	**v.** 요구하다, 필요하다
hurt	**v.** 아프게 하다, 아프다
abdominal respiration	복식 호흡

thoracic respiration	흉식 호흡
chest	**n.** 가슴, 흉곽, 큰 상자
swell	**v.** 붓다, 부풀어 오르다
fall	**v.** 떨어지다, 넘어지다

The **chest swells** and **falls**.
가슴이 부풀어 올랐다 내렸다 한다.

diaphragm	**n.** 횡경막, 가로막
rise	**n.** 증가, 상승 **v.** 증가하다, 오르다
rib	**n.** 갈비뼈, 늑골
forward ↔ backward	**adv.** 앞쪽으로 ↔ 뒤쪽으로
keep	**v.** (동작·상태를) 유지하다, 계속하다
touch	**v.** 만지다, 건드리다
heel	**n.** 발뒤꿈치, 뒷발굽, 하이힐 구두
reduce	**v.** 줄이다, 감소시키다, 줄어들다
easier	(easy의 비교급) ~보다 더 쉬운

It really is **easier** to run when you do as Spot says.
스폿 말대로 하니까 달리기가 정말로 더 쉽다.

Chapter 6

- The Science in the Long Jump
- The Science in Throwing
- The Science in the Pole Vault

the long jump	멀리뛰기
emergency	**n.** 비상(사태), 응급
go off (과거: went off)	자리를 뜨다, (경보기 등이) 울리다
trickle	**v.** (액체가 가늘게) 흐르다 **n.** 실개천
get away from	~에게서 벗어나다
at risk	~의 위험이 있는, 위험에 처한

They're after me and I'm with you guys, so you're **at risk**, too.
그들은 나를 쫓고 난 너희와 함께 있으니, 결국 너희 역시 위험에 처한 셈이지.

rescue	**v.** 구출하다 **n.** 구출, 구조
trap	**v.** 가두다 **n.** 함정, 덫

ditch   **n.** 배수로, 도랑

There's a **ditch** behind us.
우리 뒤는 도랑이야.

run-up   **n.** 도움닫기, 상승, 급등

as fast as   ~한 만큼 빨리

Do the **run-up as fast as** you can!
도움닫기는 최대한 빠르게 해!

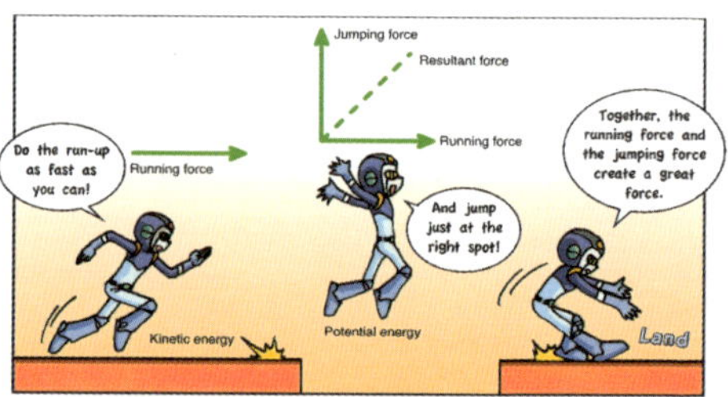

kinetic energy   운동 에너지

potential energy   위치 에너지

resultant force   합성력, 합력

spot   **n.** 점, 반점, 얼룩, 장소

acceleration   **n.** 가속, 가속도

courageous   **adj.** 용감한, 용기 있는

at least   적어도, 최소한

throwing	n. (육상 경기) 던지기
enough	adj. 충분한 adv. ~에 필요할 정도로
elastic	adj. 고무로 된, 탄력 있는 n. 고무 밴드
rubber band	고무 밴드, 고무줄
further	(far의 비교급) 더 멀리, 더 한층

> If you do a run-up, you can throw **further** because you gain **acceleration**.
>
> 도움닫기를 하면 가속도가 생겨 더 멀리 던질 수 있다.

mass	n. 질량, 덩어리
javelin	n. (투창 경기용) 창, (the ~) 창던지기, 투창
relatively	adv. 비교적, 상대적으로
light	adj. 가벼운 n. 빛
resistance	n. 저항, 저항력, 반항
wind	n. 바람, 관악기
suitable	adj. 적당한, 적절한
angle	n. 각도, 기울기, 관점
critical	adj. 비판적인, 비평의, 중대한
space	n. 공간, 장소, 우주

spin	**v.** 회전하다, 빙빙 돌리다 **n.** 회전
around	**prep.** 둘레에, 주위에
centrifugal force	원심력

Even if there isn't too much **space**, you can throw far using **centrifugal force**.

비록 장소가 너무 좁더라도 원심력을 이용하면, 멀리 던질 수 있다.

the shot put	포환던지기
discus	**n.** 원반
the discus throw	원반던지기
hammer	**n.** 망치, 해머
the hammer throw	해머던지기
radius	**n.** 반지름, (범위) 반경
rotation	**n.** 회전, 순환, 자전

The greater the **mass**, the faster the **spin**, and the bigger the **radius** of **rotation**, the greater the centrifugal force.

원심력은 물체의 질량이 클수록, 회전이 빠를수록, 회전 반경이 클수록 커진다.

motion	**n.** 운동, 움직임, 동작
rotary motion	회전 운동
timing	**n.** 타이밍, 시간
tendency	**n.** 성향, 동향, 경향, 추세
pole	**n.** 막대기, 장대, 기둥, 극, 극지
vault	**v.** 뛰다, 도약하다 **n.** 뛰기, 도약
the pole vault	장대높이뛰기
hurry	**v.** 서두르다, 급히 하다, 재촉하다
dead end	막다른 곳(골목)
on purpose	고의로, 일부러

Don't worry. I came this way **on purpose**.
걱정하지 마. 일부러 이쪽으로 왔으니까.

reason	**n.** 이유, 원인, 이성
crash	**v.** 충돌하다 **n.** (충돌) 사고

We're going to **crash**!
충돌하겠어!

brave (비교급: braver)	**adj.** 용감한, 용맹한
practice	**v.** 연습하다 **n.** 실행
calm down	진정하다, 흥분을 가라앉히다
horizontally	**adv.** 수평으로, 가로로
float	**v.** (물·공기에) 뜨다, 떠다니다

Anyone can **float** on water!
누구나 물에 뜰 수 있어!

affect(ed)	**v.** 영향을 주다 (**adj.** 영향을 받은)
buoyancy	**n.** 부력, (액체의) 부양성
iron	**n.** 철, 쇠, 다리미
sink	**v.** 가라앉다, 침몰하다

depending on   ~에 따라

density   **n.** 밀도, 조밀도, 농도

volume   **n.** 용량, 용적

consider   **v.** ~이라고 여기다, 고려하다

specific gravity   (물리) 비중

leg artery   다리 동맥

liver   **n.** 간, 간장

nail   **n.** 손톱, 못

toenail   **n.** 발톱

fat   **n.** 지방 (조직), 기름 **adj.** 뚱뚱한

flat   **adj.** 평평한 **adv.** 평평하게

If you lie **flat**, the abdomen **floats** and the legs **sink**.
평평하게 누우면, 배 부분은 뜨고, 다리 쪽은 가라앉는다.

generally   **adv.** 일반적으로, 대개, 보통

The body **generally** sinks in water, but can float **depending on** breathing or posture.
신체는 일반적으로 물에서 가라앉지만, 호흡이나 자세에 따라 뜰 수 있다.

sick   **adj.** 아픈, 병든, 메스꺼운

trouble	**n.** 문제, 골칫거리 **v.** 괴롭히다, 애먹이다
kick	**v.** 발로 차다 **n.** 발길질
be different from	~와 다르다
vacuum	**n.** 진공 **v.** 진공 청소기로 청소하다
struggle	**v.** 허우적거리다, 분투하다

> Thus, in outer space, which is almost a **vacuum**, you can't move forward, no matter how much you **struggle**.
>
> 그래서, 거의 진공 상태인 우주 공간에서는 아무리 허우적거려도 앞으로 나아갈 수 없다.

intensity	**n.** 강도, 강렬함
flail	**v.** (팔 등을) 마구 휘두르다, 매타작하다
blindly	**adv.** 앞이 안 보인 채, 무턱대고, 맹목적으로
purposefully	**adj.** 목적의식이 있는, 결단력 있는, 결의에 찬
specialty	**n.** 전공, 특기, 장기, 특수성

breaststroke	**n.** 평영, 개구리헤엄
pros and cons	장단점
freestyle	**n.** 자유형
unregulated	**adj.** 규제(통제·조정)되지 않은
competition	**n.** 경쟁, 경기

Freestyle is an **unregulated** swimming form used in swimming **competitions**.

자유형은 수영 경기에 이용되는 규제 없는 수영의 형태다.

crawl	**n.** (수영) 크롤 영법
backstroke	**n.** 배영, 받아치기
at all times	항상, 언제든지
alternate	**adj.** 번갈아 하는, 교대의
be divided into	~로 나뉘다
submerge	**v.** 잠수하다, 잠기다
contract ↔ expand	**v.** 수축하다 ↔ 팽창하다
harmony	**n.** 조화, 화합
butterfly	**n.** 접영, 나비
wave	**n.** 파도, 물결

be compared to ~와 비교하다, ~와 비교되다

The motion in which the two arms stretch forward, pulling the water down, **is compared to** that of a butterfly.

두 팔을 동시에 앞으로 뻗쳐 물을 아래로 끌어당기는 동작이 나비의 동작과 비교된다.

curious **adj.** 궁금한, 호기심이 많은

swimmer **n.** 수영 선수, 헤엄치는 사람

wear **v.** 입다, 착용하다, 쓰다, 신다

full body swimsuit 전신 수영복

friction **n.** 마찰, 마찰 저항, 불화

fabric **n.** 직물, 천, 구조

keep ~ from ~ing ~하는 것을 막다

Doesn't the **friction** between the **fabric** and the water **keep** you **from moving** fast?

옷과 물 사이의 마찰이 빨리 나아갈 수 없게 하는 거 아닙니까?

shave **v.** 면도하다, 깎다, 밀다

actually **adv.** 실제로, 사실은, 정말로

material **n.** 소재, 재료, 원료

technology **n.** (과학) 기술, 공학

scale **n.** 비늘, 규모, 눈금, 축적 **v.** 오르다

denticle	n. 이 모양의 돌기, 작은 이
surface	n. 표면, 표층, 수면
mimic	v. 흉내를 내다
exert	v. (힘·지식을) 쓰다, (압력을) 가하다, 노력하다
regulation	n. 규정, 규칙, 법규, 조절
ban	v. 금지하다 n. 금지(령)
controversy	n. 논란, 논쟁, 갈등, 문제
hypothermia	n. 저체온(증), 냉각법
be exposed to	드러나다, ~에 노출되다
symptom	n. 증상, 징후, 조짐
disturbance	n. 방해, 장애, 소란, 동요
consciousness	n. 의식, 자각
poorly	adv. 형편없이, 가난하게, 빈약하게, 초라하게
pulse	n. 맥박, 고동, 박자
wipe down	~을 말끔히 닦다
wrap	v. 포장하다, 감싸다, 두르다
breeze	n. 산들바람, 미풍

shooting	n. 사격
island	n. 섬
still	adv. 아직도, 여전히 adj. 고요한
real	adj. 진짜의, 실제의
hide	v. 숨다, 숨기다, 감추다
protective	adj. 보호하는, 보호용의, 방어적인
gear	n. (특정 목적을 위한) 장비(복장), 톱니바퀴, 기어
against	prep. ～에 맞서, ～에 반대하여

In actual paintballl games, **protective gear** must be worn at all times and care must be taken **against** injury in short distance **shooting**.

실제 서바이벌 게임에서는 항상 보호 장구를 착용해야 하고, 근거리 사격에서는 부상에 대비하여 주의해야 한다.

content	**n.** 속에 든 것(들), 내용(물)
modify	**v.** 수정하다, 바꾸다
gun	**n.** 총, 총기, 포
lousy	**adj.** 몸이 안 좋은, 엉망인, 형편없는
fire	**v.** 총을 쏘다 **n.** 불, 화재
dodge	**v.** (몸을) 재빨리 움직이다, 피하다

We don't even need to **dodge**…

피할 필요도 없네….

hit	**v.** 때리다, 치다 **n.** 치기, 타격
be good at	～을 잘하다, 능숙하다
part	**n.** 부품, 부분, 부위
backsight	**n.** (총의) 가늠자, (측량) 후시
foresight	**n.** (총의) 가늠쇠, 선견지명, 통찰(력)
decoration	**n.** 장식, 꾸밈, 장식물

Aren't they just for **decoration**?

그것들은 그저 장식 아닌가?

aim	**v.** 목표하다, ～을 대상으로 하다 **n.** 목적, 목표

miss	**v.** 놓치다, 빗나가다, 그리워하다
align	**v.** 일직선으로 하다, 가지런히 하다
straight line	직선
surrender	**v.** 항복하다, 포기하다, 넘겨주다
retreat	**v.** 후퇴하다, 퇴각하다 **n.** 퇴각, 철수
far away	저 멀리, 멀리 떨어져
villain	**n.** 악당, 악한, 악인
hold	**v.** 잡다, 유지하다, 억누르다
gunpoint	**n.** 총부리, 총구

A long **gunpoint** is better for hitting the mark.
총구가 길수록 과녁을 맞히는 데 더 좋다.

bullet	**n.** 총알, 탄환, 작은 공

The longer the gunpoint, the straighter it keeps the **bullet** as it moves forward.
총구가 길수록 총알이 앞으로 나아감에 따라 더 곧게 유지해 준다.

spiral	**n.** 나선, 나선형 **adj.** 나선의, 나사 모양의
groove	**n.** 홈, 리듬
barrel	**n.** 총열, 통 **v.** 쏜살같이 달리다

air gun	공기 소총, 소총
rifle	**n.** 라이플총, 소총
compressed	**adj.** 압축된, 간결한

An **air gun** fires bullets by means of **compressed** air or other gas.
공기 소총은 압축된 공기나 다른 가스의 힘으로 총알을 발사한다.

piston	**n.** 피스톤
operate	**v.** 조작하다, 조종하다
coil(ed)	**v.** 감다, 휘감다 **n.** 고리, 전선 (**adj.** 휘감긴)
pressurized	**adj.** 가압된, 기밀 구조의
nitrogen	**n.** 질소
chamber	**n.** 방, 실, 공간, 회의실
utilize	**v.** 활용하다, 이용하다
source	**n.** 원천, 근원, 출처 자료
projectile	**n.** (총알 같은) 발사체 **adj.** 추진하는, 발사되는
range	**n.** 범위, 사거리
weapon	**n.** 무기, 병기, 공격, 수단

launch	**v.** 발사하다, 시작하다, 출시하다
velocity	**n.** 속도, 빠른 속도
burning	**adj.** 불타는 **n.** 연소
propellant	**n.** 압축가스, 추진 연료
noisy	**adj.** 시끄러운, 떠들썩한
vibrate	**v.** 진동하다, 흔들리다

A **rifle**, though it has a longer **range** than an air pistol, is **noisy** and the **barrel vibrates** more after shooting.

라이플총은 공기 권총보다 사거리가 길지만 소음이 있고, 사격 후 총열이 더 흔들린다.

cover   **v.** 엄호하다, 덮다

Let me **cover** for you while you go out through the back.

내가 엄호할 테니 그 사이 너희는 이 뒤로 빠져나가.

Chapter 9

archery	**n.** 활쏘기, 양궁, 궁술
field	**n.** 경기장, 들판, 논밭
stick (과거분사: stuck)	**v.** (뾰족한 것을) 찌르다, 찔리다
arrow	**n.** 화살, 화살표
fly	**v.** 날아가다 **n.** 파리
arc	**n.** 원호, 둥근 모양

> The **arrow flies** in an **arc**, so you must aim higher
> than the target.
>
> 화살은 포물선을 그리며 날아가기 때문에 표적보다 위를 목표로 해야 한다.

actual	**adj.** 실제의, 현실의, 사실상의
track	**n.** 길, 진로, 궤도, 자국
set up	～을 설치하다, ～을 세우다

scarecrow	**n.** 허수아비, 허깨비
elasticity	**n.** 탄성, 탄력성
bow	**n.** 활 **v.** (허리를 굽혀) 절하다
pulling force	견인력
reach	**v.** ~에 이르다, 도달하다
furthest	(far의 최상급) 가장 멀리
tilt	**v.** 기울다, (뒤로) 젖혀지다, 갸우뚱하다
off aim	오조준
bowstring	**n.** 활시위, (악기 활의) 현
arrowhead	**n.** 화살촉
fletching	**n.** 화살깃

Why is there **fletching** on the arrow?

화살에는 왜 깃이 있는 걸까?

latter part	후단, 뒷부분
shaky	**adj.** (병·감정·노쇠로) 떨리는, 휘청거리는

unstable

adj. 불안정한, 변하기 쉬운

A long object, like an arrow, is **unstable** when it flies.

화살같이 긴 물체는 날아갈 때 불안정하다.

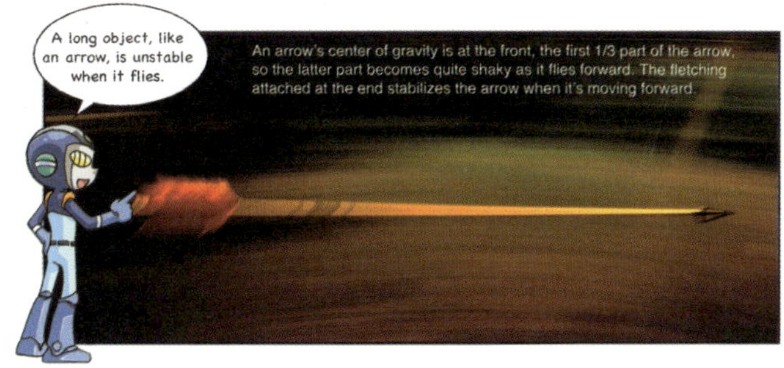

attach(ed)　**v.** 붙이다, 첨부하다 (**adj.** 덧붙여진, 첨부된)

stabilize　**v.** 안정되다, 안정시키다

shaking　**n.** 진동, 동요 **adj.** 흔들리는, 떨리는

inconsistent　**adj.** 부합하지 않은, 일관성 없는

damaged　**adj.** 손해(피해)를 입은, 하자가 생긴

tail wing　꼬리 날개

wing　**n.** 날개

demonstrate　**v.** (행동으로) 보여 주다, 증명하다

n. 설명, 시범, 시위

amazing　**adj.** (감탄스럽도록) 놀라운, 굉장한

mark	**n.** 표시, 자국, 과녁 **v.** 표시하다, 기념하다
dangerous	**adj.** 위험한
Of course!	물론이지!
penetrate	**v.** 뚫고 들어가다, 관통하다
bulletproof vest	방탄조끼

Arrows can **penetrate** even a **bulletproof vest**.

화살은 방탄조끼도 뚫을 수 있다.

densely	**adv.** 밀집하여, 빽빽하게
glass fiber	유리 섬유
weave (과거분사: woven)	**v.** 짜서(엮어서) 만들다
web	**n.** (복잡하게 연결된) 망, 거미줄
absorb	**v.** 흡수하다, 받아들이다 **n.** 흡수

Chapter 10

equipment	**n.** 장비, 설치
manager	**n.** 관리인, 관리자
speed up	속도를 높이다
pedal	**n.** 페달 **v.** 페달을 밟다
shift	**v.** 옮기다, 이동하다, 바꾸다
force point	힘점
fulcrum	**n.** 받침점, 지렛목, 지주, 버팀대
point of application	작용점
wheel	**n.** 바퀴, 자동차 핸들
axle	**n.** (바퀴의) 차축, 회전축
contrary	**n.** 반대 **adj.** 반대되는

start out	시작하다
uphill ↔ downhill	**adv.** (언덕·비탈) 위로 ↔ 아래로
velodrome	**n.** 경륜장
generate	**v.** 발생시키다, 만들어 내다
arena	**n.** 경기장, 무대
steeply	**adv.** 가파르게, 급경사로
irregularly	**adv.** 불규칙적으로
cyclist	**n.** 자전거 타는 사람, 사이클 선수
drag	**v.** 끌다 **n.** 장애물, 항력
helmet	**n.** 헬멧, 안전모, 투구
pointy	**adj.** 끝이 뾰족한
glide	**v.** 미끄러지듯 움직이다 **n.** 미끄러짐

The air in the back **glides** by smoothly.
뒤에 있는 공기가 매끄럽게 미끄러지듯이 흐른다.

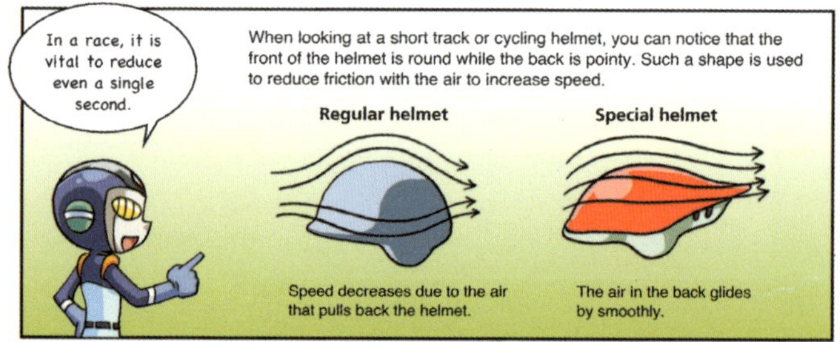

chase	v. 뒤쫓다, 추적하다
minimize	v. 최소화하다
figure skating	피겨 스케이팅
blade	n. (칼·도구 등의) 날
speed skating	스피드 스케이팅
veer	v. 진행 방향이 갑자기 바뀌다
slippery	adj. 미끄러운, 미끈거리는
momentarily	adv. 잠깐 (동안), 곧, 즉각
instant(ly)	n. 순간 adj. 즉각적인 (adv. 즉각, 즉시)
pour	v. 쏟아붓다, 따르다
artificial	adj. 인공의, 인조의

suddenly	**adv.** 갑자기, 별안간
environment	**n.** (주변의) 환경, 주변
droplet	**n.** 작은 (물)방울
crystallize	**v.** 결정체를 이루다(이루게 하다)
ride ∼ down	∼을 타고 내려가다
rascal	**n.** 악동, 개구쟁이, 녀석, 악당
scared	**adj.** 겁먹은, 깜짝 놀란, 무서운

Don't be **scared** and bend your body keeping your legs straight.

겁먹지 말고 다리를 일직선을 유지하면서 몸을 구부리도록 해.

athletic	**adj.** 강건한, 육상의, 운동선수의
slight	**adj.** 약간의, 조금의, 경미한
Inflection point	변곡점
inward	**adv.** 안쪽으로, 내부에
centripetal force	구심력
motor nerve	운동 신경
lock	**v.** 잠그다 **n.** 자물쇠, 잠금장치
password	**n.** 비밀번호, 암호(말)

Chapter 12

basketball	**n.** 농구
continue	**v.** 계속하다, 지속시키다
hoop	**n.** (농구의) 링, 굴렁쇠, 테
consecutive	**adj.** 연이은, 연속되는

You pass the test only if you make three **consecutive** baskets.
연속 3득점을 해야만이 테스트에서 합격이다.

start over	다시 시작하다
bummer	**n.** 실망(스러운 일), 게으름쟁이
score	**n.** 득점, 점수 **v.** 득점을 올리다
scope	**n.** 범위, 기회 **v.** 자세히 살피다
vertical	**adj.** 수직의, 세로의

snap	**n.** 찰칵하는 소리 **v.** 딱 (하고) 부러뜨리다
wrist	**n.** 손목, 손목 관절
sufficiently	**adv.** 충분히
soar	**v.** 하늘 높이 날아오르다, 솟구치다
crouch	**v.** 쭈그리다, 몸을 웅크리다
backboard	**n.** (농구 골대의) 백보드
backspin	**n.** (공의) 역회전
bump	**n.** 혹, 타박상, 돌기 **v.** 쿵하고 부딪치다
slip away	미끄러지다, 사라지다, 슬그머니 떠나다
accuracy	**n.** 정확, 정확도
tame	**v.** 길들이다, 억누르다 **adj.** 길들여진
frictional force	마찰력
soccer	**n.** 축구
goalpost	**n.** 골대, 골포스트
obstacle	**n.** 장애물, 장애, 방해
shoe	**n.** 신발(한 짝을 가리킴), 구두
take off	이륙하다, 날아오르다, 벗다

boundary	**n.** 경계선, 한계선
fluid	**n.** 유체, 유동체 **adj.** 유동성의
incense	**n.** 향, 향료
opponent	**n.** 상대, 반대자
triangle	**n.** 삼각형, 삼각자, 3인조
penalty kick	페널티 킥

A **penalty kick** is made 11 m away from the goal line.

페널티 킥은 골라인으로부터 11미터 떨어진 곳에 정해진다.

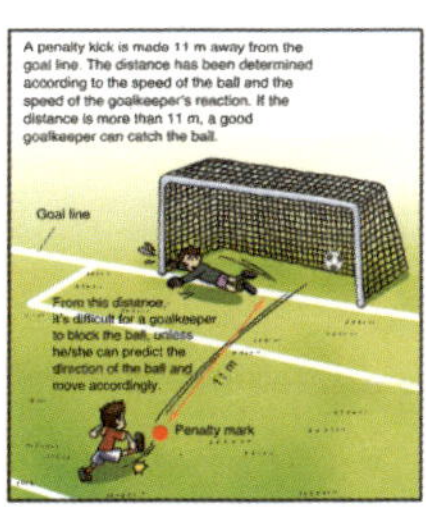

predict	**v.** 예측하다
accordingly	**adv.** 그에 맞춰, 따라서
feint	**n.** 상대방을 속이는 동작, 속임 동작
deceive	**v.** 속이다, 기만하다
pentagon	**n.** 오각형
hexagon	**n.** 육각형
spherical	**adj.** 구 모양의

Chapter 13

- The Science in Volleyball
- The Science in Baseball

volleyball	**n.** 배구
court	**n.** 코트, 법정, 법원, 뜰
successive	**adj.** 연이은, 연속적인, 계속적인
contact	**n.** 접촉 **v.** 연락하다, 접촉하다
throw	**v.** 던지다, 버리다
net	**n.** 네트, 골대, 그물
bounce	**v.** 튀어 오르다, 뛰다 **n.** 튐, 튀어 오름
waste	**v.** 낭비하다 **n.** 낭비, 쓰레기
awesome	**adj.** 경탄할 만한, 엄청난
weird	**adj.** 기이한, 기묘한, 불가사의한
calculate	**v.** 계산하다, 산출하다

imagine	v. 상상하다, 생각하다
mistake	n. 실수, 잘못 v. 잘못 판단하다, 오해하다
attitude	n. 태도, 사고방식
falling speed	침강 속도
running speed	주행 속도
block	v. 막다, 차단하다 n. 사각형 덩어리, 구역
coincidence	n. 우연의 일치
make an effort	노력하다
toss	v. (가볍게) 던지다 n. (배구) 토스
defense	n. 방어, 수비, 방위
setter	n. (배구) 세터
baseball	n. 야구, 야구공
motorcycle	n. 오토바이
pitcher	n. (야구) 투수
right-handed	adj. 오른손잡이인
left-handed	adj. 왼손잡이인
random	adj. 무작위의, 닥치는 대로

batter   **n.** (야구) 타자

catcher   **n.** (야구) 포수

characteristic   **adj.** 특유의 **n.** 특징, 특질

core   **n.** 속, 심, 핵, 근원

stitch   **n.** 바늘땀, 코 **v.** 바느질하다, 꿰매어 깁다

grip   **n.** 꽉 붙잡음, 통제 **v.** 꽉 잡다, 움켜잡다

Baseball pitches differ depending on how the **pitcher grips** the ball.

야구의 투구는 투수가 공을 잡는 방법에 따라 다르다.

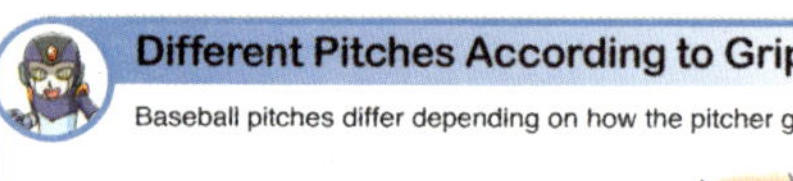

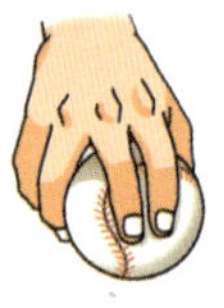

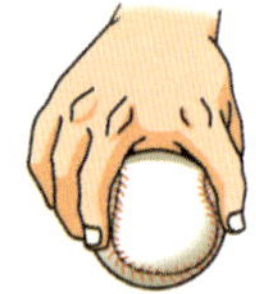

pattern   **n.** 양식, 형, 형태, 무늬

analyze   **v.** 분석하다, 해석하다

signal   **v.** 신호를 보내다, 시사하다 **n.** 신호, 징후

skinny	**adj.** 마른, 말라 빠진
dimple	**n.** 보조개, 옴폭 들어간 곳 **v.** 보조개를 짓다
nick	**n.** 칼자국(새김눈) **v.** 칼자국을 내다
scratch	**n.** 긁힌 자국, 찰과상 **v.** 긁다
leap	**n.** 높이뛰기, 도약 **v.** 뛰어오르다, 급등하다

Golf balls can make a double **leap**.

골프공은 2단 도약이 가능하다.

challenge	**n.** 도전 **v.** 도전하다
incline	**n.** 경사(면) **v.** ~쪽으로 기울다
slant	**v.** 기울다, 기울게 하다 **adj.** 비스듬한
keep in mind	~을 마음에 담아 두다, 명심하다

indicate	v. 나타내다, 가리키다
unit	n. 단위, 구성 단위
pound	n. (무게 단위) 파운드
knock down	넘어뜨리다, 때려 부수다
strike	n. (볼링) 스트라이크, 때리기 v. 치다, 부딪치다
embarrassing	adj. 부끄러운, 쑥스러운, 당황스러운
phase	n. 단계, 국면, 양상 v. 단계적으로 하다
stride	n. 걸음, 활보, 발전 v. 성큼성큼 걷다

If you make big **strides**, you will lose balance.
보폭을 크게 하면, 몸의 균형을 잃는다.

| pendular movement | 진자 운동 |

offset	**v.** 상쇄하다, 벌충하다
gutter	**n.** 홈, 배수로, 물받이
remember	**v.** 기억하다, 문득 떠올리다
floor	**n.** (나무·콘크리트·대리석 등으로 된) 바닥
had better	~하는 게 더 낫다(좋다)
split	**n.** (볼링) 스플릿, 분할, 분열 **v.** ~으로 쪼개다
theoretically	**adv.** 이론상, 이론적으로는
crash into	~와 충돌하다
repel	**v.** 쫓아버리다, 물리치다
virtually	**adv.** 사실상, 거의, 가상으로
win the lottery	복권에 당첨되다
attempt	**n.** 시도, 도전 **v.** 시도하다, 애쓰다
accurately	**adv.** 정확히, 정밀하게
expect	**v.** 기대하다, 예상하다

This time, you can **expect** a **strike** for sure!
이번에는 확실히 스트라이크를 기대해도 좋다!

Chapter 16

The Science in Tennis

racket	n. 시끄러운 소리(소음), (테니스 등) 라켓
string	n. 끈, 줄, 실
observe	v. ~을 보다, 목격하다, 관찰하다
approach	v. 다가가다, 착수하다 n. 접근법, 다가감
moist	adj. 촉촉한, 습기 있는
scatter	v. 뿌리다, 흩어지게 하다
crack	n. 금, 틈 v. 갈라지다, 금이 가다
freezing point	어는점
iceberg	n. 빙산
salinity	n. 염분, 염도
flavor	n. 맛, 향미

Chapter 17

- The Science in Table Tennis
- The Science in Badminton
- The Science in Gliding

table tennis	탁구
greedy	**adj.** 탐욕스러운, 욕심 많은
crush	**v.** 으스러뜨리다, 부수다
stack	**n.** 더미, 무더기, 굴뚝 **v.** 겹쳐 포개다
instantaneous	**adj.** 즉각적인, 순간적인
shuttlecock	**n.** (배드민턴 공) 셔틀콕
comparison	**n.** (～와) 비교함, 비유
charm	**n.** 매력, 아름다운 용모, 마력
feather	**n.** (새의) 깃털
smash	**n.** (테니스 등) 스매시 **v.** 박살내다, 부딪치다
elbow	**n.** 팔꿈치

gliding	**n.** 활공, 글라이더 경기
tracking device	추적 장치
no matter what	어떠한 일이 있어도

Because the doctor programmed me to train you first, **no matter what**.

어떠한 일이 있더라도 박사님은 너 먼저 훈련하도록 날 프로그램하셨다.

propeller	**n.** 프로펠러, 추진기
lift force	양력
electric power	전력
initial	**adj.** 처음의, 초기의
altitude	**n.** 해발 고도, 높이
head wind	역풍, 맞바람
give up	포기하다, 중도에 그만두다
in the middle of	~의 중앙에
experience	**v.** 겪다, 경험하다 **n.** 경험, 체험

weather   **n.** 날씨, 기상, 일기

The **weather** is very important in **gliding**.
글라이딩에서 날씨는 매우 중요하다.

rely on   ～에 의존하다

current   **n.** 흐름, 기류, 해류 **adj.** 현재의

sunlight   **n.** 햇살, 햇빛, 일광

intense   **adj.** 강렬한, 극심한

updraft   **n.** 상승 기류, 공기의 상승

beginner   **n.** 초보자, 초심자

mild   **adj.** 가벼운, 온화한, 순한

valley   **n.** 계곡, 골짜기

You should avoid the back of mountains or **valleys**.
산 뒤쪽이나 계곡은 피해야 한다.

irregular   **adj.** 고르지 못한, 불규칙적인

safe   **adj.** 안전한, 무사한

Chapter 18

judo	**n.** 유도
base	**n.** 기지, 맨 아래 부분, 기초
path	**n.** 길, 통로, 방향
narrow	**adj.** 좁은, 편협한, 한정된
back door	뒷문
figure out	알아내다, 이해하다, 계산하다
dare	**v.** 감히 ～하다 **n.** 감히 함, 도전
feed	**v.** 공급하다, 먹이를 주다
technique	**n.** 기술, 기법, 기교
trip	**n.** 여행, 발을 헛디딤 **v.** 발을 걸어 넘어뜨리다
leverage	**n.** 지렛대, 영향력, 효력

destabilize	**v.** 불안정하게 하다
throw	**n.** (유도) 메치기
prowess	**n.** (절묘한) 기량, 솜씨, 용기, 역량
pin down	꼼짝 못하게 잡다
forehead	**n.** 이마, 앞부분, 앞면
suppress	**v.** 진압하다, 숨기다, 억누르다
counterattack	**n.** 역습, 반격 **v.** 반격하다
twist	**n.** (유도) 꺾기 **v.** 비틀다
wring	**v.** ~을 짜다, 비틀다
pain	**n.** 고통 **v.** 고통스럽게 하다
joint	**n.** 관절, 이음매 **adj.** 공동의
critical point	한계점, 임계점
fulfill	**v.** 수행하다, 끝내다
mission	**n.** 임무, 사명

I haven't **fulfilled** my **mission** of rescuing you, Doctor.
박사님, 저는 당신을 구하는 임무를 끝내지 못했습니다.

deformation	**n.** 변형, 기형

blunt	**adj.** 무딘, 뭉툭한, 무뚝뚝한
momentum	**n.** 운동량, 힘, 기세, 타력
buffer effect	완충 효과
firmly	**adv.** 단호히, 확고히
instead of	~를 대신하여
destructive	**adj.** 파괴적인, 해를 끼치는
indeed	**adv.** 정말, 확실히, 참으로
fist	**n.** 주먹, 움켜쥠 **v.** (주먹을) 쥐다
external	**adj.** 외부의, 밖의, 외계의
weave	**v.** (권투) 위빙하다, 상체를 좌우로 흔들다
impact	**v.** 영향(충격)을 주다, 충돌하다
use up	다 쓰다, 소진하다
chin	**n.** 턱

Why can't he move his legs, when he was hit on the **chin**?
턱을 맞았을 때 그는 왜 다리를 움직이지 못한 거죠?

cerebellum	**n.** 소뇌
mesencephalon	**n.** 중뇌

cerebrum	**n.** 대뇌
go overboard	지나치게 열중하다, 극단에 흐르다
make up for	~을 만회하다, 벌충하다
injure	**v.** 부상을 입히다, 손상하다
contusion	**n.** 타박상, 좌상
concussion	**n.** (뇌)진탕, 진동, 충격
sprain	**v.** 삐다, 접지르다 **n.** 삐기, 염좌
ligament rupture	인대 파열
shoulder dislocation	어깨 탈골
accident	**n.** 사고, 사건, 우연
instruction	**n.** 설명, 지시, 명령
dismount	**v.** (차, 자전거 등에서) 내리다
complete	**adj.** 완벽한 **v.** 완료하다
take first aid measures	응급 처치를 하다

If someone has broken a bone or lost consciousness, you should call the hospital right away and **take first aid measures**.

누군가가 뼈가 부러지거나 의식을 잃었다면, 바로 병원에 알리고, 응급 처치를 해야 한다.

| nosebleed | **n.** 코피(가 남) |

artificial respiration	인공호흡
airway	n. (코에서 폐까지의) 기도, 항공로
nutrition	n. 영양, 영양 섭취, 영양물
pay attention	주목하다, 유의하다
breakfast	n. 아침 식사
digestion	n. 소화, 소화력, 이해
ingest	v. (음식·약 등을) 삼키다, 먹다
nutrient	n. 영양소, 영양분
vitamin	n. 비타민
mineral	n. 미네랄, 무기물
intake	n. 섭취(량), 흡입구
mental	adj. 정신의, 마음의
fall in love	사랑에 빠지다
confident	adj. 자신감 있는, 확신하는
work out	운동하다, (일이) 잘 풀리다
relieve	v. (고통 등을) 완화하다 누그러뜨리다, 해소시키다

tease	**v.** 괴롭히다, 놀리다, 집적거리다
rebirth	**n.** 부활, 갱생, 소생
slip	**v.** (재빨리) 놓다, (슬며시) 넣다
commotion	**n.** 소란, 소동, 동요
Good to see you again!	다시 만나서 반가워!
install	**v.** 설치하다, 설비하다, 장치하다
headquarter(s)	**v.** ~에 본부를 두다 (**n.** 본부, 본사)
orphanage	**n.** 고아원

These are all for you, from the children at the **orphanage**.
이것들 모두 고아원의 아이들이 당신에게 보낸 것입니다.

gratitude	**n.** 고마움, 감사
sincerity	**n.** 성실, 정직, 진실

2013년 2월 28일 1판 1쇄 발행

회장 | 나춘호   펴낸이 | 나성훈   펴낸곳 | (주)예림당
등록 | 제4-161호
주소 | 서울시 강남구 삼성동 153
구매 문의 전화 | 예림M&B 561-9007   팩스 | 567-9660
책 내용 문의 전화 | 3404-8459
홈쇼핑 문의 전화 | 3404-9286
http://www.yearim.co.kr

문제를 내 주신 선생님

정명숙

경상대학교 영어영문학과를 졸업하고 숙명여대 SMU–TESOL
과정을 마쳤습니다. 20여 년간 외국어학원, 초등학교 등에서 영어
를 가르쳤으며, 영어교육프로그램을 기획하였습니다. 현재 대학교
평생교육원에서 영어를 가르치고 있으며, English Teacher
Trainer, 영어독서전문가로 활동하고 있습니다.

Design by Creative House
sweetspot

2013년 2월 28일 1판 1쇄 발행

회장 | 나춘호
펴낸이 | 나성훈
펴낸곳 | (주)예림당
등록 | 제4–161호
주소 | 서울시 강남구 삼성동 153
구매 문의 전화 | 예림M&B 561–9007
팩스 | 567–9660
책 내용 문의 전화 | 3404–8459
홈쇼핑 문의 전화 | 3404–9286
http://www.yearim.co.kr
© 2013 예림당

Original title: Why? Sports Science
Copyright © 2013 by YeaRimDang Publishing Co., Ltd.